❧ TREASURED ❧
Amish &
Mennonite
RECIPES

Published in cooperation with
Mennonite Central Committee

Foreword by Alan Giagnocavo

Introduction by Carole Roth Giagnocavo

Fox Chapel
PUBLISHING

© 2011 by Fox Chapel Publishing Company, Inc., East Petersburg, PA.

Published in cooperation with Mennonite Central Committee.

Foreword by Alan Giagnocavo.
Introduction by Carole Roth Giagnocavo.

Treasured Amish & Mennonite Recipes is an original work, first published in 2011 by Fox Chapel Publishing Company, Inc. Portions of the text were previously published by Fox Chapel Publishing Company, Inc., in *Treasured Mennonite Recipes* (1992) and *More Treasured Mennonite Recipes* (1996). Marked recipes on pages 8, 84, 130, 174, 180, 182, 183, 214, 215, 217, 286, 293, and 303 were previously published by Pathway Publisher's Corporation in *Amish Cooking* (1977).

ISBN: 978-1-56523-599-1

Library of Congress Cataloging-in-Publication Data

Treasured Amish & Mennonite recipes / foreword by Alan Giagnocavo ; introduction by Carole Roth Giagnocavo.

    p. cm.
"Published in cooperation with Mennonite Central Committee."
Includes index.
ISBN 978-1-56523-599-1 (pbk.)
1. Amish cooking. 2. Mennonite cooking. 3. Cookbooks. I. Mennonite Central Committee. II. Title: Treasured Amish and Mennonite recipes.
TX715.T76827 2011
641.5'66--dc23

2011015393

To learn more about the other great books from Fox Chapel Publishing, or to find a retailer near you, call toll-free 800-457-9112 or visit us at *www.FoxChapelPublishing.com*.

Note to Authors: We are always looking for talented authors to write new books. Please send a brief letter describing your idea to Acquisition Editor, 1970 Broad Street, East Petersburg, PA 17520.

Printed in China
First printing: October 2011

Acquisition editors:
Peg Couch and
Alan Giagnocavo

Copy editors:
Paul Hambke and
Heather Stauffer

Cover and page designer
Jason Deller

Layout designer:
Chanyn Wise

Editor:
Katie Weeber

Proofreader:
Lynda Jo Runkle

Indexer:
Sandy Blood

TABLE OF CONTENTS

FOREWORD: HOW THIS BOOK WAS WRITTEN

When I worked as a bookseller many years ago near New Hamburg, Ontario, the site of one of the largest Mennonite Central Committee (MCC) relief sales, cookbook collectors would frequently ask for a little blue hand-bound collection of MCC relief sale recipes. This book was available in limited quantities on the day of the relief sale, and was so popular that few of the collectors would be successful in their quest, the copies having run out hours earlier.

Years later, I moved back to Pennsylvania to start a publishing company, Fox Chapel Publishing. As a young, idealistic, and optimistic entrepreneur, I set a lofty goal for myself in terms of the charitable contributions I would soon like to make. After producing a net profit of $96 after my first year in business, I looked more intently at a way of leveraging my meager cash flow to achieve my goal of helping others. Some previous studies in the fields of poverty and international development left me very impressed with the way MCC approached these problems. After deciding that MCC was to receive the donations from Fox Chapel, I suddenly remembered the little blue cookbook from New Hamburg.

All the recipes from that little blue cookbook were typed into the computer. Blessed with the aid of Beverly DeWit, a professional cookbook editor, Fox Chapel was able to expand and complete the recipes, making them accessible for any cook. After this round of professional editing and design, Fox Chapel's first Mennonite cookbook, *Treasured Mennonite Recipes: All-Time Favorite Recipes from the Mennonite Community Relief Sales*, was released in 1992. It was well received, both inside and outside the Mennonite community.

After the first volume was on bookstore shelves for several years, it seemed like the time to produce a follow-up volume from scratch. While *Treasured Mennonite Recipes* drew primarily from the Swiss-German Mennonite tradition native to Waterloo County, Ontario, and Lancaster County, Pennsylvania, the second cookbook, *More Treasured Mennonite Recipes: Food, Fun, and Fellowship From the Mennonite Relief Sales*, published in 1996, included recipes from various Russian-Mennonite traditions. Surprising to those unaware of the diversity of Mennonite churches, (cont'd on pg. vii)

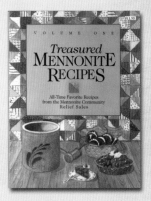

Fox Chapel's first Mennonite Cookbook was published in 1992.

The second Fox cookbook arrived four years after the first volume.

THE UNIQUE PLACE OF RELIEF SALES IN COMMUNITY LIFE

Mennonite Central Committee (MCC) relief sales were and are an important, but overlooked, part of Amish and Mennonite community life. In so many ways, these events represent the best of community spirit. They're fun, focused on serving others outside the bounds of denomination or geography, and welcoming to everyone and anyone. And of course, the food is very good, even spectacular at times. Relief sale food is freshly made and pours forth from kitchens that come to life long before sunrise. Fresh strawberry pie was the local favorite when I was growing up, followed closely by potato donuts and specialty breads. Each relief sale has its own list of favorites, depending on tradition and season. But beyond the food, MCC relief sales serve as a common meeting ground for the many different groups of Amish and Mennonites. They act as a safe "showcase" to the broader local community, without the need for Mennonites to appear aggressive or proud.

In my teen years, I worked at three farmer's markets in Amish/Mennonite communities in southern Ontario. Each had a distinctive character and drew different groups of tourists and locals. The Thursday market, held near St. Jacobs, attracted the most Plain members—horse and buggy Mennonites, Old Order Amish, and Markham "black bumper" Mennonites, driving chrome-less cars.

Saturday's Waterloo Farmer's Market drew a few of the same groups, but for the most part attracted far more liberal groups—"Muppies" (Mennonite yuppies) and prosperous well-educated urban Russian-Mennonites, only a generation away from the horrors of their parents' flight from Russia. The Tuesday market in Aylmer, Ontario, although less than a 2-hour drive from St. Jacobs, was quite different. The crowd was a mix of first-generation Holland/Dutch immigrants, members of the small Old Order Amish community headquartered outside the town, and a large contingent of Mexican Mennonites, who had recently arrived in Canada. The Pennsylvania Dutch of Kitchener-Waterloo was rarely heard, replaced by the Low German *Plautdietsch*, spoken by the Russian Mennonites.

Altogether, I'm glad to have friends and acquaintances among more than a dozen varieties of Amish and Mennonite groups. The one thing that all of these groups have in common, however, is that they look to MCC for help in reaching out to others through relief work. Putting aside the finer points of theology and doctrine, MCC focuses on addressing basic human needs at a practical and tangible level. By sticking to these basics, MCC has achieved acceptance and respect among the very different Amish and Mennonite groups that may otherwise interact infrequently.

'What for a name is that?'

For those who grew up in Mennonite and Amish households, any book written by a person with my last name is immediately suspect. Giagnocavo is not a "Mennonite" name.

Because this Mennonite tradition of giving a quick snapshot of one's genealogy is such an expected part of introductions, let me offer some reassurance as to the authenticity of my heritage. My mother's maiden name was Martin. Her family came to the United States in the late 1700s from Switzerland. My grandfather, Emmanuel Martin, moved his family from Pennsylvania to Ontario, only to return a few years later. He is thus known as "Ontario" Emmanuel Martin to Pennsylvanian Mennonites who know their genealogy, and likewise as "Pennsylvania" Emmanuel Martin to Ontario Mennonites.

Grandfather Giagnocavo came to the United States in the late 1800s from the region of Italy best described as "the heel of the boot." He converted from Catholicism to the Mennonite faith later in life. The precise date of his conversion is unknown, but it was after my father—the youngest of thirteen children—was born.

The late poet Millen Brand included several poems about my grandfather in *Local Lives: Poems about the Pennsylvania Dutch*. Never having met my grandfather, the poems give a sense of who he was and the world from which he came.

Giagnocavo at Church*

Giagnocavo, convert to the brotherhood
and faith of Menno Simons,
dressed in his Sunday black—white
tieless collar drawing him
close to the simple elevation
of deacons and minister—
walks down the Bally chapel's men's side
to the front to hear.
The air is still. Old Mennonites
gather: on one side,
the dark suits of men
and on the other, the white
head coverings of women.
As the pews fill, babies
are comforted though a few still cry
in the plain church of plaster walls
and plaster ceiling. Giagnocavo
sits straight and waits...

*Brand, Millen. "Giagnocavo at Church." In Local Lives: Poems about the Pennsylvania Dutch, edited by Jonathan Brand, 152-154. New York: Clarkson N. Potter, Inc., 1975.

(cont'd from pg. iv) *More Treasured Mennonite Recipes* even included Laotian, Cambodian, Vietnamese, Mexican, and Central American dishes from more recently formed immigrant Mennonite communities.

With recipes coming in from all over North America, it is no exaggeration to credit MCC staffer Brenda Wagner as the real creator of the second volume. Brenda brought order to a huge undertaking, leading to the success of the second volume. Freelance writer Grace Palsgrove also helped gather and rewrite recipes and stories from the various contributors and relief sale committees.

The two original volumes have been out of print for a number of years. This latest edition takes the most popular recipes from those two books and puts them into one convenient and redesigned volume. We like to think we have selected the "best of the best."

We've made a few changes by popular request. To begin with, an expanded index and cross-reference will make finding recipes much easier, and a lay-flat binding will allow you to keep this book open while you cook. New paper and binding materials should make wiping off spatters much easier than with the first two volumes. Courtesy of some Amish MCC supporters from both Canada and the United States, we have also included many Amish-style recipes, appearing for the first time in this edition.

Because we found the earlier two cookbooks often ended up in some surprising places around the world, we've included "A Brief History of the Amish and Mennonites," for those learning about these groups for the first time. Finally, updated information on MCC relief sales and thrift shops will hopefully encourage you to attend your first, or perhaps a new, relief sale for this year, and to visit your local MCC thrift shop.

As a result of the sales of the first two cookbooks, more than $75,000 was raised to further the work of MCC. It is our hope that this new edition can generate even more as the needs of the world grow greater from year to year.

Alan

Alan Giagnocavo
LANCASTER COUNTY, PENNSYLVANIA
SPRING 2011

Fifteen recipes from *Amish Cooking* appear in this book. To order copies of *Amish Cooking*, please send a letter to Pathway Publishers, 258ON-25OW, LaGrange, IN 46761 or Pathway Publishers, RR4, Aylmer, ON N5H2R3.

The Best Memories of Food and Family

by Carole Roth Giagnocavo

I suppose any good cookbook comes from a series of relationships—with past mentors and teachers, with the food, and of course with friends around the table enjoying the meal.

While this collection contains all those types of relationships as a starting point, it keeps going. As I sit down to write this almost 20 years after Fox Chapel Publishing produced its first Mennonite cookbook, I'm finally able to see and appreciate the much richer and wider circles of relationships that are somehow connected to MCC, growing up Mennonite, and the wider world.

My mother definitely forms the primary and innermost circle of the relationships I think of as I read through these pages. Now in her 80s, she is still going strong, despite the passing of my father several years ago. She has always been known for doing three things well. In terms of enjoyment, I'd guess gardening would come first, then cooking, and then sewing.

My mother's love for gardening lives on in my children, and every summer since they were little, we have spent 2 weeks in Nebraska soaking in the life and traditions of their grandparents. The rich loose black soil of the garden has always been appealing to them. When my son was only 3 years old, he came in from the garden and announced that he had been working with Grandpa because "…that is what men do." As toddlers, my kids loved just digging in the dirt. Helping out, picking flowers, and gathering up the potatoes

Because "…that is what men do." Learning life from Grandpa in the garden.

Grandpa turned up with his pitchfork were highlights of their summer. Now, their love for the garden remains the same, but their involvement has changed. They are the ones who dig up the potatoes, water the flowers, and help pick the beans.

My mother is just as good in the kitchen as she is in the garden. She is the epitome of a great Mennonite cook, just as her mother was before her. Whenever any of my brothers now living in Pennsylvania visit her, they know they will be sent home with several cases containing our mother's specialties. These goodies include canned beef—glass jars of top-grade Nebraska beef cooked

and canned in rich genuine no-preservatives beef broth—and jars of bright red cinnamon pickles, brilliantly colored from the addition of Red Hots candies during canning.

Both of my children are excellent bakers. This is due in no small part to watching, while perched on a countertop, and later helping, Grandma Roth bake her signature cinnamon rolls, bread, and donuts. No one makes a better fresh cabbage slaw or roast beef dinner, and my mother's canned pickles and ketchup are amazing. Some of Grandma Roth's best recipes were included in the original Mennonite cookbooks, and now they are part of this larger collection.

When my mother is not gardening or cooking, she can often be found sewing. When I was a child, most of her talent for sewing was used to make clothing for our family. Now she is much more active in the sewing circle at her church and uses her time to attend the local quilting bees and finish quilting projects on her own at home.

While our small Nebraska community wasn't very cosmopolitan, I grew up with a strong sense of world citizenship and a global perspective on how my country and I fit into the rest of the world. MCC played a big part in this. Nebraska's annual MCC relief sale started several years after I moved out of the area, so my only connection to MCC while growing up was through the meat-canning project held in our area every year. Volunteer labor processed tons of meat over several days. My father volunteered every year for decades, sometimes staying past midnight to help finish. Mom still helps and volunteers at the Nebraska Relief Sale. As a child, I was fascinated by watching the cans of meat, labeled "For Relief," form huge mountains.

Grandma enjoys sharing her love of food and gardening.

Gardening and cooking is still in their blood, even as our children grow up.

Digging in the dirt. This photo is such a universal representation of the connections between the earth, food, and family.

I was curious about the people who would be on the receiving end, and wondered where in the world, literally, the cans were going.

Many years later, when I spent 3 months in the Middle East as a college student, I ran across the familiar labels while visiting schools serving a range of disadvantaged Muslim, Jewish, and Christian children. My mind went back to when I was a child in Nebraska, never dreaming I would see one of these cans or its appreciative recipient at its final destination.

For this third Fox Chapel cookbook, Assistant Editor Katie Weeber took on the Herculean task of organizing and combining the recipes, allowing me more time to reflect on the meaning and stories behind them. When working on the first cookbook, I was also busily preparing for marriage to Alan and attending to the details of our upcoming wedding. My contribution to the second cookbook was that of recipe sleuth—filling in any gaps in the various recipe sections.

This time, having the chance to reminisce over these pages and recipes has been such a pleasure. I know that each one of the hundreds of contributors and thousands of readers will have his or her own set of stories and memories as well. Knowing that brings me even greater pleasure.

Carole

Carole Roth Giagnocavo
LANCASTER COUNTY, PENNSYLVANIA
SPRING 2011

MCC canned beef tins labeled "Food for Relief: Beef Chunks," on the shelves of a Middle Eastern school in the 1980s.

A Brief History of the Amish and Mennonites

Amish and Mennonite food is often thought of as good old-fashioned stick-to-your-ribs comfort food. It is associated with a time when families were closely connected to the land, raising, growing, and harvesting everything they consumed. But Amish and Mennonite dishes do not solely consist of well-known classics like chicken pot pie and whoopie pies. The recipes reflect the history and culture of these religious groups. They collectively tell a story of struggle and religious persecution and emphasize the strong bonds of family and community that are such an important part of Amish and Mennonite life. To truly understand the scope and importance of Amish and Mennonite food, you must first understand the history and culture of these groups.

Who are the Amish and the Mennonites?

The Amish and the Mennonites are part of a religious group whose members are found throughout the United States, Canada, and many other countries.

The Mennonite church began in Switzerland in the early sixteenth century during the time following the Protestant Reformation. The reformation, led by Martin Luther in Germany, was a protest against the perceived corruption and heretical practices of the Roman Catholic Church. The reformation sought a return to the teachings of scripture and a focus

on Jesus Christ. Around the same time that Martin Luther was nailing his ninety-five theses to the door of the Castle Church in Wittenberg, Germany, Urlich Zwingli was leading a similar movement in Switzerland.

Several of Zwingli's followers, however, believed that Zwingli and Luther had not taken a bold enough stand against the church and had fallen short of their goal of making scripture a central focus for believers. This small sect began to hold secret meetings in the homes of fellow members and to solidify their views.

The group members maintained two central beliefs that set them apart from the popular reformers of the time. First, they turned away from infant baptism, declaring that a Christian community could only be made up of adults who could knowingly and voluntarily confess their faith and then choose to be baptized. Second, the group believed that the church should be a separate entity from the state.

These were radical concepts for the sixteenth century, but members of the group felt strongly enough about these beliefs that they decided to act. In January 1525, Conrad Grebel led members of the Swiss group as they confessed their faith and baptized each other. Their actions were not only religiously radical, they were illegal.

As a result of their actions, the group members were titled Anabaptizers, or re-baptizers, by other reformers, as well as the Catholic Church, both of whom refused to listen to the Anabaptists' arguments that their actions were fully supported by scripture. Instead, the group was heavily persecuted, and many of its leaders were killed.

This persecution led many Anabaptists to flee their homes and seek refuge in other countries, resulting in a spread of the movement. In the Netherlands, a catholic priest named Menno Simons struggled with questions and doubts he had about the mass and infant baptism. His questioning eventually led him to a deep and thorough study of the Bible. He joined the Anabaptist movement in 1536 and became a major force behind it. Simons worked tirelessly to organize at-home church groups

and spent a great deal of time preaching and writing about the group's concepts for reform.

Soon, many began to call Simons' followers Menists (translated as Mennonite), a term that would eventually replace the name Anabaptist and be applied to all members of the movement. The members themselves, however, preferred the name *Taufgesinnt*, which translates, "those who baptize on confession of faith."

A similar instance led to the development of the term Amish. The name comes from Jacob Ammann, a bishop who had a great influence over the movement in the late 1600s and early 1700s.

When persecution in Europe grew to be too great, many Mennonites fled to the New World. In 1683, German-speaking immigrants established a Mennonite community in Pennsylvania, making it the first of such communities on American soil. Over the next several decades, many more Mennonites, including those belonging to the conservative segment known as the Amish, made their way to America. Eventually, members of the Mennonite community moved west, establishing a presence throughout the country.

Many of the Mennonites who remained in Europe moved into Prussia (Poland) and the south of Russia. During the nineteenth and twentieth centuries, however, many chose to move to the United States, Canada, and even South America.

The Old Order Amish have also spread throughout America, establishing a presence in about twenty states. These Mennonites, following the most conservative teachings of the church, strive to maintain a simple and pure lifestyle. They seek to separate themselves from the rest of the world in order to strengthen their beliefs and values. They therefore live without the creature comforts that many of us are accustomed to, such as electricity, running water, and cars.

What Are Their Beliefs?

The Amish and Mennonites, although part of the same religious group, sometimes differ in their

fundamental beliefs about dress, their connection to mainstream society, and other similar religious and cultural matters. The Amish choose to dress simply, in a manner they believe is called for in the scriptures. Women wear head coverings, or bonnets, and do not cut their hair. All Amish clothing, both men's and women's, is made of solid colors and lacks any ostentatious adornments, such as buttons. This style of dress is an effort to maintain simplicity and modesty in a world where glamor and immodesty are often the emphasis of the fashion world.

The Amish are also known for their policy of nonviolence and nonresistance. This belief comes directly from the biblical message to turn the other cheek.

Finally, the Amish believe in community and communal support. They see it as their responsibility, and no one else's, to support and assist members of their faith. As a result, the Amish do not accept any kind of aid or welfare from the government or other organizations, choosing instead to depend on those around them for aid.

While the Amish strictly adhere to and follow these beliefs, their practices are not typical of the larger less-conservative segment of the Mennonite church. Most Mennonites have immersed themselves in modern society, living in houses with electricity and driving cars to get to and from work. What makes modern believers Mennonites is their continued adherence to the values of the Swiss reformers.

Mennonites today still recognize the importance of maintaining a separation between church and state. They emphasize the scriptures and the teachings of Jesus Christ as part of their belief system and values, and still believe that baptism, as well as church membership, needs to be voluntary.

Connecting Mennonite Food and Culture

Along with their religious beliefs, the Mennonites have also maintained much of their European cultural heritage. Many Amish communities, for example, continue to speak a form of German most commonly referred to as Pennsylvania Dutch. Perhaps the most well-known aspect of Mennonite heritage, however, is their food. Mennonite dishes typically have a strong connection to the European countries in which group members lived before immigrating to America. The Mennonites were widely scattered, and their food is equally varied, reflecting culinary tastes from countries such as Switzerland, Germany, Russia, Prussia, Hungary, and many more.

Mennonite recipes also demonstrate the agricultural heritage of the group. Most Mennonite families were farmers, and all their food was produced from what they were able to raise and grow on the farm. Ingredients lists for Mennonite dishes often call for garden produce, fresh meats, and dairy products. It is not unexpected to come across an unusual or surprising ingredient, as many recipes were developed with what was readily available. Substitutions and variations are typical; if one ingredient was not on hand, recipes were adapted to work with what was accessible at the time.

For the most part, recipes were not written down, and there was no measuring involved. Cooks in Mennonite kitchens added ingredients as they saw fit until they were satisfied with the result.

Mennonite dishes will often serve large numbers of people, reflecting the need to feed large hard-working families with big appetites, and to provide the occasional meal for the community as a whole at events such as barn raisings or quilting bees.

The Mennonites Today

Mennonites today can be seen following all these traditions of food, family, and religious faith. In an effort to bring the biblical concepts of peace, love, and community to others, many Mennonites have become involved in peace-building efforts, as well as disaster relief and aid. Mennonite Central Committee (MCC) is responsible for organizing and promoting many of these efforts, and they often do so by bringing people together in the sharing of food.

Mennonite Central Committee was founded in 1920 in an effort to provide efficient and organized aid to members of the Mennonite community in Russia and the Ukraine. During the 1920s, Russia experienced a massive famine, which was spurred on by the effects of World War I and the disruption of agriculture. In 1920, four members from Mennonite villages in the afflicted area arrived in the United States to request aid for their families and communities. Seven Mennonite conferences and relief organizations combined their efforts to respond by sending food and aid. MCC would eventually send several relief workers to Russia to help with the relief effort.

It was quickly realized that funds would be needed if MCC's relief efforts were to continue. To raise money, a "relief" sale was held on the John K. Warkentin Farm in Reedley, California. Items were auctioned, raising more than $200 for Russia. With these extra funds, MCC was able to complete its first development project, sending fifty Fordson tractor-plow outfits to Russia so that farming could begin again. Six weeks after the tractors and plows arrived in Russia, more than 4,300 acres of land were plowed.

More than 90 years later, MCC serves in more than fifty countries around the world, reaching out to those who have been struck by war, famine, and natural disaster by providing food and other aid. Their commitment to partnering with organizations in the affected regions, such as local churches and

relief groups, has enabled them to ensure they can continue to provide aid for months, or even years, as it is needed.

Just as MCC has grown, the fundraising efforts used to support it have also grown. Today, relief sales are held in forty-five locations throughout the United States and Canada. The sales combine fellowship with charity, often centered around an auction of quilts, crafts, food, and even livestock.

Volunteers work year round to plan the sales, and people often travel from miles away to attend. Auction bidders raise the prices on everything from exquisite handcrafted furniture to loaves of bread. The money paid rarely reflects the true value of the goods, as the bidders are often seeking to do more than purchase an item; they wish to reach out to others as well.

Those who donate items to be sold also do their part for the MCC's relief efforts. They lovingly stitch quilts, cook and bake food, create crafts, and donate heirlooms.

Those who attend relief sales come to share food, friendship, and the hope that they can do their part to support MCC. Each year, these relief sales raise close to five million dollars for the support of MCC's relief efforts around the world. Almost all of the recipes in this book were collected from relief sales, and include some of the favorite dishes from those events.

Today, there are about 150,000 Amish living in the United States. There are also more than one million members of the Mennonite church worldwide. The Mennonites, with their strong sense of community, have found fulfillment and joy in a world often struck by tragedy and sadness by reaching out to others around them. It is likely that they will continue to grow, as they have before, passing their rich history of tradition, belief, and community on to the future generation.

—K. W.

PUNCHES AND DRINKS

BLACK CURRANT DRINK

- ❖ ¾ cup currants
- ❖ ½ cup sugar
- ❖ Cold water

Take as many quart jars as you need. Add to each ¾ cup currants and ½ cup sugar. Then fill each jar with cold water. Steam for 10 minutes. (Count time when water in steamer is rolling.) These should stand for 1 month before using.

BLACK CURRANT LEMONADE

- ❖ 4 quarts currants
- ❖ 1 cup water
- ❖ 1 cup sugar

Cover the currants with the water and boil until fruit is soft. Strain. Reheat juice and add the sugar to make a syrup. (Don't add sugar until fruit is soft. Adding it too soon makes the currants tough and they lose their flavor.) Seal.

To serve, use equal parts of the syrup and water with ½ lemon to each serving.

JUICE

Always use real juice for these recipes, not juice substitutes. You'll enjoy the flavor that much more.

CRANBERRY PUNCH

- 1 package cranberries
- 3 quarts water
- 2 cinnamon sticks
- Juice of 6 oranges and 2 lemons
- 2 cups sugar

Cook the cranberries and cinnamon sticks in the water (bottled juice can be used instead of the cranberries). Put through a sieve. Add the sugar and the juice from the oranges and lemons. Heat all to boiling point. Add ginger ale or lemon-lime soda at serving time.

DANDELION DRINK

- 4 quarts boiling water
- 1 quart dandelion blossoms
- 4 quarts water, cold
- 4 cups sugar
- 4 lemons, thinly sliced

Pour the boiling water over the dandelion blossoms. Let stand 24 hours. Strain. Add the sugar and lemons to the cold water. Boil 5 minutes. Add dandelion liquid. Return to boil and seal in sterile jars.

EGGNOG

- 4 eggs
- 4 cups cold milk
- ⅓ cup sugar
- ⅛ teaspoon nutmeg
- ⅛ teaspoon salt
- ½ teaspoon vanilla

Beat all together until frothy.

FOR THE PUNCH BOWL

- 1 cup sugar
- 2 cups water
- 2 6-ounce cans frozen orange juice
- 2 6-ounce cans frozen grapefruit juice
- 2 28-ounce bottles ginger ale
- ⅔ cup grenadine (purchase at grocer's)

Boil the sugar and water. Cool. At serving time, mix with the remaining ingredients.

CB

FRIENDSHIP TEA

- 3 packages Tang
- ⅓ cup instant tea
- 1 package lemonade mix
- ½ cup sugar
- 1 teaspoon cloves
- 1 teaspoon cinnamon (ground)

Mix. To use, put 2-3 teaspoons in a cup and fill with boiling water.

FRUIT PUNCH

- 1½ quarts pineapple juice
- 1 6-ounce can frozen lemonade
- 1 12-ounce can frozen orange juice
- 1 quart cranberry juice
- 1½ quarts cold water
- 1 cup sugar
- Half of a 3-ounce package cherry gelatin dissolved in 1 cup boiling water

Add additional red coloring if desired. Mix all together. At serving time, add 1 quart ginger ale or lemon-lime soda. Add orange or lemon sherbet if desired.

Serves 35.

THERE IS NO PLACE MORE DELIGHTFUL THAN HOME.

FRUIT PUNCH FOR FIFTY

- 3 cups sugar
- 3 cups water, cold
- ¼ cup tea or mint leaves
- 3 cups boiling water
- 3 cups orange juice
- 3 cups pineapple juice
- 1 cup lemon juice
- 1½ quarts ginger ale

Combine the sugar and the cold water and boil to make a syrup. Cool. Steep the tea (or mint) in the boiling water for 7 minutes. Strain and cool. Mix the fruit juices together. Mix together the syrup, tea, and juices. Add the ginger ale at serving time.

ॐ

Party Fruit Punch

- 3 quarts pineapple juice
- 1½ cups lemon juice
- 3 cups orange juice
- ⅓ cup lime juice
- 2½ cups sugar
- 1 cup lightly packed fresh mint leaves
- 2 large bottles ginger ale
- 1 large bottle carbonated water
- 1 pint fresh strawberries, quartered

Combine juices, sugar, and mint. Chill. Just before serving, add remaining ingredients and pour over cake of ice in punch bowl.

Makes 75 4-ounce servings.

Quantity Fruit Punch

- 2 46-ounce cans pineapple juice
- 3 6-ounce cans frozen orange juice
- 2 6-ounce cans frozen lemonade
- 12 ounces frozen strawberries
- 1 orange, cut into thin slices
- 1 tray ice cubes

Mix the first three ingredients. Before serving, add the strawberries and ice cubes. Garnish with the orange slices.

Serves 25.

Golden Punch

- 1 can (46 ounces) pineapple juice
- 1 can (12 ounces) frozen orange juice, thawed
- 1 can (12 ounces) frozen lemonade, thawed
- 1-1½ quarts water
- 1 bottle (28 ounces) ginger ale

Mix together all ingredients except ginger ale. If desired, freeze part of this liquid in a ring mold to place in the punch bowl for chilling. Place fruit juice mixture in punch bowl and add ginger ale just before serving.

Serves 50.

Martha Tschetter
Freeman, South Dakota
Minn-Kota MCC Relief Sale
Sioux Falls, South Dakota

GRAPE JUICE

- ❖ 1 cup grapes, washed and stemmed
- ❖ ¾ cup sugar

Put the grapes into a sterile 1-quart sealer. Add the sugar and slowly fill with boiling water (jars crack easily if water is poured too fast). Seal and store. In a month you can pour off a lovely juice to serve as it is or mix it with lemon and ginger ale to taste.

GRAPE JUICE ON THE STOVE

- ❖ Grapes, washed and stemmed
- ❖ Water
- ❖ Sugar

Put the grapes in a large kettle. Add water until just below the level of the grapes. Boil 5 minutes. Strain. To each 4 cups grape juice, add 1 cup sugar. Bring to boiling point again and seal.

HOMEMADE RHUBARB JUICE

- ❖ 3½ quarts (18 cups) rhubarb, washed and cut
- ❖ 12 cups hot water
- ❖ 2 cups sugar
- ❖ ½ teaspoon red color

Simmer rhubarb and water for 40 minutes. Strain through sieve and put onto heat. Add sugar and coloring. When it boils, it may be bottled in sterile jars. When making punch, add equal parts of pineapple juice, a tray of ice, and red and green cherries.

Makes 4 32-ounce bottles.

HOT SPICED APPLE CIDER

- ❖ 4 teaspoons whole cloves
- ❖ 4 teaspoons whole allspice
- ❖ 4 cinnamon sticks
- ❖ 2 gallons apple cider

Tie spices together in cheesecloth. Add spice bag to cider and heat to desired temperature (do not boil). Serve hot. Add ½-1 cup brown sugar if cider is too tart.

Ken Snyder
Salem, Oregon
Oregon MCC Fall Festival, Albany

&

LEMON-ORANGE CONCENTRATE

- 3 lemons
- 4 oranges
- 8 cups white sugar
- 1½ quarts boiling water
- 2 ounces citric acid (available at drugstores)

Grate rinds and squeeze juice from the lemons and oranges. Strain juices if desired. Add the boiling water and citric acid (available at drugstores) to the white sugar to make a syrup. Cool. Mix the syrup and the juices. Bottle and refrigerate. Good mixed with water or as a base in a punch bowl.

LEMONADE

- 1 container (20 ounces) powdered lemonade mix
- 1 can (6 ounces) frozen orange juice, thawed
- 2 gallons cold water

Mix ingredients well and chill thoroughly.

Makes 2 gallons.

Ken Snyder
Salem, Oregon
Oregon MCC Fall Festival, Albany

MINT TEA

- 1 tea bag
- 6 stems mint, slightly crushed
- Dash cayenne pepper
- 2 cups boiling water
- 1 cup sugar
- ½ cup lemon juice

Steep the tea bag and mint in boiling water with cayenne pepper. Strain. Add the sugar and lemon juice. Refrigerate. Dilute with equal parts of water when ready to serve.

PINEAPPLE PUNCH

- 1 can (12 ounces) frozen orange juice
- 1 can (6 ounces) frozen lemonade
- 1 quart water
- 1 quart 7-Up (half a 2-liter bottle)
- 2 quarts pineapple sherbet
- 1 quart vanilla ice cream

Mix juices and water. Add 7-Up just before serving and stir in sherbet and ice cream.

Lisa Kauffman
Pleasant View Mennonite Church
Goshen, Indiana

QUICK ROOT BEER

- 2 cups white sugar
- 1 gallon lukewarm water
- 4 teaspoons root beer extract
- 1 teaspoon dry yeast

Use some hot water to dissolve sugar. Mix all. Put in jars. Cover and set in sun for 4 hours. Chill before serving. Ready to serve the next day. No need to bottle.

From Amish Cooking, *published by Pathway Publishers Corporation*

RASPBERRY VINEGAR

- 4 quarts raspberries
- Vinegar
- Sugar

Put the raspberries in a crock and cover with vinegar. Let stand in a cool place for 24 hours. Heat to boiling point and strain. Add 1 cup sugar to each cup of juice. Boil 15 minutes and seal in sterile jars.

RHUBARB JUICE

- 10 cups chopped rhubarb
- 10 cups water
- 2 cups sugar

Boil rhubarb in the water until very soft. Strain. Stir sugar into strained juice and bring to a boil. Pour into hot sterilized jars and seal, or cool and freeze. Make punch, if desired, by adding 2 large bottles 7-Up, Sprite, or ginger ale and 1 large can (12 ounces) frozen orange juice, thawed.

SPICY BEVERAGE

- 2 quarts hot milk
- 1 cup Spiced Syrup (see ingredients below)
- ⅛ teaspoon salt

Spiced Syrup:
- 2 cups water
- 1½ tablespoons cloves
- ½ cup red cinnamon candies
- ½ cup sugar

To prepare the spiced syrup, combine ingredients in saucepan. Simmer 15 minutes, stirring occasionally. Strain and discard cloves. Use 2 tablespoons syrup to flavor 1 cup milk. To prepare the spicy beverage, mix hot milk, spiced syrup, and salt. Serve in mugs topped with marshmallows or whipped cream.

Makes 8 servings.

Mrs. Helen Schmidt
Marion, South Dakota
Minn-Kota MCC Relief Sale
Sioux Falls, South Dakota

Swiss Tea

- ½ cup green tea (preferably Tender Leaf tea)
- 2 sticks cinnamon, broken in pieces
- ½ teaspoon (or big pinch) saffron
- 1½ cups sugar (more or less to taste)

Add tea, cinnamon, and saffron to 1 quart boiling water. Simmer 15-20 minutes. Strain. Add enough hot water to make 1 gallon tea. Stir in the sugar until dissolved.

Ohio Relief Sale

Tomato Juice

- 11-quart basket tomatoes
- 1 stalk celery
- 3 onions
- ½ cup sugar
- 2 tablespoons salt
- 2 tablespoons vinegar

Cut tomatoes coarsely. Boil with celery and onions for 30 minutes and strain. Bring juice to a boil and add sugar, salt, and vinegar. Boil 5 minutes and seal.

Veranda Punch

- ½ cup water
- ½ cup sugar
- 1 cup tea
- 3 lemons
- 2 oranges
- 1 pint ginger ale
- 1 pint soda water
- Orange and lemon slices

Boil the sugar in the water for 5 minutes. Steep a cup of tea. Cool each. Squeeze the juice from the lemons and oranges. Mix all together. Add the ginger ale and soda water at serving time. Garnish the punch bowl with orange and lemon slices.

Try a dash of kindness with a pinch of love today. Top it off with a bit of cheerfulness and add a touch of goodwill. See how much better the day can be!

Appetizers and Dips

AMISH-STYLE DEVILED EGGS

- 12 eggs
- 2 tablespoons mayonnaise
- 1 heaping tablespoon yellow mustard
- 4 ounces chopped olives
- Dash salt and pepper

Bring a large pan of water to a boil, then turn off heat. Prick the end of the shell of each egg and drop gently into the hot water. Cover and let sit for 20 minutes. Pour out water. Rinse eggs in cold water. Peel. Halve eggs and remove yolks. Place in medium bowl and mash. Mix in mayonnaise, mustard, olives, salt, and pepper. Stuff eggs with mixture.

Brunetta Lloyd Martin
Houston Mennonite Church, Texas

WASH A STYROFOAM EGG CARTON AND USE IT
AS A CARRYING CASE FOR DEVILED EGGS.

APPLE DIP

- 8 ounces cream cheese, softened
- ¾ cup brown sugar
- ¼ cup granulated sugar
- 2 teaspoons vanilla

Mix all ingredients well to blend. Serve with raw apple slices.

Mrs. Kenneth (Christine) Folkers
Flanagan, Illinois
Salem Evangelical Mennonite Church
Gridley, Illinois
Illinois Mennonite Relief Sale, Peoria

'THE BEST YOU EVER HAD' DIP

- 2 packages (8 ounces each) cream cheese
- 4 tablespoons milk
- 1 cup sour cream
- 1 jar (15 ounces) chipped beef, shredded
- 2 tablespoons chopped onion
- 2 tablespoons chopped green pepper
- ½ cup chopped nuts
- ¼ teaspoon pepper

Mix cream cheese and milk. Stir in remaining ingredients. Place in small ovenproof casserole dish and bake at 350° for 15 minutes. Serve warm with crackers, chips, or vegetables.

Virginia Gindlesperger
Johnstown, Pennsylvania
MCC Quilt Auction and Relief Sale, Johnstown

CHEESE BALL

- 1 package (8 ounces) cream cheese
- 1 jar (5 ounces) Kraft Old English sharp processed cheese spread
- ½ teaspoon Worcestershire sauce
- ¼ teaspoon garlic salt
- ½ cup chopped English walnuts

Bring cheeses to room temperature. Mix until well combined. Stir in Worcestershire sauce and garlic salt. Form into a ball. Roll in chopped nuts.

Nila Kauffman
Pleasant View Mennonite Church
Goshen, Indiana

HAM BALLS

Ham Balls:
- 1-1½ pounds ground ham
- 1-1½ pounds ground beef
- 2 eggs, beaten
- 2 cups bread crumbs
- 1 cup milk
- Salt and pepper to taste

Sauce:
- 1½ cups brown sugar
- 1 tablespoon dry mustard
- ½ cup vinegar
- ½ cup water

Mix together ingredients for ham balls. Form into about 25 small balls. Place in a roaster. Mix together sauce ingredients. Pour over ham balls. Cover and bake at 350° for 2 hours.

BAKED HAM BALLS

Sauce:
- 6 cups brown sugar
- 6 teaspoons dry mustard
- 3 cups vinegar
- 3 cups water

Ham Balls:
- 6 pounds ham, ground
- 9 pounds pork, ground
- 12 eggs, beaten
- 6 cups milk
- 12 cups bread crumbs

Mix sauce ingredients together and heat to dissolve sugar. Mix ingredients for ham balls together well. Form into small balls. Place in baking pans. Pour sauce over top. Bake at 325° for 1½-2 hours or until done. Baste frequently.

Makes 80 ham balls.

Ham Dip

- 2 cups ground ham
- 1 package (8 ounces) cream cheese
- 1 cup sour cream
- ½ cup salad dressing
- 2 green onions, chopped, with tops
- ½ teaspoon seasoned salt
- 1 loaf French or round rye bread

Mix all ingredients (except bread). Refrigerate until ready to serve. Cut top third off bread. Hollow out loaf, leaving a shell about 1 inch thick. Cut up removed portion of bread into 1-inch cubes. Set aside. When ready to serve, toast bread shell at 400° for 3 minutes. Place ham dip in shell. Serve with reserved bread cubes and vegetable sticks. One package (10 ounces) frozen chopped spinach can be added if desired.

Ardith Epp
Henderson, Nebraska
Nebraska Mennonite Relief Sale, Aurora

Salad Dressing

Throughout this book, you might see "salad dressing" appear on the ingredients list. This term does not refer to French, Honey Dijon, or your own favorite salad dressing, but rather to Miracle Whip salad dressing or your favorite equivalent brand. Use this or mayonnaise when the ingredients list calls for salad dressing.

Vietnamese Spring Rolls

- 1 package (8 ounces) bean thread noodles
- 1 pound very lean coarsely-ground pork (preferably ground at home)
- 1 cup minced onion
- 1 cup finely shredded carrot
- 2 cups shredded jicama
- 1 teaspoon sugar
- 1 teaspoon monosodium glutamate (MSG)
- 1 tablespoon fish sauce
- ¼ teaspoon salt
- 1½ teaspoons coarse black pepper
- 4 dozen egg roll wrappers
- Oil for frying

Soak bean thread noodles in warm water for 30 minutes. Drain. Cut into 1-inch sections (you should have about 1½ cups) and place in a large bowl. Combine noodles with remaining ingredients (except egg roll wrappers and oil). Using both hands, mix filling until well blended. Set aside. Place egg roll wrappers on a smooth surface. Drop 1 heaping tablespoon of filling 1 inch from lower edge. Shape filling into a roll 3 inches wide. Fold bottom edge of wrapper over filling, roll once, then fold in both side edges. Finish rolling (loosely, because the filling will expand during cooking) to form a neat cylinder. Wrap rolls carefully, taking care not to tear the wrappers (holes let the filling drop out during cooking). Set finished rolls on a platter seam side down. Heat oil over medium-high heat in a large nonstick frying pan. Heat until oil is very hot, but not smoking (360°). Put a few rolls in the pan folded edge down so the rolls won't open during cooking. Leave a little space between rolls. Use tongs or long chopsticks to turn rolls occasionally and fry until light golden brown all over. Watch carefully so they don't overcook or get too brown. Line a large bowl with several layers of paper towels. Transfer cooked rolls to bowl. Lean upright against rim of bowl to drain.

Makes about 4 dozen.

Soups, Salads, and Dressings

BORSCHT

- 1 2-pound soup bone
- 2 quarts cold water
- 2 carrots, chopped (optional)
- 1 medium head cabbage, finely chopped
- 2 medium potatoes, cubed
- 1 medium onion, minced
- 1 teaspoon salt
- Half a star aniseed (optional)
- 1 small bay leaf
- 10 whole allspice
- 1½ tablespoons chopped parsley
- Bunch dill
- 1-1½ cups whole tomatoes
- Cream (optional)

Bring soup bone and water to a boil. Simmer briskly for at least 1½ hours. Add more water as it boils away to keep broth at 2 quarts. Add vegetables (except tomatoes) and seasonings. Cook until vegetables are done (20-30 minutes). Add tomatoes and bring just to a boil. If desired, add cream just before serving

Serves 6-8.

BORSCHT WITH POTATOES

- 50 pounds bones and meat (pork and beef)
- Water
- Fresh dill and parsley, tied in large bunches
- 12 pounds onions, chopped or sliced
- 1 bunch celery, chopped or sliced
- 5 pounds carrots, chopped or sliced
- 5 bell peppers (preferably red), cored, seeded, and chopped or sliced
- 3 cans (48 ounces each) tomato soup
- 100 ounces tomato juice
- 50 ounces (or less) ketchup
- 2 cups (or less) salt
- 2 tablespoons crushed chilies
- 25 pounds potatoes, chopped or sliced
- 22 pounds cabbage, chopped or sliced
- 100 ounces fresh tomatoes

Boil bones and meat in a 20-gallon cauldron with big bunches of dill and parsley for 3 hours. Remove everything from cauldron. Separate stock from meat and bones and discard herbs. Clean cauldron and return stock to it. Separate meat from bones. Cut up or shred into bite-size pieces. Reserve meat. Add onions, celery, carrots, peppers, and seasonings (tomato soup, juice, ketchup, salt, and chilies) to stock in cauldron. Cook until vegetables are partly done. Add potatoes, cabbage, then tomatoes. Return cut-up meat to cauldron when vegetables are tender. Cook until heated through.

Makes 20 gallons.

Anni Giesbrecht
Kelowna, British Columbia

Chicken Borscht

- 1 chicken
- 10 cups water
- 1½ teaspoons salt
- 3 cups diced potatoes
- 3 cups diced carrots
- ¾ cup onion
- 3 cups cooked tomatoes
- 6 cups shredded cabbage
- 6-10 peppercorns
- 3-4 bay leaves
- 4-6 whole allspice
- Chicken bouillon to taste

Cook chicken in salted water until tender. Remove skin and debone chicken. Cut up meat and set aside. Skim fat off broth. Add potatoes, carrots, and onion. Cook until almost tender. Add reserved chicken, tomatoes, and cabbage. Place peppercorns, bay leaves, and allspice in cheesecloth bag or spice holder and add to soup. Simmer until cabbage is tender. Remove spices. Add chicken bouillon to taste. Add more water to make a thinner soup. Add a few drops of vinegar to each portion after ladling it into the bowl for additional taste.

Serves 8-10.

Rocky Ford MCC Relief Sale

Bread Soup

- 1 tablespoon butter
- 2 slices bread, cut into
  ¾-inch squares
- Pinch of salt
- ½ cup (or more) boiling water
- ¼ cup cream

Melt butter and add bread cubes. After bread is browned, put in a dish and add salt, water, and cream.

TRIUMPH IS JUST A LITTLE "TRY" AND A LOT OF "UMPH."

ଔ

Broccoli-Cauliflower-Cheese Soup

- 3 chicken bouillon cubes
- 3 cups water
- ½ cup diced celery
- ½ cup diced green pepper
- ½ cup diced carrots
- ¼ cup diced onion
- 1 cup cauliflower, cut into flowerets
- 1 cup broccoli, cut up
- 6 cups milk
- ½ cup melted butter
- ½ cup flour
- 1 cup cubed Velveeta cheese

Dissolve bouillon cubes in water in soup kettle. Add celery, green pepper, carrots, and onion. Cook until partly tender. Add cauliflower and broccoli. Cook until all vegetables are tender. Add milk to soup. Heat, but do not boil. Blend together butter and flour in separate saucepan. Cook until frothy, but not browned. Remove from heat and blend with small amount of the soup broth to thin mixture. Add to soup kettle. Stir until well blended. Add cheese. Heat soup gently and stir to prevent sticking until cheese melts. Do not let soup boil.

Ruby Waltner
Marion, South Dakota
Minn-Kota MCC Relief Sale
Sioux Falls, South Dakota

Butter Soup with Angel Food Dumplings

- 1 onion
- Salt
- 2 bay leaves
- 4 small potatoes
- 4 pepper kernels

Dumplings:
- 1 cup all-purpose flour
- 2½ teaspoons baking powder
- ¼ teaspoon salt
- ⅓ cup milk
- 1 egg

Combine soup ingredients. Cover and cook for 1 hour. Sift dry ingredients for dumplings. Beat egg and add milk. Add to dry ingredients. Drop by spoon into boiling soup. Let rise until puffed (about 5 minutes). Cover and cook gently for about 15 minutes. Add cream and 1 teaspoon butter.

Cabbage Beef Soup

- ❖ 1 pound beef with bone
- ❖ 2 quarts water
- ❖ 2 tablespoons salt
- ❖ 2 parsley roots
- ❖ 2 bay leaves
- ❖ 1 teaspoon dill or dillweed
- ❖ 6 cups shredded cabbage
- ❖ 1 medium-large onion, chopped
- ❖ 2 cups sliced carrots
- ❖ 5 cups cubed potatoes
- ❖ 1 quart whole tomatoes
  or tomato soup

Cover beef with water. Add salt, parsley roots, bay leaves, and dill. Cook until meat is almost done. Add cabbage, onion, carrots, and potatoes. Add more water if necessary to cover vegetables. Simmer slowly until vegetables are almost tender. Add tomatoes and heat to boiling. Serve plain or with cream.

Serves 8.

Mary B. Duerksen
Mountain Lake, Minnesota
Minn-Kota MCC Relief Sale
Sioux Falls, South Dakota

Cabbage Cheese Soup

- ❖ 2 tablespoons butter
- ❖ 1 cup chopped onion
- ❖ 4 cups chopped cabbage
- ❖ 1 cup sliced celery
- ❖ 2 cups diced potatoes
- ❖ 1 can (13 ounces) chicken broth
- ❖ 1 teaspoon salt
- ❖ ¼ cup butter
- ❖ ¼ cup flour
- ❖ ¼ teaspoon paprika
- ❖ ¼ teaspoon pepper
- ❖ 4 cups milk
- ❖ 1½ cups shredded cheddar cheese
- ❖ Dash dillweed

Melt 2 tablespoons butter in large saucepan. Add onion and sauté until soft. Add cabbage, celery, potatoes, chicken broth, and salt. Cover and bring to a boil. Reduce heat and simmer until vegetables are tender (about 20 minutes). Melt ¼ cup butter in a 4-quart saucepan. Blend in flour, paprika, and pepper. Remove from heat and stir in milk. Heat to boiling, stirring. Boil 1 minute. Remove from heat and add cheese, stirring until it melts. Add vegetables and their liquid to cheese mixture. Return soup to stove and warm over low heat. Sprinkle dillweed over top before serving.

Makes 10-12 cups.

Lena Sala
Hollsopple, Pennsylvania
MCC Quilt Auction and Relief Sale
Johnstown, Pennsylvania

CHICKEN CORN SOUP

- 1 6-pound stewing chicken
- 1 pound extra-fine noodles
- 3 packages (10 ounces each) frozen corn
- 1 medium onion, chopped
- 1 tablespoon chopped parsley
- Pinch saffron
- 2 teaspoons Accent seasoning
- ½ teaspoon black pepper
- Salt to taste
- 4 hard-boiled eggs, chopped

Cook chicken in enough water to cover until tender. Remove meat from bones, chop, and return to broth. Add remaining ingredients (except eggs) with more water if needed. Bring to a boil. Reduce heat to low and cook 45 minutes. Watch carefully so that soup does not scorch. Remove from heat. Stir in chopped eggs and serve. To store, let cool uncovered in a cool place for about 1 hour. Cover and refrigerate. Keep very cold.

Makes 10 quarts.

Rhoda Petersheim
Contributed by Irene Zimmerman
Pennsylvania Relief Sale, Harrisburg

CHICKEN NOODLE SOUP

- Chicken
- Cinnamon
- Parsley
- Bay leaves
- Whole ginger
- Onion

Cut chicken in serving pieces. Cover with cold water in fairly large pot. Simmer for 3 hours. Add spices and onion. Continue to simmer for another 30 minutes. Cook noodles in this broth.

CHILI

- 12 ½ pounds ground beef
- 1 gallon cooked beans (chili, kidney, or a mixture)
- 2 gallons tomato juice
- Brown sugar
- Chili powder
- Minced onion
- Salt and pepper to taste

Brown ground beef. Place in large electric roaster along with remaining ingredients.

Fay Kliewer
Nebraska MCC Relief Sale, Aurora

FAMILY-STYLE CHILI

- 1½-2 pounds ground beef
- Salt to taste
- 1 can kidney beans
- 1 can tomato soup
- 2 cups water
- 1 pint homemade
  chili sauce (recipe below)
- Chili powder to taste

Brown ground beef and add salt to taste. Add beans, soup, water, chili sauce, and chili powder. Simmer 20 minutes. Serve with crackers.

Serves 10.

Vivian Gering
Freeman, South Dakota
Minn-Kota MCC Relief Sale
Sioux Falls, South Dakota

SAUCE FOR MAKING CHILI

- 1½ cups chopped onions
- 1 cup chopped green peppers
- 1½ cups chopped celery or
  1½ teaspoons celery seed
- 6 quarts chopped tomatoes
- ⅓ cup vinegar
- ⅓ cup sugar or honey
- 1 tablespoon salt
- 1 quart water
- 1 tablespoon whole allspice
- 1 tablespoon whole cloves
- 1 2-inch cinnamon stick
- 2 bay leaves
- 1 teaspoon ginger
- 1 teaspoon chili powder
- 1 clove garlic, chopped

Combine onions, green peppers, celery, tomatoes, vinegar, sugar, salt, and water in a large kettle. Tie spices in a cheesecloth bag and add to kettle. Bring vegetables to a boil. Reduce heat and simmer slowly for about 1½ hours. Remove spice bag. Ladle into hot sterilized pint jars and seal.

Makes about 6 pints.

Vivian Gering
Freeman, South Dakota
Minn-Kota MCC Relief Sale
Sioux Falls, South Dakota

CHINESE SOUP

- 1 package Lipton's
  Chicken Noodle Soup
- ½ cup frozen peas
- 1 cup mushrooms
- 1 egg, well beaten

Prepare the soup as directed on package. Add the peas and mushrooms. Drizzle the egg into the soup. Garnish with sliced green onion tops if desired.

℃℞

CORN CHOWDER

- ❖ 5 slices bacon
- ❖ 1 medium onion, chopped
- ❖ 2 diced potatoes
- ❖ ½ cup water
- ❖ 1-2 cups corn
- ❖ 2 cups milk
- ❖ 1 teaspoon salt
- ❖ Dash of pepper

Brown bacon and onion in a large skillet. Add potatoes and water and cook until potatoes are tender. Add remaining ingredients, heat, and serve.

Betty Hartzler
Belleville, Pennsylvania

CREAM OF BEAN SOUP

- ❖ 2 cups yellow beans, soaked overnight
- ❖ 1 quart rich milk
- ❖ Salt to taste
- ❖ ½ cup celery
- ❖ ½ cup grated carrot
- ❖ ¼ cup finely minced onion
- ❖ 2 slices lean side bacon

Cook yellow beans slowly until very soft and mushy. Put through fruit press. Add milk and salt to taste. Fry the vegetables and bacon until the vegetables are tender, but not soft. Add to beans and milk. Heat to scalding point and serve with toasted bread cubes or crackers.

GARLIC

Garlic is not only a vegetable, but is also very good for medicinal uses. It aids digestion, relieves dyspepsia and colic, and acts as an intestinal antiseptic and blood purifier. It destroys round and thread worms. It is a good nerve tonic and is very beneficial as a treatment for colds and coughs. It is also very rich in vitamins and minerals.

Dutch Potato Soup

- 2 cups diced potatoes
- ½ cup diced onion (optional)
- 3 cups water
- 1 teaspoon salt
- 1 cup chopped celery
- ½ cup grated carrot
- 1 quart milk
- 2 tablespoons butter
- 3 hard-boiled eggs, chopped
- 1 tablespoon chopped fresh parsley

Bring potatoes, onion, water, and salt to a boil. Simmer briefly. Add celery and carrot when potatoes are partially cooked. Heat milk in separate saucepan. Add to soup mixture when potatoes are soft. Stir in butter, eggs, and parsley just before serving.

Irene Zimmerman
Brownstown, Pennsylvania

THIS RECIPE SERVES FOUR—OR TWO IF THE DINERS ARE FARMERS!

Grene Schauble Suppe (Green Bean Soup)

- 6-7 quarts chunked potatoes
- 7-8 quarts green beans (fresh or frozen)
- 7 cups chopped onions
- 1 quart sliced (or grated) carrots
- 5 teaspoons salt
- Clump of summer savory 1 inch thick and 4 inches long, wrapped and tied in cloth
- 6 pounds boneless ham, cut in ½-inch cubes
- 5 cups sour cream

Cover potatoes, beans, onions, carrots, salt, and savory with water. Bring to a boil. Add cubed ham and reduce heat to a simmer. Cook until vegetables are tender. Ladle several cups of the hot broth into the sour cream. Mix well. Stir sour cream mixture into soup. (This process keeps sour cream from curdling.) Remove from heat.

Makes 5 gallons.

THE FIRST GREEN BEANS OF THE SUMMER ALWAYS GO INTO A SOUP.
SERVE THIS SOUP WITH FRESH BREAD FOR A WHOLESOME MEAL.

ॐ

GREEN BEAN SOUP

- 1½-2 pounds ham bones and meat
- 4-5 sprigs summer savory
- 2 cups diced potatoes
- 4 cups cut green beans
- 1 teaspoon salt
- 2 tablespoons ham base
- 2 cups sour cream

Place ham bones and summer savory in cooking pot. Cover with water and cook about 2 hours. Remove ham from bones. Chop meat and return to pot. Add potatoes, beans, salt, and ham base. Cook until vegetables are tender. Stir in sour cream just before serving.

Serves 8.

Ardith Epp
Henderson, Nebraska
Nebraska MCC Relief Sale, Aurora

HAM AND BEAN SOUP

- 4 pounds large navy beans
- 4 pounds picnic ham, chopped fine
- 1 onion, minced
- 4 stalks celery, chopped
- 2 carrots sliced on cabbage cutter
- Salt, pepper, onion salt, and garlic salt to taste

Soak beans overnight. Add remaining ingredients and enough water to make 10 quarts of soup. Bring to a boil. Reduce heat and simmer until beans are soft (about 2 hours).

Makes about 10 quarts.

Sadie Weaver

MEATBALL SOUP

- 1 medium onion, sliced
- 2 stalks celery, sliced
- 1 grated carrot
- 4 potatoes, peeled and cubed
- 1 bay leaf
- Salt and pepper
- 2½ quarts water
- ½ cup sour cream

Meatballs:
- 1 pound ground beef
- 1 egg
- 1 small onion, chopped
- 1 small potato, grated
- Salt, pepper, and chopped parsley

Cook vegetables, bay leaf, and seasonings in water in large stock pot. Cook until vegetables just begin to get tender. Mix ingredients for meatballs. Form into balls and drop into soup. Continue boiling for 20 minutes. Reduce heat to a simmer. Remove from heat and stir in sour cream when ready to serve.

Susana Siemens
Winnipeg, Manitoba
MCC Manitoba Relief Sale

MENNONITE BEAN SOUP

- ❖ 2 cups assorted dried beans
- ❖ 1¾ quarts water
- ❖ 1 ham bone
- ❖ 1 onion, chopped
- ❖ 3 stalks celery, chopped
- ❖ 3 carrots, chopped
- ❖ 4 cups canned tomatoes
- ❖ Salt and pepper to taste

In the evening, soak beans in water. Transfer to a crockpot before bedtime. Turn pot on low. Next morning, add remaining ingredients to pot. Warm through and serve.

Relief Sale Recipe
Houston Mennonite Church, Texas

MRS. EICHELBERGER'S HAMBURGER VEGETABLE SOUP

- ❖ 3 cups water
- ❖ 4 beef bouillon cubes
- ❖ 3 peeled carrots, chopped
- ❖ 2 medium potatoes, chopped
- ❖ 1 cup chopped celery
- ❖ 2 medium onions, chopped
- ❖ ½ cup chopped green pepper
- ❖ 1 pound ground beef
- ❖ 1 teaspoon Kitchen Bouquet
- ❖ 1 teaspoon salt
- ❖ ½ teaspoon pepper
- ❖ 1 bay leaf
- ❖ ⅛ teaspoon dried basil leaves
- ❖ 1 can (16 ounces) stewed tomatoes
  (or substitute tomato juice)

Bring water and bouillon cubes to a simmer. Stir to dissolve cubes. Add carrots, potatoes, celery, onions, and green pepper to broth. Simmer. Brown ground beef and drain off any fat. Add browned meat and remaining ingredients to soup pot. Cover and simmer until vegetables are tender.

Makes 6 generous servings.

Mrs. Roger (Lavonne) McGuire
Morton, Illinois
First Mennonite Church, Morton
Illinois MCC Relief Sale, Peoria

OYSTER SOUP

- ❖ 1½ cups milk
- ❖ 3 or 4 oysters
- ❖ Salt, pepper, and butter to taste

For each bowl of soup, heat 1½ cups milk. When hot, add 3-4 oysters (or more) to each bowl. Season with the salt, pepper, and butter. Heat until oysters are hot and curl a bit.

☘

PLUMA MOOS

- 1½ cups dried prunes
- 1½ cups dried apricots
- 1½ cups raisins
- 1 cinnamon stick 1-1½ inches long
- 4 quarts water
- 1 cup sugar (or less)
- ¼-½ cup flour
- ½ cup cream
- ¾ cup milk

Soak dried fruits and cinnamon stick overnight in the water. The next morning, cook fruit in soaking water until soft (simmering 30 minutes to 1 hour). Mix together sugar, flour, cream, and milk to form a paste. Very slowly add to the hot fruit. Simmer 10 minutes more or until thickened. (Mixture will thicken more as it cools.) Cool. If you do not want a creamy moos, substitute same amount of water for the cream and milk.

Makes 1 gallon.

Cleo Friesen
Mountain Lake, Minnesota

PLUMAMOUSSE

- 1 cup dried prunes
- ¾ cup raisins
- 3 heaping tablespoons flour
- ½ cup sugar
- ¾ cup cream or canned milk
- 2 cups milk
- ½ teaspoon cinnamon (optional)
- 1 tablespoon vinegar (optional)

Cook prunes in 3 cups of water until well done. Mash the prunes. Add raisins and 2 more cups of water. Cook a little longer. Mix flour and sugar together. Blend in cream. Stir the paste into hot fruit mixture. Add milk and bring to a boil. Add cinnamon and vinegar.

Makes about half a gallon.

Mrs. G. B. Huebert
Submitted by Kathy Heinrichs Wiest
Kingsburg, California

PLUMI MOOS

- 3 cups chopped and mixed dried fruits
- 4 quarts water
- 1½ cups sugar
- 4 tablespoons cornstarch
- 1 package cherry-flavored gelatin

Cook fruit in the water until very tender. Mix sugar with cornstarch. Stir in enough water to make a thin paste. Add paste to hot fruit mixture. Cook a few minutes to take away starchy taste. Remove from heat. Stir in cherry-flavored gelatin.

Makes 1 gallon.

Hilda Patkua
Clavet, Saskatchewan

Cherry Moos

- 1 quart pitted sour cherries and juice
- 1 quart water
- 6 tablespoons flour
- 1½-2 cups sugar
- 1 cup sweet cream
- 1 quart milk

Bring cherries, their juice, and the water to a boil in a 5-6 quart saucepan. Make a paste of the flour, sugar, cream, and milk. Stir in paste when cherries are boiling. Bring to a boil again. Cook until mixture thickens. Stir and watch carefully to prevent burning. Serve hot or cold.

Makes 1 gallon.

Cleo Friesen
Mountain Lake, Minnesota

Smoked Sausage Potato Soup

- 4 large potatoes, peeled
- 1 pound smoked sausage
- 1 tablespoon onion, finely chopped (optional)
- ¼ teaspoon salt
- Milk
- Parsley

Cut sausage in ¼-inch pieces. Place in 3-quart pan with 2 inches water. Cube potatoes. Add to pan with sausage. Add onion and ¼ teaspoon salt. Cover and bring to boil. Cook over medium heat, stirring frequently to prevent sticking and burning bottom of pan. Cook 20-30 minutes until potatoes are soft. Cover with milk. Add a few sprinkles of dried or freshly chopped parsley if desired. Cover and let stand 5 minutes. It should be very thick.

Serves 4-6.

ONLY HE WHO ATTEMPTS THE RIDICULOUS
CAN ACHIEVE THE IMPOSSIBLE.

VEGETABLE SOUP

- 4 pounds beef
- 25 quarts tomato juice
- 1 pound barley
- 30 pounds potatoes
- 14 pounds baby lima beans
- 14 pounds peas
- 14 pounds carrots
- 6-8 quarts green beans
- 8 medium heads cabbage
- 30 large onions
- 6 bunches celery
- 12 pounds corn
- 2¼ cups salt
- 2¼ cups sugar

Cook beef in plenty of water until tender. Remove from broth and cut into small pieces. Set aside. Add tomato juice and barley to beef broth. Cook until barley just begins to get tender. Clean all vegetables and cut into small pieces. Add to soup pot along with salt and sugar. Cook until vegetables are tender.

Makes about 30 gallons.

Kathryn L. Suter
Virginia Relief Sale, Fisherville

WILD RICE SOUP WITH CHICKEN DUMPLINGS

- 1 cup wild rice
- ¼ cup butter
- 2 cups finely diced carrots
- 2 cups finely diced celery
- 1 large onion, finely diced
- ⅓ cup oil
- ½ cup flour
- 3 cups cream or whole milk
- 5 cups chicken stock
- Salt and pepper to taste

Dumplings:
- 1 cup ground chicken pieces
- 1-2 eggs
- Salt and pepper

Precook the wild rice (it will take about an hour). Set aside. Melt butter in a heavy frying pan. Add carrots, celery, and onion. Sauté. Set aside. Make a white sauce with the oil, flour, and cream in a large stock pot. Add the chicken stock. Whisk until smooth. Add sautéed vegetables. Cook until vegetables are tender (about 15 minutes). Stir soup and watch it carefully so it doesn't burn. Season to taste. Add reserved wild rice and simmer a few minutes more. Make dumpling mixture by using a blender to blend chicken until very fine. Add eggs and seasonings. Drop dumpling mixture by teaspoons into the soup shortly before serving. Simmer a few minutes until dumplings cook through.

Contributed by Susana Siemens
Winnipeg, Manitoba
MCC Manitoba Relief Sale

Wiener Potato Soup

- 1 cup chopped onion
- 3 cups potatoes, peeled and diced
- 3 cups boiling water
- 4 chicken bouillon cubes
- 3 tablespoons butter
- 1 cup milk
- 1 cup light cream
- 1 teaspoon salt
- ¼ teaspoon pepper
- ½ pound wieners

Cook the onion and potatoes in the boiling water. Cook until very tender. (Put them through a sieve if you like.) Add the vegetables (including the water in which they were cooked) to a mixture of the bouillon cubes, butter, milk, cream, salt, and pepper. Stir well and heat to almost boiling. Cut the wieners into thin slices and add a generous spoonful to each bowl of soup.

Serves 6.

Zucchini Soup

- 2 tablespoons chopped shallots or onions
- 1 clove garlic, minced
- 2 tablespoons butter
- 1 teaspoon curry powder
- 1 pound cleaned unpeeled zucchini, chopped
- 1¾ cups chicken broth (or water plus 3 chicken bouillon cubes)
- ½ cup coffee cream
- ½ teaspoon salt (optional)

Sauté shallots and garlic in butter in heavy saucepan until soft, but not browned. Add curry powder, zucchini, and broth. Cook 10-20 minutes, stirring to keep from burning. Transfer soup to blender when zucchini is tender. Blend. (Divide soup into small batches to fit in blender if necessary). Stir in cream. Taste and add salt if desired. Serve hot with croutons or cold with chives.

Serves 2-4.

Cleva Waltner
Freeman, South Dakota
Minn-Kota MCC Relief Sale
Sioux Falls, South Dakota

APPLE SALAD

- ❖ Apples
- ❖ 1 beaten egg
- ❖ 1 tablespoon flour
- ❖ 1 teaspoon vinegar
- ❖ ½ cup water
- ❖ ½ cup sugar
- ❖ 1 tablespoon butter
- ❖ Pinch of salt
- ❖ Sliced bananas, nuts, and marshmallows (optional)

Boil all ingredients together until thickened. Cool, and add 1 cup whipped topping. Pour over apples that have been chopped and sugared. Add sliced bananas, nuts, and marshmallows as desired. Do not prepare far in advance as apples will become brown and mushy.

R. Beiler
Quarryville, Pennsylvania

TASTY APPLE SALAD

- ❖ 2 cups diced apples
- ❖ Orange or pineapple juice (enough to cover apples)
- ❖ 2 cups diced celery
- ❖ 2 cups diced carrots
- ❖ 2 cups raisins
- ❖ 1 cup unsalted dry-roasted peanuts (broken into halves)
- ❖ 1 cup unsalted sunflower seeds
- ❖ Yogurt (plain or vanilla-flavored)

Dice apples directly into enough fruit juice to cover them. Let sit while dicing, measuring, and preparing remaining salad ingredients. Drain juice from apples. Combine with remaining ingredients, using enough yogurt to form a dressing.

Mianna Geissinger
Mountain Lake, Minnesota
Minn-Kota MCC Relief Sale
Sioux Falls, South Dakota

BROCCOLI DELIGHT SALAD

- ❖ 1 large bunch fresh broccoli, cut into pieces (4-5 cups)
- ❖ 1 cup raisins
- ❖ ¼ cup diced red onion (optional)
- ❖ 10 strips bacon, fried and crumbled
- ❖ 1 cup sunflower seeds

Dressing:
- ❖ 3-4 tablespoons sugar
- ❖ ½ cup light mayonnaise
- ❖ 1 tablespoon vinegar

Put washed and drained broccoli in large glass bowl. Add raisins, onion, bacon, and sunflower seeds. Mix dressing ingredients. Pour over salad. Chill before serving if desired.

Serves 6.

Tillie Janzen
Mountain Lake, Minnesota
Minn-Kota MCC Relief Sale
Sioux Falls, South Dakota

Cabbage Salad

- 1 onion, finely chopped
- 1 small head cabbage, shredded
- 1 cup sugar
- 1 teaspoon salt
- ½ cup vinegar
- ⅜ cup oil, or less to taste
- 1 teaspoon celery seed
- 1 teaspoon prepared mustard
- ⅛-¼ teaspoon turmeric

Combine the onion and cabbage. Add sugar and salt. Mix. Heat the vinegar to boiling point. Add the oil, celery seed, mustard, and turmeric. Add all to shredded cabbage. Add green and red pepper or shredded carrots for color. Store 3-4 hours before serving.

California Salad

- 1 cup sour cream
- 1 cup marshmallows
- 1 cup crushed pineapple, drained
- 1 cup shredded coconut
- 1 can mandarin orange segments

Mix together and let set a few hours. Half a cup of green and red seedless grapes may be added.

Chicken Salad

- 2 cups cooked chicken, cubed
- 1 cup pineapple tidbits
- 1 cup orange sections
- 1 cup chopped celery
- 2 tablespoons orange juice
- 1 teaspoon marjoram
- ½ teaspoon salt
- 1 teaspoon vinegar
- ¼ cup mayonnaise

Mix all ingredients (except mayonnaise) and put in refrigerator for 1 hour before serving. Add mayonnaise and mix.

CHICKEN/TURKEY SALAD

- ❖ 3 cups chopped cooked chicken or turkey
- ❖ 2 cups ring macaroni, cooked
- ❖ 2 cups frozen peas, cooked and cooled
- ❖ ¼ cup sliced almonds
- ❖ ¼ cup sliced stuffed olives
- ❖ ¼ cup chopped sweet pickles
- ❖ 1 cup finely chopped celery
- ❖ ¼ cup ground onion
- ❖ 2 hard-cooked eggs, chopped
- ❖ ½-¾ teaspoon salt
- ❖ ¼ teaspoon pepper
- ❖ 2 cups canned shoestring potatoes

Dressing:
- ❖ 2-3 cups salad dressing
- ❖ ½ cup sour cream

Combine all ingredients except shoestring potatoes and dressing. Mix well. Mix salad dressing and sour cream when ready to serve. Combine with salad ingredients. Stir in shoestring potatoes immediately before serving.

Serves 12-16.

Rita Ann Graber
Freeman, South Dakota
Minn-Kota MCC Relief Sale
Sioux Falls, South Dakota

COLE SLAW

- ❖ 2 gallons shredded cabbage
- ❖ 1 quart shredded carrots
- ❖ 1 cup diced green pepper

Relief Sale Salad Dressing:
- ❖ 2½ cups sugar
- ❖ 1½ cups vinegar
- ❖ 4 teaspoons dry mustard
- ❖ 4 teaspoons salt
- ❖ 1 cup salad oil
- ❖ 4 teaspoons grated onion
- ❖ 1 tablespoon celery seed

Combine the vegetables in a large bowl and mix well. To prepare dressing, dissolve sugar in vinegar and add remaining ingredients. Mix well by hand or in a blender. Pour dressing over vegetables. Toss to mix thoroughly. Refrigerate until ready to serve.

Makes 70 servings (4 cups dressing).

Sherry Troyer
Mio, Michigan

CREAMY CABBAGE SLAW

- 2 hard-boiled eggs, diced
- ¼ cup finely grated carrots
- 3 cups shredded cabbage

Dressing:
- 1 cup Miracle Whip
- ¼ cup half-and-half
- 1 tablespoon sugar
- 2 tablespoons vinegar
- ½ teaspoon salt
- ¼ teaspoon pepper

Mix dressing ingredients and refrigerate overnight. Just before serving, add to cabbage, carrots, and eggs.

CREAMY COLE SLAW DRESSING

- 1 cup mayonnaise
- 1 cup cream (sweet or sour)
- ½ cup sugar
- ½ cup vinegar
- Salt to taste

Mix all ingredients together well. Recipe makes enough dressing for 1 medium head cabbage.

Adella (Stutzman) Gingrich
Albany, Oregon

CORNBREAD SALAD

- 1 large onion, diced
- 4 tomatoes, diced
- 1 green pepper, diced
- 4-5 stalks celery, diced
- 2 cups cauliflower
  (broken into small pieces)
- 1 cup mayonnaise
- 1 tablespoon sugar
- 1 tablespoon sweet pickle relish
- 1 box Jiffy cornbread mix,
  baked the day before

Toss vegetables in a large bowl. Combine mayonnaise, sugar, and relish. Stir into vegetables. Cut cornbread into bite-size pieces and add to salad before serving.

Joan Belsley
Morton, Illinois
Bethel Mennonite Church, Pekin
Illinois Mennonite Relief Sale, Peoria

CRANBERRY FRUIT MEDLEY

- 2 cups fresh cranberries
- 2 medium-large apples, cored, but not peeled
- 2 medium-large bananas
- ¾ cup granulated sugar

Coarsely chop cranberries and apples. Dice bananas and add to cranberry-apple mixture along with sugar. Stir well. Cover tightly and place in refrigerator for at least 3 hours or overnight to blend flavors. Add 2 cups miniature marshmallows with the fruit and stir in 1 cup whipped topping if desired.

Makes 6 servings.

Faye Claassen
Albany, Oregon
Oregon MCC Fall Festival, Albany

CRANBERRY SALAD

- 1 package cranberries (1 pound)
- 4 apples
- 2 oranges or ½ cup crushed pineapple
- 2 cups sugar
- 3 packages raspberry gelatin
- 3 cups hot water
- 3 cups cold water
- ½ cup nuts

Wash and grind cranberries in food chopper. Pare and core apples and chop or grind. Add chopped oranges, nuts, and sugar. Dissolve gelatin in hot water. Add cold water. When cool and beginning to congeal, add salad mixture.

CREAMY WALDORF SALAD

- 2 packages (3 ounces each) lemon-flavored gelatin
- 2 cups boiling water
- 1 cup cold water
- 1 package (3½ ounces) instant vanilla pudding mix
- 2 cups milk
- 1 cup diced apples
- ½ cup chopped celery
- ½ cup chopped nuts

Prepare lemon-flavored gelatin using the boiling and cold water. Set aside until partly set. Prepare pudding mix using the milk. Cool. Mix gelatin and pudding together. Add apples, celery, and nuts. Chill well before serving.

Amy Cable
Hollsopple, Pennsylvania
MCC Quilt Auction and Relief Sale, Johnstown

CREAM CHEESE SALAD

- 1 3-ounce package lime gelatin
- 2 cups boiling water
- 2 cups pineapple, drained
- 1 tablespoon unflavored gelatin
- ½ cup cold water
- 1 cup pineapple juice
- 6 ounces cream cheese
- 1 cup whipped cream
- 1 package red gelatin
- 1 ¾ cups boiling water

Dissolve the lime gelatin in 2 cups boiling water. Cool until syrupy. Add the pineapple. Pour into 2-quart mold. Set in refrigerator until firm. Dissolve unflavored gelatin in cold water. Heat pineapple juice. Add the gelatin and stir until dissolved. Remove from heat and cool. Mash up cream cheese and blend into the juice with beater. Stir in whipped cream. Pour this on top of lime gelatin and let set until firm. Dissolve red gelatin in 1 ¾ cups boiling water. Cool well and pour over firm cheese layer. Set until all is firm. Serve on glass plate and decorate with whipped cream and mayonnaise. Sprinkle with grated coconut, nuts, or grated cheese if desired.

EMMA'S BEAN SALAD

- ½-1 cup sugar
- ½ cup lemon juice
- 1 small can kidney beans, drained
- 1 small can lima beans, drained
- 1 small can yellow beans, drained
- 1 small can green beans, drained
- 1½ cups chopped onion
- ½ cup chopped celery
- ½ cup chopped green pepper

Bring sugar and lemon juice to a boil. Remove from heat and cool slightly. Mix together remaining ingredients. Pour dressing over top. Toss well to coat all ingredients with dressing. Refrigerate overnight or longer.

Sally Ann Reddecliff
Johnstown, Pennsylvania
MCC Quilt Auction and Relief Sale, Johnstown

REMEMBER THE STEAM KETTLE—ALTHOUGH UP TO
ITS NECK IN HOT WATER, IT CONTINUES TO SING.

Far East Fruit Plate

- 1 20-ounce can pineapple chunks
- 1 11-ounce can mandarin oranges, drained
- 2 large bananas, sliced
- ½ cup chopped dates
- 2 tablespoons vinegar
- ¼ cup salad oil
- 1 teaspoon curry powder
- ¼ teaspoon salt
- 2 pounds cottage cheese
- ½ cup chopped salted peanuts or almonds
- Crisp salad greens

Drain pineapple, reserving ½ cup syrup. Combine pineapple and next 3 ingredients in large bowl. Combine reserved syrup with next 4 ingredients in jar. Cover and shake well. Pour over fruit and marinate 30 minutes. Arrange greens in bowl. Spoon cheese onto greens and top with fruit mixture. Sprinkle with peanuts.

Serves 6.

Festive Party Salad

- 6 ounces lime gelatin
- 2 cups boiling water
- 2 cups cold water
- 1 teaspoon unflavored gelatin
- 1 11-ounce can mandarin oranges
- 1 4-ounce package white cream cheese, room temperature
- ¼ cup chopped walnuts or pecans
- 1 cup finely chopped inner celery stalks

In a medium-sized bowl, soak the unflavored gelatin in ¼ cup cold water for 5 minutes. Add the lime gelatin and boiling water. Stir well. Add the remaining 1¾ cups cold water. Stir and chill until partially set. Cream the cheese in a small bowl. Shape into small balls and roll in nuts. Fold the balls, drained orange sections, and celery into the gelatin. Turn into a mold. Chill until set.

THE TIME TO MAKE FRIENDS IS BEFORE YOU NEED THEM.

Frozen Fruit Salad

- 1 8-ounce package softened cream cheese
- ¾ cup sugar
- 1 pint frozen strawberries
- 1½ cup grapes
- 1 cup blueberries
- 11 ounces mandarin oranges, drained
- 8 ounces pineapple, crushed and drained
- 1 8-ounce container Cool Whip or non-dairy whipped topping

Blend cream cheese and sugar. Fold in Cool Whip, then fruit. Pour into an 8x8-inch square pan. Freeze. Remove 1 hour before serving. Cut into squares of desired size. Add marshmallows or nuts if desired.

Eileen D. Wenger
Leola, Pennsylvania

Fruit Salad with Sweet Dressing

- 1½ pounds pink grapes
- 1 large can pineapple rings
- 3 oranges
- 3 apples

Dressing:
- 1 tablespoon flour
- ½ cup sugar
- 1 cup scalded milk
- 1 egg, well beaten
- 1 tablespoon butter
- ½ pint whipping cream, whipped

Halve and seed grapes. Dice pineapple. Peel and dice oranges and apples. Combine fruits and set aside. Prepare dressing by combining flour and sugar. Add scalded milk and bring to a slow boil. Stir in beaten egg and butter. Cool. Fold in whipped cream. Pour dressing over drained fruit mixture just before serving. Toss gently to mix.

Ruth Beckley Felix
MCC Quilt Auction and Relief Sale
Johnstown, Pennsylvania

Fruited Cheese Salad

- 3 cups creamed style cottage cheese
- 1 quart frozen whipped topping, thawed
- 1 3-ounce package each of orange and pineapple gelatin
- 1 can pineapple tidbits, drained
- 1 small can mandarin oranges, drained

In mixer, blend cottage cheese and whipped topping. Stir in dry gelatin. Fold in pineapple tidbits and oranges and put in mold. Chill several hours.

Serves 12.

ം

GELATIN SALAD

- ❖ 1 package lemon gelatin
- ❖ 1 teaspoon sugar
- ❖ 1 cup boiling water
- ❖ 1 cup milk
- ❖ 1 cup mini-marshmallows
- ❖ 2 tablespoons salad dressing
- ❖ 1 can fruit cocktail, well drained

Mix gelatin, sugar, and boiling water. Let stand until cooled, but not jelled. Add milk, marshmallows, and salad dressing. Let stand until starting to set. Add fruit cocktail. Stir in gelatin and let set.

HORSERADISH SALAD

- ❖ 2 scant cups beets, shredded
- ❖ 2 cups liquid from beets and water
- ❖ 1 package gelatin
- ❖ 5 tablespoons white sugar
- ❖ 1¼ teaspoons salt
- ❖ 1 tablespoon horseradish
- ❖ 1 tablespoon lemon juice

Mix all ingredients and serve in a bowl.

HOT MUSHROOM SALAD

- ❖ 1 tablespoon melted butter
- ❖ 1 pound fresh mushrooms, sliced
- ❖ 1 small onion, thinly sliced
- ❖ 1 green pepper, cut in thin strips
- ❖ 1-1½ tablespoons soy sauce
- ❖ 1-1½ tablespoons teriyaki sauce
- ❖ Lettuce
- ❖ 3 slices bacon, cooked and crumbled

Combine all ingredients (except lettuce and bacon) in skillet or wok. Cook, stirring frequently, until mushrooms and onions are tender. Spoon onto lettuce and garnish with bacon. Serve immediately.

Serves 4.

Bev Kennell
Roanoke, Illinois
Cazenovia Mennonite Church

Hot Potato Salad

- 4 cups hot diced potatoes
- 1 cup chopped celery
- 1 teaspoon chopped parsley
- 1 onion, chopped
- ½ teaspoon pepper
- 2 tablespoons salad oil or lard
- 1½ teaspoons salt
- 1 tablespoon flour
- ⅓ cup vinegar
- ⅓ cup sugar
- ⅔ cup water

Fry chopped onion in hot lard until light brown. Add flour and blend. Add salt, sugar, vinegar, and water. Bring to a boil, stirring constantly. Pour dressing over the potatoes. Mix in celery and parsley. Sprinkle with pepper and paprika and serve hot.

Serves 6.

Hot Slaw

- 1 cup finely diced celery
- 1 medium head cabbage, shredded
- 3 tablespoons solid vegetable shortening or margarine
- Dash salt
- 2 teaspoons flour
- 1 tablespoon sugar
- 1 tablespoon vinegar
- 2 tablespoons sour cream

Cook celery in a little water in a small saucepan. Place cabbage in a large skillet. Pour celery and water over top. Add shortening and salt. Cover and steam 10 minutes. Sprinkle flour over top. Stir to mix well with cabbage. Also stir in sugar and vinegar. Add a bit more flour if sauce is too thin. Stir in sour cream. Cook 2 minutes.

Mary Kaufman
Johnstown, Pennsylvania
MCC Quilt Auction and Relief Sale, Johnstown

Lemon-Lime Gelatin Salad

- 1 package lemon gelatin
- 1 package lime gelatin
- 2 cups boiling water
- 2 cups cold water
- 20 ounces crushed pineapple
- 2 cups mini-marshmallows
- 2-3 bananas, sliced
- 2 ounces slivered almonds (optional)

Dissolve gelatin in boiling water. Stir in cold water. Chill partially. Drain pineapple, reserving juice for another use. Fold pineapple, sliced bananas, marshmallows, and almonds into gelatin. Pour into 7x12-inch pan. Chill until firm. Orange gelatin may be used as a substitute.

CB

SOUPS, SALADS, AND DRESSINGS

Marinated Carrot Salad

- 1 pound carrots, diagonally sliced
- 1 medium onion, thinly sliced
- 1 medium green pepper, cut in strips
- Half a 10-ounce can tomato soup
- ½ cup sugar
- ½ cup salad oil
- ½ teaspoon dry mustard
- ⅓ cup vinegar
- ¼ teaspoon salt
- ¼ teaspoon pepper

Cook carrots just until tender (about 8 minutes). Do not overcook. Drain. Add onion rings and green pepper strips. Whip remaining ingredients until blended. Pour over vegetables. Marinate several hours or overnight in refrigerator. To serve, lift vegetables out of dressing and place in lettuce-lined serving dish.

Serves 6-8.

Macaroni Salad

- 2 cups macaroni
- ½ cup chopped celery
- 1 medium onion. chopped
- 1 teaspoon parsley
- 1 grated carrot
- 6 hard-boiled eggs
- 1 teaspoon celery seed

Dressing:
- 1½ cups granulated sugar
- 1 scant cup flour
- ¼ teaspoon salt
- 1½ cups water
- ½ cup vinegar
- ¼ cup mustard
- 1 cup mayonnaise

Cook macaroni in salt water. Drain and rinse with cold water. Add vegetables and eggs. Cook first 5 dressing ingredients together until thickened. Cool. Add mustard and mayonnaise. Mix with macaroni mixture.

Verna Stoltzfus
Bird-In-Hand, Pennsylvania

What wisdom can you find that is greater than kindness?

Mexicali Salad Ring

- 1 can red kidney beans
- 1 can mandarin oranges
- ½ cup chopped onion
- ¼ cup chopped parsley
- ¼ cup salad oil
- 2 tablespoons cider vinegar
- 1 teaspoon sugar
- ½ teaspoon salt
- Lettuce

Drain kidney beans and orange segments. Toss onion with parsley in a small bowl. Mix salad oil, vinegar, sugar, and salt in a cup. Line a serving bowl with lettuce. Spoon beans in a ring around edge and mandarin oranges next to beans. Pile onion mixture in center. Drizzle dressing over top.

Old-fashioned Bean Salad

- 1 quart plain canned green and yellow beans
- 1 onion
- 1 teaspoon vinegar
- 1 teaspoon sugar
- Salt and pepper

Let all stand 2-3 hours. At serving time, add ¾ cup sour cream and 2 hard-cooked eggs.

Orange Banana Salad

- 1 6-ounce package banana-orange gelatin
- ⅓ cup sugar
- 2 cups boiling water
- ⅛ teaspoon salt
- ½ cup orange juice
- 1 teaspoon grated orange rind
- 1 ¼ cups cold water
- 1 cup diced orange sections
- 1 banana, sliced
- ½ cup cream

Dissolve the gelatin, sugar, and salt in the boiling water. Add orange juice, orange rind, and cold water. Measure 2 cups of mixture and chill to slightly thickened (set the remainder aside and chill until slightly thickened). Fold in orange sections and banana. Spoon into 6-cup mold and chill until almost firm. Whip cream and fold into remaining gelatin. Spoon over gelatin in mold. Chill until firm.

Serves 8-10.

ORIENTAL SALAD

- 1-2 heads Napa cabbage
- 2-3 bunches green onions
- 2 packages (3 ounces each) Ramen noodles
- Butter
- 1 package (2¼ ounces) sliced almonds
- ⅓ jar sesame seeds
- ½ cup sugar
- ¾ cup oil
- ¾ cup vinegar
- 2 tablespoons soy sauce

Chop cabbage and onions. Crumble 1 package of the Ramen noodles and mix with cabbage and onions. Set aside. Melt some butter in a frying pan. Add almonds, sesame seeds, and remaining package noodles. Brown. Mix sugar, oil, vinegar, and soy sauce in a small saucepan. Add browned almond mixture. Heat to boiling and pour over cabbage mixture. Toss well to mix. You can add a few stalks of chopped celery to the cabbage-green onion mixture if desired.

Sharon Dirst
East Peoria Mennonite Church
Illinois Mennonite Relief Sale, Peoria

POTATO SALAD

- 1 quart boiled diced potatoes
- 1 pint cabbage and celery
- 2 hard-boiled eggs
- ½ teaspoon salt
- A little pepper

Dressing:
- 1 heaping tablespoon butter, melted
- 1 egg, well beaten
- ½ cup vinegar
- 1 cup sour cream
- ½ teaspoon mustard
- ½ cup sugar

Mix first 5 ingredients well. Boil dressing ingredients until thick. Add to potato mixture.

GOOD TALKERS HAVE LITTLE TROUBLE GETTING JOBS, BUT ONLY GOOD DOERS KEEP THEM!

Potato and Macaroni Salad

- ❖ 12 cups shredded potatoes, cooked
- ❖ 1 medium onion, chopped
- ❖ ¾ cup celery, chopped
- ❖ 12 hard-boiled eggs
- ❖ 3 cups cooked macaroni
  or 1½ cups dried
- ❖ 1 cup shredded carrots

Dressing:
- ❖ 3 cups mayonnaise
- ❖ ¼ cup vinegar
- ❖ 2 tablespoons salt
- ❖ 6 tablespoons prepared mustard
- ❖ 1½ cups sugar
- ❖ 1¼ cups milk

Combine potatoes, macaroni, eggs and vegetables. In a separate bowl, combine dressing ingredients. Pour over potato and macaroni mixture. Let set overnight in the refrigerator.

Frances H. Martin
Quarryville, Pennsylvania

Raw Cauliflower and Broccoli Salad

- ❖ 2 cups broccoli,
  broken into small pieces
- ❖ 2 cups cauliflower,
  broken into small pieces
- ❖ 1 cup frozen peas, thawed
- ❖ ½ cup chopped onion

Dressing:
- ❖ 3 tablespoons lemon juice
- ❖ 3 tablespoons vinegar
- ❖ 1 teaspoon salt
- ❖ ½ teaspoon sugar
- ❖ ¼ teaspoon pepper

Combine salad ingredients. Combine dressing ingredients. Pour dressing over salad. Let marinate in refrigerator at least 1 hour (preferably overnight). Stir well before serving.

Mrs. Silas (Verlyn) Waltner
Marion, South Dakota

SALAD OF GREENS

- 4 cups greens (dandelion, endive, spinach, or greens of choice)
- 2-3 hard-boiled eggs

Dressing:
- 3 slices bacon
- 2 tablespoons flour
- 2-4 tablespoons sugar
- ¼ cup vinegar
- ½-¾ cup cream (milk or water can also be used)

Prepare dressing by cutting bacon into pieces and frying. Blend flour into hot bacon. Reduce heat and add sugar, vinegar, and cream. Bring dressing to a boil. Toss with greens and eggs, or toss with greens and shred egg over top to garnish. Serve at once. Do not allow to fully wilt.

SAUERKRAUT SALAD

- 32 ounces sauerkraut, drained
- 1 cup celery
- 1 green pepper, diced
- 1 sweet pepper
- 1 pimiento
- 1 cup sugar
- ⅓ cup salad oil
- ⅓ cup white vinegar
- ¼ cup water
- 1 teaspoon salt
- Onion

Mix all ingredients and let stand for 1 hour.

TACO SALAD

- 20 pounds ground beef
- 1 gallon tomato sauce
- 4 cups taco seasoning
- 1 case taco chips
- 6 heads lettuce, shredded
- 6 quarts sliced tomatoes
- 5 pounds shredded cheese

Cook meat until all traces of pink are gone and drain well. Add tomato sauce and taco seasoning. Mix well. Cook until thoroughly heated. Remove from heat and cool. Layer 1 cup crushed chips, ¾ cup shredded lettuce, several slices tomato, 4 ounces taco-flavored meat, and 1 ounce cheese when ready to serve.

Makes 80 servings.

Bertha Stark
Freeman, South Dakota
Bethany Mennonite Church
Minn-Kota MCC Relief Sale
Sioux Falls, South Dakota

Easy Taco Salad

- 1 head lettuce, broken into little pieces
- ½ pound ground beef, browned and drained
- 1 small can red beans, washed
- Tomatoes
- Corn chips
- Grated cheese
- French dressing

Toss all ingredients together and serve.

Alpha Mae Mumaw
Yellow Creek Mennonite Church
Goshen, Indiana

Tangy Slaw

- 10 cups shredded cabbage
- 1½ cups chopped green pepper
- 1½ cups shredded carrot
- ¼ cup chopped onion

Dressing:
- 1 cup salad oil
- ¼ cup vinegar
- ½ cup sugar
- ½ teaspoon salt
- ¼ teaspoon pepper

Combine vegetables in a bowl and toss to mix well. Mix dressing ingredients in a small bowl. Add to cabbage about 30 minutes before serving. Toss to mix.

Pam Hofer
Carpenter, South Dakota

Tuna Salad

- 1 cup tomato juice
- 2 packages unflavored gelatin
- ¼ cup mayonnaise
- 2 cans tuna or 1 large can salmon
- 3 tablespoons hot dog relish
- 1 chopped onion (small)

Heat tomato juice and add gelatin. Add mayonnaise to tomato-gelatin mixture when partially cooked. Let set. Mix tuna, hot dog relish, and onion with gelatin. Pour in mold.

FRUIT CREAM DRESSING

- 3 tablespoons sugar
- 2 tablespoons flour
- 2 eggs
- 2 tablespoons vinegar
- 1 cup pear or pineapple juice
- 1 lemon rind and juice
- 1 cup cream or whipped topping substitute

Mix in order given and cook over boiling water until thick. Before serving, add cream, whipped stiff, or whipped topping substitute.

MAYONNAISE

- 1 cup white sugar
- 2 eggs
- ¼ teaspoon salt, pepper
- 2 teaspoons dry mustard
- 2 teaspoons flour
- Scoop of butter the size of an egg
- ¾ cup vinegar
- ¾ cup water
- Cream

Mix all together and cook over a slow fire. When ready to use, mix equal parts of cream with mayonnaise.

MUSTARD

- 1 egg, beaten
- ¼ cup sugar
- 1 teaspoon cornstarch
- 4 teaspoons dry mustard
- 1 cup vinegar
- Salt

Mix all together and boil.

HOT MUSTARD

- 1 cup flour
- ¾ cup brown sugar
- ¾ teaspoon salt
- 5 tablespoons dry mustard
- 5 tablespoons prepared mustard
- 1 cup vinegar

Mix all together and store in jar.

Homemade French Dressing

- ½ cup sugar
- ¾ cup ketchup
- ¼ cup vinegar
- 1 cup salad oil
- ¼ cup water
- ½ teaspoon onion salt
- ½ teaspoon salt
- 1 teaspoon celery seed

Put all ingredients in a quart jar. Shake very well or use a blender to mix all ingredients.

Quick French Dressing

- ½ cup sugar
- 1 teaspoon paprika
- 1 teaspoon salt
- ¼ cup cider vinegar
- ⅓ cup ketchup
- ¼ cup salad oil
- Juice of half a lemon

Put all ingredients into a 20-ounce jar with lid and shake well. Serve.

Salad Dressing

- ½-1 cup sugar
- ½-1 cup vinegar (start with ½ cup and add more to taste if desired)
- 1 cup salad oil
- 1 can (10¾ ounces) tomato soup (undiluted)
- 1 teaspoon dry mustard
- 1 teaspoon salt
- ½ teaspoon garlic powder
- 1 teaspoon celery seed
- 1 teaspoon pepper
- 1 clove (optional)

Combine all ingredients in a quart jar. Shake well to combine. Store covered in the refrigerator.

Susana Siemens
Winnipeg, Manitoba
MCC Manitoba Relief Sale

ॐ

BOILED SALAD DRESSING

- 3 eggs
- 5 tablespoons sugar
- 4 teaspoons flour
- 1 teaspoon mustard
- 1 cup water
- 1 teaspoon salt
- Pinch of pepper
- 1 cup vinegar
  (cider vinegar preferred)

Mix all ingredients and boil, stirring continually until thick. Take off heat and cool. Can be used warm or stored in jars.

RUSSIAN SALAD DRESSING

- 1½ cups salad dressing
  (Miracle Whip)
- ¼ cup ketchup
- 4 tablespoons sweet pickle relish
- ½ teaspoon garlic salt
- ½ teaspoon pepper

Mix well. Add 1 cup evaporated milk.

ST. ANTHONY SALAD DRESSING

- 1 cup ketchup
- 1 cup salad oil
- ½ cup grated cheese (cheddar preferred)
- 2 onions, chopped
- 1 cup white sugar
- ½ cup vinegar

Mix and shake in quart jar.

Sweet and Sour Salad Dressing

- 1 medium onion, finely chopped
- 1 cup sugar
- 1 teaspoon salt
- 3 teaspoons prepared mustard
- 1 teaspoon pepper
- 1 teaspoon celery seed
- ⅓ cup vinegar
- 1 cup corn oil
- 2 tablespoons salad dressing

Put all ingredients together in a jar and shake well (or use an egg beater). For best results, let stand a few hours before serving.

Makes 1 pint.

Ammon and Rebecca Stoltzfus
New Providence, Pennsylvania

Whipped Cream Topping for Gelatin Salads

- ½ cup sugar
- 3 tablespoons flour
- 1 cup pineapple juice
- 1 egg, slightly beaten
- 1 tablespoon butter
- ½ cup whipping cream or whipped topping
- ¼ cup shredded cheese
- 2 tablespoons Parmesan cheese

Combine sugar and flour in saucepan. Stir in juice and egg. Cook over low heat until thickened. Add butter. Cool. Fold into whipped cream and use to frost gelatin salads. Sprinkle with cheese.

MAIN DISHES AND CASSEROLES

BIG CATCH CASSEROLE

- 1 10-ounce can
  cream of celery soup
- ½ cup salad dressing
- ¼ cup milk
- ¼ cup grated cheese
- 1 12-ounce package frozen peas or
  1 can peas, juice included
- 1 7½-ounce can salmon or tuna
- 4 ounces (2 cups) noodles, cooked
- 1 tablespoon chopped onion

Heat oven to 350°. Cook noodles in salted water and drain. Combine soup, salad dressing, milk, and cheese. Blend well. Add peas, salmon, onion, and noodles and mix lightly. Pour into a 1½-quart casserole. Bake 25 minutes. Serve with salad and rolls.

BREAKFAST BAKE

- 16 slices white bread,
  crusts removed
- 8 slices deli ham
- Shredded mozzarella, Swiss,
  or American cheese
- 6 eggs
- 3 cups milk
- ½ teaspoon onion salt
- ½ teaspoon pepper
- ½ teaspoon dry mustard
- ½ cup (1 stick) butter, melted
- Cornflakes

Grease a 9x13-inch baking pan. Cover bottom of pan with 8 slices of the bread. Layer ham over bread. Layer cheese over ham. Top with the remaining 8 slices bread. Beat together eggs, milk, onion salt, pepper, and mustard. Pour over layers in baking pan. Refrigerate overnight. Remove casserole from refrigerator 1 hour before baking. When ready to bake, pour melted butter over casserole and top with cornflakes. Bake at 350° for 1¼ hours. Let stand 10 minutes before cutting and serving.

Florence Blough
Hollsopple, Pennsylvania
MCC Quilt Auction and Relief Sale, Johnstown

TRY THIS RECIPE FOR SUNDAY BREAKFAST
WITH ORANGE JUICE AND FRESH FRUITS.

MAIN DISHES AND CASSEROLES

Breakfast Casserole

- 1 pound sausage
- ¼ cup (half a stick) butter or margarine, melted
- 6 slices bread
- 1½ cups shredded cheddar cheese
- 5 eggs
- 2 cups half-and-half
- 1 teaspoon dry mustard
- ½ teaspoon salt

Cook sausage. Drain well and set aside. Place melted butter in 13x9-inch baking pan. Cut bread into small squares (remove crusts or not, as desired). Spread over butter. Spread drained sausage over bread. Cover with cheese. Beat eggs, half-and-half, mustard, and salt together. Pour over ingredients in baking pan. Chill 8 hours or overnight. Bake at 350° for 40-50 minutes.

Sally Ann Reddecliff
Johnstown, Pennsylvania
MCC Quilt Auction and Relief Sale, Johnstown

Cheese and Bread Casserole

- 2 cups soft bread crumbs
- Strong yellow cheese, thinly sliced or grated
- 3 eggs
- 1 teaspoon salt
- 2 cups scalded milk

Layer bread crumbs and cheese in a greased casserole until dish is filled. Beat together eggs, salt, and milk. Pour over crumbs and cheese (milk should fill dish). Bake at 350° until golden brown.

Chicken and Dressing Casserole

- 1 3-4 pound chicken
- 2 cans (10¾ ounces each) cream of mushroom soup
- 1 medium onion, diced
- ¾ teaspoon poultry seasoning
- Salt and pepper to taste
- 20 slices dried bread, cubed
- Chicken broth
- 2 eggs, beaten

Cook chicken and remove meat from bones. Combine meat and mushroom soup. Set aside. Combine onion, seasoning, salt, pepper, and bread cubes with enough broth to moisten. Spread half the dressing over bottom of a 13x9-inch baking pan. Add chicken mixture. Add beaten eggs to remaining dressing. Spread over top of casserole. Bake at 350° for 45 minutes.

Jo Ann Swearengin
Missouri MCC Relief Sale, Harrisonville

CHICKEN ETTI

- 8-ounce package spaghetti, broken into 2-inch pieces
- 3-4 cups of sliced chicken
- ¼ cup pimento
- ¼ cup green pepper
- 2 cups mushroom soup
- 1 cup chicken broth
- ¼ teaspoon celery salt
- ¼ teaspoon pepper
- 1 grated onion
- ¾ pound grated Velveeta cheese

Keep back some cheese to sprinkle on top of casserole. Bake at 350° for 1 hour.

Eunice Sauder

CHICKEN VEGETABLE CASSEROLE

- 2 cups cut-up cooked chicken
- 2 cans (10¾ ounces each) cream of mushroom soup
- 1 can (8 ounces) water chestnuts
- 1 small can mushrooms
- 1 bag (16 ounces) California mixed frozen vegetables
- 1 tablespoon finely chopped onion
- 4 ounces cheddar cheese

Mix together all ingredients in order given in a casserole dish. Bake covered at 350° for 1 hour. Uncover and bake 15-20 minutes longer.

Serves 8.

Mrs. Arthur (Beverly) Carlson
Odin, Minnesota
Minn-Kota MCC Relief Sale
Sioux Falls, South Dakota

CHICKEN WITH RICE CASSEROLE

- 1 3-pound chicken, cut up, or 3 pounds chicken legs or breasts, uncooked
- 1 cup uncooked rice
- 4 cups hot water
- 1 package onion soup mix
- 1 can mushroom soup
- 1 package chicken with rice soup mix or 1 tablespoon chicken broth concentrate

In the bottom of an oblong casserole, put rice, then chicken pieces. Dissolve soup mixes in water and pour over top. Sprinkle paprika over top if desired. Bake at 350° for 2 hours.

Chicken-Bean Casserole

- 1 box Croutettes stuffing mix
- 1 can (14½ ounces) french-cut green beans
- 2-3 cups cooked diced chicken or turkey
- 1 package (2 ounces) slivered almonds (optional)
- 1 can (10¾ ounces) cream of chicken soup
- 1 cup chicken broth or milk

Spread half the package of croutettes over bottom of a casserole. Spread drained beans over. Layer with chicken and almonds. Mix soup with broth or milk. Pour over ingredients in casserole. Cover with remaining croutettes. Bake at 350° for about 1 hour.

Serves 6 to 8.

Rita Ann Graber
Freeman, South Dakota
Minn-Kota MCC Relief Sale
Sioux Falls, South Dakota

Chicken-Broccoli Casserole

- 1 cup uncooked rice
- 1 package (20 ounces) frozen broccoli
- 1 jar (16 ounces) Cheese Whiz processed cheese sauce
- 1 can (10¾ ounces) cream of chicken soup
- 3 cups deboned chicken
- Buttered bread crumbs

Cook rice. Cook broccoli and drain. Combine. Mix in cheese sauce, soup, and chicken. Put into a buttered 13x9-inch baking pan. Top with crumbs. Bake at 350° for 45 minutes to 1 hour.

Mary Glanzer
Freeman, South Dakota
Minn-Kota MCC Relief Sale
Sioux Falls, South Dakota

Chicken-filled Shells

- 2 cups cubed cooked chicken
- 1 cup cooked peas
- ½ cup mayonnaise
- ⅓ cup onion, finely chopped
- 1 package (16 ounces) jumbo shells, cooked and drained
- 1 can (10¾ ounces) condensed cream of mushroom soup
- ½ cup water

Mix together chicken, peas, mayonnaise, and onion. Stuff into shells. Arrange shells in a single layer in a baking dish. Stir soup and water together. Pour over stuffed shells. Cover with aluminum foil and bake at 325° for 25 minutes.

Virginia Gindlesperger
Johnstown, Pennsylvania
MCC Quilt Auction and Relief Sale, Johnstown

CHICKEN-MACARONI CASSEROLE

- 2 cups uncooked elbow macaroni
- 2 cups diced cooked chicken or turkey
- 1 package (8 ounces) Velveeta processed cheese spread
- 2 cans (10¾ ounces each) cream of chicken soup
- 2 cups milk
- 4 diced hard-cooked eggs

Mix all ingredients together. Place in casserole. Cover and refrigerate overnight. Remove from refrigerator 1 hour before baking. Bake at 350° for 1 hour.

FESTIVE MEXICAN CHICKEN

- 1 can broth
- 1 can cream of chicken soup
- 1 can cream of mushroom soup
- Cooked chicken
- 1 medium onion, diced
- 1 package corn chips, crushed
- 2 cups shredded cheddar cheese
- Chopped black olives and red peppers for garnish

Mix together broth and soups. Set aside. Cut up chicken and spread over bottom of a 13x9-inch baking pan. Top with layers of onion, crushed chips, and cheese in order given. Pour soup mixture over all. Top with olives and peppers. Bake at 350° for 20-30 minutes.

Jean Shaw
Missouri MCC Relief Sale, Harrisonville

QUICK SAUCY CHICKEN CASSEROLE

- 3 cups cut-up cooked chicken
- 2 cans (10¾ ounces each) cream of mushroom soup
- 1 box frozen mixed vegetables
- 1 teaspoon poultry seasoning (optional)
- ½ teaspoon garlic salt
- 2 cups baking mix
- 1½ cups milk
- 1 teaspoon parsley
- 1 cup shredded cheddar cheese

Mix chicken, soup, mixed vegetables, and seasonings. Spread over bottom of a 13x9x2-inch baking dish. Stir together baking mix and milk. Pour over chicken mixture. Spread cheese and parsley over top of casserole. Bake at 450° for 30-35 minutes.

Serves 8-10.

Lena Sala
Hollsopple, Pennsylvania
MCC Quilt Auction and Relief Sale, Johnstown

CORN CASSEROLE

- 2½ cups corn (cooked or raw)
- ⅓ cup celery, cut fine
- 1¼ cups cracker crumbs
- ½ cup diced cheese
- 1⅔ cups milk
- Half an onion, chopped
- 3 tablespoons melted butter
- ½ teaspoon salt
- 3 eggs, separated

Beat egg yolks with milk. Add all other ingredients except egg whites. Beat egg whites until stiff and fold in last. Put in a greased casserole or baking dish. Top with a bit of bread or cracker crumbs and sprinkle with paprika. Bake 45 minutes to 1 hour at 350°.

DUTCH GOOSE CASSEROLE

- 2 cups cubed bread
- 2 cups diced cooked potatoes
- Dressing seasonings to taste
- 1 pound sausage, fried and cut up
- 1 egg, beaten
- Milk

Combine bread, potatoes, seasonings, and sausage. Beat together egg and enough milk to moisten the dressing ingredients. Pour over casserole and toss to mix. Bake in a moderate oven for 30-40 minutes.

Mary Kaufman
Johnstown, Pennsylvania
MCC Quilt Auction and Relief Sale, Johnstown

EASY SAUSAGE CASSEROLE

- 1 cup diced carrots, cooked
- 2 cups diced potatoes, cooked
- 1 medium onion
- 8 bread slices broken into pieces
- 2 beaten eggs
- 2 cups milk
- 1 pound sausage

Mix ingredients together and bake at 350° for 1 hour.

Nancy Beiler
Kinzer, Pennsylvania

NO MAN (OR WOMAN) WILL EVER BE A GREAT LEADER WHO DOES NOT TAKE GENUINE JOY IN THE SUCCESS OF THOSE UNDER HIM.

MAIN DISHES AND CASSEROLES

FETTUCINI CASSEROLE

- 8 ounces fettucini noodles, cooked
- 2 cups cubed ham
- ¼ cup chopped onion
- 3 cups milk
- 1 cup sour cream
- 1 small carton dry-curd cottage cheese
- Salt and pepper to taste

Mix together all ingredients in a casserole. Bake at 350° for 30 minutes.

Deb Roth
Henderson, Nebraska
Nebraska MCC Relief Sale, Aurora

HAM AND NOODLE BAKE

- 8 ounces noodles
- 3 cups cubed ham
- 1 medium onion, chopped
- 1 teaspoon salt
- Dash pepper
- 1 can (10¾ ounces) cream of chicken soup
- 1½ cups milk
- 1 cup sour cream
- 1 cup grated cheese

Cook noodles following package directions and drain. Brown ham and onion. Season with salt and pepper. Mix soup, milk, sour cream, and cheese together. Combine with noodles, ham, and onion in a casserole dish. Bake at 350° for 30 minutes.

Serves 6.

Daphne Epp
Crete, Nebraska
Nebraska MCC Relief Sale, Aurora

HAM AND WILD RICE CASSEROLE

- 1 package (6 ounces) long grain and wild rice
- 1 bag (20 ounces) frozen chopped broccoli
- 2 cups (about 12 ounces) cubed ham
- 1¼ cups shredded cheddar cheese
- 1 can (10¾ ounces) cheddar cheese soup
- 1 cup mayonnaise or Miracle Whip salad dressing
- 2 teaspoons dry mustard

Cook rice following directions on package. Spread over bottom of 13x9-inch pan. Top with a layer of broccoli, then ham, then 1 cup of the shredded cheese. Mix together soup, mayonnaise, and mustard. Spread over casserole. Sprinkle remaining cheese over top. Bake at 350° for 40-45 minutes.

Sharon Dirst
East Peoria Mennonite Church
Illinois MCC Relief Sale, Peoria

Ham, Potato, and Cheese Casserole

- 1 medium onion, chopped
- 3 tablespoons chopped green pepper (optional)
- ¼ cup (half a stick) butter or margarine
- 2½ tablespoons flour
- 2 cups milk
- Salt and pepper to taste
- 3 cups cooked cubed potatoes
- 3 cups cooked cubed ham
- ¾ cup shredded cheese

Cook onion and green pepper in butter for 5 minutes. Add flour and stir. Add milk. Cook until thickened. Season with salt and pepper. Add potatoes and ham. Put in 2-quart casserole. Top with cheese. Bake at 350° for 25-30 minutes.

Serves 6 easily.

Trella Harshberger
Johnstown, Pennsylvania
MCC Quilt Auction and Relief Sale, Johnstown

Piggy Casserole

- 4 cups cooked diced potatoes
- 5 cups cubed bread
- 2 pounds ground pork
- 1½ cups milk
- 2 eggs
- 2 tablespoons salt
- 1 teaspoon black pepper

Cook potatoes with jackets, then peel and cube. Mix with bread and ground pork, which should be broken into small pieces. Add milk, eggs, salt, and pepper. Bake in casserole for about 1½ hours at 325° or until nicely browned.

There is as much greatness in acknowledging
a good turn as in doing it.

HAMBURGER-CORN BAKE

- 1½ pounds ground beef
- 1 onion, chopped
- 1 package (12 ounces) medium noodles
- 1 can (12 ounces) whole kernel corn
- 1 can (10¾ ounces) cream of mushroom soup
- 1 can (10¾ ounces) cream of chicken soup
- 1 cup sour cream
- ¼ teaspoon pepper
- ¾ teaspoon salt (optional)
- ½ teaspoon monosodium glutamate (optional)
- ¼ cup chopped canned pimientos (optional)
- 2 cups soft bread crumbs mixed with 4 teaspoons melted butter (optional)

Brown ground beef with onions and drain. Cook noodles following package directions and drain. Mix all ingredients (except bread crumbs) together. Place in a casserole. Top with buttered bread crumbs. Bake at 350° for 1-1½ hours.

Serves 10-12.

Martha Tschetter
Freeman, South Dakota

HAMBURGER-GREEN BEAN CASSEROLE

- 1 pound ground beef
- 1 onion, chopped
- Salt and pepper to taste
- 1 can (14½ ounces) green beans, drained
- 2 small cans (8 ounces each) tomato sauce or 1 can (10¾ ounces) tomato soup
- Mashed potatoes

Brown beef and onion. Season to taste. Spread over bottom of baking dish. Layer beans over meat mixture. Pour tomato sauce over beans. Spread mashed potatoes on top of everything. Bake at 350° for 30-40 minutes.

LaVerna Friesen
Freeman, South Dakota
Minn-Kota MCC Relief Sale
Sioux Falls, South Dakota

HAMBURGER TOMATO CASSEROLE

- 1 pound hamburger
- 1 quart canned tomatoes
- ¾ cup uncooked rice
- Salt and pepper to taste
- Cheese slices for top

Combine hamburger, tomatoes, and rice. Pour into casserole and bake for 1½ hours at 350°. About 30 minutes before serving, top with cheese slices and return to oven to finish cooking.

SEVEN LAYER DINNER

- 1-2 inch layer of raw sliced potatoes
- 1 layer sliced raw onions
- 1 layer sliced raw carrots
- ¼ cup quick-cooking rice
- 1 can peas and their liquid
- 1 pound link-style pork sausages
- 1 10-ounce can tomato soup
- 1 can water
- Salt and pepper

Arrange all ingredients in layers in deep greased casserole. (Salt and pepper each layer.) Cover and bake 1 hour at 350°. Uncover and bake 15-30 minutes longer. One and a half pounds ground beef can be substituted for pork sausages.

TUNA NOODLE CASSEROLE

- 1 chopped onion
- 1 tablespoon butter
- 1 can cream of mushroom soup
- ½ cup milk
- 1 7-ounce can tuna, drained
- 1 cup cooked noodles
- ½ cup drained cooked peas
- ½ cup shredded cheddar cheese

Cook onion in butter until browned. Combine with soup, milk, tuna, noodles, and peas. Pour into 1-quart casserole and top with cheese. Bake uncovered at 375° for 25 minutes until hot and bubbling.

TURKEY PIE WITH ENGLISH PASTRY

Pie Filling:

- ❖ 3-4 cups cut-up cooked turkey
- ❖ 2 large potatoes, cubed
- ❖ 2 carrots, sliced
- ❖ 1 package frozen peas
- ❖ 1 onion, chopped
- ❖ Leftover gravy made from broth in which turkey was cooked
- ❖ Cream of chicken or cream of mushroom soup

English Pastry:

- ❖ 2 cups flour
- ❖ 2 teaspoons baking powder
- ❖ 1 teaspoon salt
- ❖ ⅔ cup shortening
- ❖ ½ cup hot water
- ❖ 1 tablespoon lemon juice
- ❖ 1 unbeaten egg yolk

To make pie filling, put all vegetables (except peas) into pot and cook until done. Add peas and pieces of turkey meat. Season with salt and pepper. Cook until peas are done, adding more water if necessary. Mix in gravy and soup. To make English pastry, sift together flour, baking powder, and salt. Mix shortening with hot water, lemon juice, and egg yolk. Stir into dry ingredients. Chill dough for easier handling. Use ¾ of dough to line a 2-quart casserole dish. Add filling and cover with remaining dough. Cut slits in dough. Bake at 425° for 25 minutes.

WIENER CASSEROLE

- ❖ 3 large potatoes
- ❖ 1 pound wieners
- ❖ Salt and pepper to taste
- ❖ 1 tablespoon flour
- ❖ ½ cup grated cheese
- ❖ 1 onion, sliced
- ❖ 1 can cream of chicken soup or cream of mushroom soup
- ❖ Sliced tomatoes

Slice potatoes and put in bottom of casserole. Add seasonings and flour. Cut wieners in ½-inch pieces and add to dish. Sprinkle with cheese and add onion. Pour soup over all and top with sliced tomatoes. (Sprinkle with more grated cheese if desired.) Bake at 350° for 1½ hours.

Serves 4.

ZUCCHINI CASSEROLE

- 1 pound ground beef
- 2 cups chopped tomatoes
- 2 cups grated or very thinly sliced zucchini
- 1 small onion, finely chopped
- ½ cup instant rice
- ¼ pound Velveeta processed cheese spread, shredded or cut in chunks
- ½ cup bread crumbs

Brown beef in skillet and drain. Add tomatoes, zucchini, onion, and rice. Transfer half the mixture to a casserole dish. Spread cheese (keeping a little for the top) and bread crumbs over bottom layer. Cover with remainder of meat mixture. Bake at 350° for 45 minutes. Add the reserved cheese to top of casserole when it's almost done.

Mary Kaufman
Johnstown, Pennsylvania
MCC Quilt Auction and Relief Sale, Johnstown

HERB SHAKER

- Garlic powder
- Basil
- Marjoram
- Thyme
- Onion powder
- Parsley flakes
- Freshly ground white or black pepper
- Paprika

Try this mixture on some of the main dishes in this section. To make the seasoning blend, thoroughly combine 1 tablespoon of each of the listed ingredients.

Sally Ann Reddecliff
Johnstown, Pennsylvania

A QUICKIE

- 1 pound hamburger
- 1 onion, diced
- 1 can creamed corn
- 1 package instant mashed potatoes

Brown hamburger with onion. Mix with corn and put in casserole. Top with instant mashed potatoes prepared as instructed on package. Bake in oven for 20 minutes.

BAKED CHICKEN WITH RICE

- 1 whole chicken
- 1½-2 cups uncooked rice
- 1 can (10¾ ounces) tomato soup
- 1 can (10¾ ounces) cream of mushroom soup
- 2 cups water
- Salt to taste

Cut up chicken and brown in frying pan. Combine rice, soups, water, and salt in roaster. Stir well. Place chicken pieces on top. Bake at 350° for 1¼-1½ hours.

Serves 5-6.

Edie Tschetter
Freeman, South Dakota
Minn-Kota MCC Relief Sale
Sioux Falls, South Dakota

Baked Fish en Papillote

- 1 pound fish fillets
- ⅓ cup melted butter
- Parsley
- Salt
- Dill weed
- Lemon juice
- Carrots, onion rings, and Swiss cheese (all optional)

Use any kind of fish fillets your family likes. Thaw if necessary. Sprinkle each fillet with salt and pepper on each side. Make a sauce of butter and other ingredients (all quantities to taste). Make squares of aluminum foil for each piece of fish. Spread with some of the butter mixture. Place a piece of fish on each and garnish with thinly sliced carrots, onion rings, and a piece of Swiss cheese if desired. Divide remaining butter sauce evenly among fish pieces, pouring an equal amount over each fillet. Fold up foil securely to make a packet. Place on baking sheet and bake at 400° for 20-40 minutes depending on thickness of fish. This can also be done covered in a flat casserole or baking dish.

Baked Ham

- 8 slices home-cured ham
- 8 tablespoons brown sugar
- 3 tablespoons dry mustard
- 2 cups milk

Bake in a covered casserole at 325° for 1½ hours.

Baked Liver

- 1-1½ pounds liver
- 2 tablespoons hot oil

Sauce:
- 1 chopped onion
- 1 teaspoon dry mustard
- 1 teaspoon paprika
- 1 tablespoon butter
- 4 teaspoons brown sugar
- Dash of hot pepper sauce
- ⅓ cup chili sauce
- 2 tablespoons vinegar

Dip liver in flour. Fry in hot oil. When browned on both sides, remove and place in an oven dish. Simmer sauce ingredients for 10 minutes. Pour over liver and bake at 300°-350° for 1 hour.

BAR-B-QUE BURGERS

- 1 pound ground beef
- 2 tablespoons fat
- 1 can chicken gumbo soup
- ½ cup water
- 1 tablespoon prepared mustard
- ½ cup chopped onion
- ½ teaspoon salt
- ⅛ teaspoon pepper
- 1 tablespoon ketchup

Cook meat and onion in hot fat until meat is browned (pour off some of the fat after the meat is partly cooked). Stir in remaining ingredients and simmer over low heat for 30 minutes. Spoon it from skillet to buns.

Makes about 8 hamburgers.

BARBECUE

- 10 pounds ground beef
- 4 cans (10¾ ounces each) tomato soup
- 2 packages dry onion soup mix
- ½ cup ketchup
- ¼ cup prepared mustard
- 1½ teaspoons salt
- 3-4 cups rolled oats

Mix together all ingredients very well. Place in large baking pan and bake at 350° for 2 hours, stirring occasionally.

Carol Tschetter
Freeman, South Dakota

BARBECUED SPARERIBS

- 3 pounds spareribs
- 1 medium onion, chopped
- 1 tablespoon butter
- 1 tablespoon vinegar
- 1 tablespoon sugar
- 2 teaspoons salt
- 3 tablespoons lemon juice
- ½ tablespoon prepared mustard
- ½ cup water
- ½ cup chopped celery
- Dash of pepper
- 1-2 tablespoons Worcestershire sauce (optional)

Wipe ribs with damp cloth and cut into serving size pieces. Place in a shallow baking pan and bake uncovered at 350° for 30 minutes. Meanwhile, lightly brown onion in butter, then add remaining ingredients. Mix well and simmer 5 minutes. Pour over the spareribs and continue baking for 1 hour longer, basting ribs from time to time with the sauce in the bottom of the pan.

Serves 5.

Barbecued Meatballs

Meatballs:
- 3 pounds ground beef
- 1 can (12 ounces) evaporated milk
- 1 cup rolled oats
- 1 cup cracker crumbs
- 2 eggs
- ½ cup chopped onion
- ½ teaspoon garlic powder
- 2 teaspoons salt
- ½ teaspoon pepper
- 2 teaspoons chili powder

Sauce:
- 2 cups ketchup
- 1 cup brown sugar
- ½ teaspoon liquid smoke (optional)
- ½ teaspoon garlic powder
- ¼ cup chopped onion

Combine all ingredients for meatballs (mixture will be soft). Shape into walnut-size balls. Place meatballs in a single layer on cookie sheets lined with wax paper. Freeze until solid. Store in bags in freezer until ready to cook. When ready to use, place frozen meatballs in a 13x9-inch baking pan. Combine all sauce ingredients. Stir until sugar is dissolved. Pour sauce over meatballs. Bake at 350° for 1 hour.

Makes about 80 meatballs.

Ladonna Waltner
Marion, South Dakota

Saucy Barbecued Meatballs

Meatballs:
- 3 pounds ground beef
- 2 cups oatmeal
- 2 cups milk
- 2 eggs, beaten
- 1 chopped onion
- 2 teaspoons salt
- ½ teaspoon pepper
- 2 teaspoons chili powder

Sauce:
- 2 cups ketchup
- 2 cups water
- 3 cups brown sugar
- 4 tablespoons liquid smoke
- 1 teaspoon garlic powder

Fix meatballs in a baking dish. Pour sauce over top. Bake at 350° for one hour.

R. Beiler
Quarryville, Pennsylvania

BLACK BEANS BRAZILIAN STYLE

- 2 cups (about 1 pound) dried black beans
- 6 cups water
- ¾ teaspoon baking soda
- 2 cups water
- 1 teaspoon salt
- Smoked pork hock, bacon, bacon fat, or smoked sausage (for flavor)
- 2 cloves garlic, minced
- 1 medium onion, chopped
- Half a green pepper, chopped (optional)
- 2 teaspoons oil, bacon fat, or butter
- 1 cup chopped tomatoes
- 1 tablespoon flour

Place beans in the 6 cups water with the soda and soak overnight. The next day, drain and rinse beans. Place in crock pot with the 2 cups water, salt, and meat. Cook about 2 hours or until beans and meat are tender. Sauté garlic, onion, and green pepper in oil in frying pan. Add tomatoes when onions are transparent. Cook until they are tender. Remove ¼ cup of the vegetable mixture and combine with the flour. Return paste to frying pan and stir well. Mix vegetable sauce into beans. Serve with rice.

Lois Thieszen Preheim
Bethesda Mennonite Church, Henderson
Nebraska MCC Relief Sale, Aurora
Contributed by Betti Harder, Alberto Kruger,
Evaldo Warkentin, and Marvin Warkentin

BEEF STROGANOFF

- 1½ pounds sliced round steak
- ¼ cup flour
- Dash of pepper
- ¼ cup margarine
- 1 4-ounce can sliced mushrooms, drained
- ½ cup chopped onion
- 1 small clove garlic, minced
- 1 can beef broth
- 1 cup sour cream
- 3 cups cooked noodles

Cut the round steak into thin strips. Dust with flour and pepper. Brown meat in a large skillet with the margarine. Add the mushrooms, onion, and garlic. Brown lightly. Stir in beef broth and cover. Cook for 1 hour or until meat is tender, stirring occasionally. Gradually stir in sour cream. Cook over low heat 5 minutes. Serve over cooked noodles.

Serves 4.

TO CLEAN YOUR BARBECUE OR OVEN RACKS, PLACE THEM ON THE GRASS OVERNIGHT OR ON A RAINY DAY. THE CLEANUP JOB IS EASIER!

Beef-Macaroni Dinner

- 1 package Cheese-and-Macaroni Dinner cooked as directed on package
- 1 can mushroom soup
- 1 can corn
- 1 can mushrooms (optional)
- 2 cups diced celery
- 1 can tomato soup
- 1 small can tomato sauce
- 1½ pounds ground beef
- 2 large onions, sliced
- 2 tablespoons butter

Brown meat and onion in butter in frying pan. Mix with remaining ingredients. Season with salt, pepper, and Worcestershire sauce. Heat in 325° oven until warm.

Best-Ever Stew

- 2 pounds chuck or round steak, cut in cubes
- 2 tablespoons oil
- 3 medium onions, cut in chunks
- 3 carrots, cut in chunks
- 4 stalks celery, cut in chunks
- 3-4 potatoes, cut in chunks
- 1 tablespoon tomato paste
- 3 tablespoons flour
- 2-3 cups beef broth
- Salt and pepper to taste

Brown meat in oil in heavy ovenproof pan. Remove and set aside. Add vegetables to pan along with additional oil if needed. Brown slightly. Stir in tomato paste, flour, and broth. Season with salt and pepper. Return meat to pan and cook on top of stove until sauce is thickened. Bake at 325° for 2 hours or until beef is tender. Store the remaining tomato paste by dropping tablespoons of the paste onto waxed paper. Freeze and store in small plastic bags. Use the next time you wish to make this stew.

Lena Sala
Hollsopple, Pennsylvania
MCC Quilt Auction and Relief Sale, Johnstown

BIEROCKS

Filling:

- ❖ 10 pounds ground beef
- ❖ 1 cup water
- ❖ 3 pounds chopped cabbage
- ❖ 1½ cups onion
- ❖ 3 tablespoons salt
- ❖ 1 tablespoon pepper
- ❖ 1 teaspoon garlic powder
- ❖ 1 cup flour

Dough:

- ❖ 1 quart warm water
- ❖ ½ cup sugar
- ❖ ½ cup shortening
- ❖ ½ cup powdered milk
- ❖ ⅓ cup yeast
- ❖ Enough flour to make a sponge
- ❖ 5 eggs
- ❖ 1½ teaspoons salt
- ❖ 10 cups flour

To prepare the filling, cook meat with water until all red is gone. Add remaining ingredients (except flour). Cook until cabbage is done. Add flour and stir until well mixed. Drain the meat to remove excess grease. Let filling cool before using. To prepare the dough, combine the warm water, sugar, shortening, and powdered milk in a blender. Pour into a mixing bowl with the yeast. Mix well with enough flour to make a sponge. Let rise until bubbles form. Add eggs and salt. Mix in enough of the flour (about 10 cups) to make a soft dough. Let rise until double in bulk. Punch down and roll out to form bierocks. Use ⅓ cup filling for each bierock.

New Hopedale Church, Meno;
West New Hopedale Church, Ringwood;
and Saron Mennonite Church, Orienta
Oklahoma MCC Relief Sale, Fairview

BREAD DRESSING

- ❖ 1 loaf bread
- ❖ ¼ pound butter
- ❖ 1 cup chopped celery
- ❖ 1 medium onion, chopped
- ❖ 3 large eggs
- ❖ 2 cups milk
- ❖ 1 cup water
- ❖ 1 tablespoon parsley
- ❖ ½ teaspoon sage
- ❖ ½ teaspoon poultry seasoning
- ❖ 1 teaspoon saffron
- ❖ 1 teaspoon salt
- ❖ ¼ teaspoon pepper

Cook onions and celery in butter over medium heat. Do not brown. Toast bread and cube. Beat eggs and add all seasonings, liquid, cooked celery, onion, and bread. Mix together. Stuff fowl or bake in casserole for 1 hour at 350°. If desired, cook onion and celery, let cool, then mix with other ingredients just before stuffing fowl.

Cabbage Rolls

- 1 very large head Savoy or regular cabbage
- 2 pounds ground chuck (beef)
- 1 pound ground pork
- ½ teaspoon pepper
- 2 teaspoons salt
- 1 teaspoon dry mustard
- ½ cup chopped onion
- ¼ cup ketchup
- 1 20-ounce can tomato soup
- 1 48-ounce can tomato juice
- ½ cup long grain uncooked rice

Remove the core from cabbage and separate leaves carefully. Pour boiling water over leaves and let stand about 2 minutes. Drain leaves very well for about 20 minutes. Mix all remaining ingredients (except tomato soup and juice). Form meatballs about the size of a large egg, put in the center of cabbage leaf, and roll up tightly. Place cabbage rolls, open side down, in roasting pan in neat layers. Mix tomato soup and juice well and pour over top. Cover and simmer in oven at 300° for 4 hours. If you enjoy sauerkraut, cabbage rolls may also be placed on a bed of sauerkraut before tomato mixture is poured over. Serve with hot crusty bread.

Calzone

- 1 loaf frozen bread dough

Filling:
- 1 cup grated parmesan cheese
- 1½ cups grated mozzarella cheese
- 1 pound ground beef, browned and drained
- 1½ cups sliced mushrooms
- ½ cup sliced black olives

Sauce:
- 2 cans (8 ounces each) tomato sauce
- 1 clove garlic, minced
- 2 teaspoons sugar
- 1 teaspoon oregano
- ¾ teaspoon basil

Thaw bread dough, but don't let it rise. Roll out into a rectangle big enough to cover the bottom and sides of a 13x9-inch pan plus enough to fold completely over the top. Fit dough into pan. Mix together all filling ingredients. Pour filling into dough-lined pan. Cover with remaining dough rectangle and seal edges. Bake at 375° for 20 minutes or until golden. Combine sauce ingredients and heat while calzone is baking. Cut baked calzone into squares and serve with sauce. Bread dough can also be divided into portions, formed, and filled to make individual calzones.

Tanya Ortman
Marion, South Dakota
Minn-Kota MCC Relief Sale
Sioux Falls, South Dakota

CHALUPA

- 1 3-4 pound pork roast
- 1 pound (3 cups) dried pinto beans
- ½ cup chopped onion
- 4-5 cups water
- 1½ tablespoons chili powder
- 1 teaspoon garlic salt
- 1 teaspoon cumin
- 1 teaspoon oregano
- 1 can green chilies

Mix together all ingredients. Place in a crockpot (slow cooker) and cook for 12 hours. Serve over taco chips with lettuce, tomato, onion, green pepper, cheddar cheese, taco sauce, and sour cream.

Sherry (Epp) Thiesen
Henderson, Nebraska
Nebraska MCC Relief Sale, Aurora

CHEESE SOUFFLÉ

- 1½ cups milk
- 2 cups soft bread crumbs
- 1½ cups grated cheese
- 1 tablespoon butter
- ⅛ teaspoon paprika
- 1 teaspoon salt
- 3 eggs, separated

Heat first 6 ingredients in top of double boiler until cheese is melted. Cool slightly. Add to well-beaten egg yolks. Beat egg whites until stiff. Fold cheese and egg mixture into stiffly-beaten egg whites. Pour into a buttered 1½-quart casserole. Place in pan of hot water and bake at 350° for 40-50 minutes. Minced chicken, ham, turkey, or a 7½-ounce can of salmon may be used instead of cheese.

GIVE A PAT ON THE BACK TODAY. ITS EFFECT GOES ON AND ON—LIKE THAT OF A PEBBLE THROWN INTO WATER.

CHINESE CHOW MEIN DINNER

Chow Mein:
- 1 small onion, diced
- Vegetable oil
- 1 head cabbage, shredded
- 2 cans bean sprouts, drained
- 2 cans (4 ounces each) mushrooms
- 2 stalks celery, diced
- 2 cups cooked chicken
  or beef, cut up
- Chinese pea pods (optional)

Fried Rice:
- 1 cup diced celery
- 1 cup diced carrots
- 1 cup peas
- 1 tablespoon margarine
- 1½-2 cups cooked rice
- 1 pound bacon, diced and fried

To make chow mein, sauté onion in oil. Add remaining ingredients and simmer about 30 minutes. To make fried rice, cook celery, carrots, and peas together in a little water until soft. Drain. Season with salt and pepper as desired. Melt margarine in a skillet. Combine all rice ingredients in skillet. Mix well and simmer about 30 minutes.

Mrs. Lonnie (Linda) Ulrich
Metamora, Illinois
Linn Mennonite Church
Illinois MCC Relief Sale, Peoria

CHICKEN BRUNSWICK STEW

- 100 pounds whole chickens
- 30 pounds onions,
  peeled and diced
- 100 pounds potatoes,
  peeled and diced
- 12 gallons tomatoes
- 12 gallons butter beans
- 1 box (¼ ounce) red pepper
- 2 pounds salt
- 1 box (8 ounces) black pepper
- 12 gallons whole-kernel corn
  (white or yellow)
- 4 pounds butter

Put chicken and enough water to cover in a large open kettle around 6 a.m. Cook until meat falls off bones. Remove bones from meat and broth. Add potatoes and onions. Add water if the stock is thickening too fast. (Add only a little water at a time.) Add tomatoes when potatoes are cooking well. Drain liquid from butter beans into a kettle and save it. (You may need to add more liquid to the stew later.) Add drained beans after pot begins to boil again. Add the box of red pepper and 1 pound of the salt. Let mixture cook until about 4 p.m., adding the black pepper and the remainder of the salt about mid-afternoon. Drain corn and add to kettle at 4 p.m. Add the butter at 4:30 p.m. Cook, stirring constantly, until 5 p.m.

Makes 50 gallons, but can be cut to size as desired.

Contributed by Bid Lloyd
Virginia Relief Sale, Fisherville

ᘓ

CHICKEN POT PIE

- 1 chicken (boiling fowl preferred)
- 4 potatoes, quartered
- Salt and pepper to taste

Dough:
- 1½ cups flour
- ½ teaspoon salt
- 2 eggs
- 3 tablespoons cream

To prepare chicken, cut into pieces. Add water to cover and cook until meat is done. Remove meat. Season broth to taste and add water to make at least 4 cups. You may need some additional commercial chicken broth mix, salt, pepper, and parsley to season it. Add potatoes. To prepare dough, push a well in flour, pour in egg and cream, and mix. Stir into a soft dough. Roll thin and cut into 2-3 inch squares. Drop carefully on surface of boiling broth. Each piece should remain flat. Cook 30 minutes in tightly covered pot. Serve in large tureen that has the warm chicken and broth in bottom.

COUNTRY-STYLE LASAGNA

- 1½ pounds hamburger
- 1 large onion
- Salt and pepper
- ½ teaspoon garlic salt
- 1 teaspoon parsley flakes
- 2 teaspoons oregano
- 1 bay leaf, crushed

Cheese Sauce:
- 4 tablespoons shortening
- ½ teaspoon salt
- 2 cups milk
- 4 tablespoons flour
- 1 small onion, chopped
- 1 cup old cheese, grated

Cover bottom of pan with oil. Brown meat, gradually adding onions and seasoning. Take off grease after hamburger is brown. Add 1 quart tomatoes (or 20-ounce can tomatoes and 1 teaspoon sugar) and 1 large can tomato paste (11 ounces) to hamburger. Simmer 45 minutes. Make sauce by adding milk and cheese to a pot with remaining sauce ingredients. Stir until cheese sauce is thick. Cook 10 wide noodles (or twice what will cover broiler pan) in a large steamer for 14 minutes, stirring as they cook. Put in a sieve and add a small amount of oil. Rinse with cold water. Add a little oil to bottom of pan. Fill with 1 layer of noodles, half of meat sauce, and all of cheese sauce. Cover this with 2 layers of noodles. Put the rest of the meat sauce on top. Cover with mozzarella cheese. Can be left or baked right away at 250° for 1 hour covered with foil.

Rustic Lasagna

- 9 lasagna noodles
- 2 cups tomato sauce
- 1 clove minced garlic
- 1 teaspoon fresh oregano or
  ¼ teaspoon dried oregano
- 1 package (10 ounces) frozen
  chopped broccoli or fresh broccoli
- 1 cup shredded carrots
- 16 ounces part-skim ricotta cheese
- ¼ cup grated parmesan cheese
- 1 cup shredded mozzarella cheese
- Fried hamburger (optional)

Cook lasagna (do not add salt). Preheat oven to 350°. Spray 13x9-inch baking dish with no-stick spray. In a small bowl, combine tomato sauce, garlic, oregano, and hamburger. Mix well. In a medium bowl, combine broccoli, carrots, ricotta, and parmesan. Mix well. Drain noodles and spread ½ cup tomato sauce in bottom of baking pan. Place 3 noodles on top of sauce. Spread half of broccoli mixture over noodles. Spread ½ cup of tomato sauce over broccoli mixture. Place 3 noodles over top. Spread remaining broccoli mixture over noodles. Top with 1 cup tomato sauce. Top with remaining noodles and tomato sauce. Sprinkle mozzarella cheese over top. Bake for 45 minutes.

Frances H. Martin
Quarryville, Pennsylvania

Dried Beef Hot Dish

- 1 can (10¾ ounces) cream of
  mushroom or chicken soup
- 1 soup can filled with milk
- 1¼ cups grated cheddar cheese
- ¼ cup finely chopped onion
- ¼ cup finely chopped green pepper
- 1 cup uncooked elbow macaroni
- 1 package smoked dried beef
- 2 hard-boiled eggs, finely chopped
- 1 package frozen peas (optional)

Mix all ingredients (except peas) together. Put in a baking dish. Cover and refrigerate overnight. Stir in the frozen peas immediately before baking. Bake at 350° for 45 minutes.

Serves 6.

Mrs. Marian Gering
Freeman, South Dakota
Minn-Kota MCC Relief Sale
Sioux Falls, South Dakota

FRANKFURTER CHEESE BOATS

- ❖ 1 10-ounce can
  cream of mushroom soup
- ❖ ½ cup milk
- ❖ 2 packages frozen green beans,
  cooked and drained
- ❖ 8 frankfurters
- ❖ 4 slices cheese, cut in strips
- ❖ 4 slices partially cooked bacon,
  cut in half

In a shallow 12x8x2-inch pan, stir soup until smooth, gradually blending in milk. Stir in beans. Slit frankfurters lengthwise to about ½ inch from each end. Stuff with cheese. Arrange wieners on beans and top with bacon. Bake at 350° for 25 minutes or until hot.

HAM LOAF

Loaf:
- ❖ 3 pounds smoked ham
- ❖ 1 pound fresh pork
- ❖ 1 pound beef
- ❖ 2 cups bread crumbs
- ❖ 4 eggs, beaten
- ❖ 1 cup tomato juice

Sauce:
- ❖ ½ cup brown sugar
- ❖ ¼ cup vinegar
- ❖ ½ cup pineapple juice

Grind together the ham, pork, and beef (or have butcher grind it together). Add bread crumbs, eggs, and tomato juice to meat. Mix well. Form into loaves. Combine sauce ingredients and pour over loaves. Bake at 350° for 1¼ hours. Baste with sauce mixture during baking.

Mildred Brenneman
Bloomington, Illinois
Bethel Mennonite Church, Pekin
Illinois MCC Relief Sale, Peoria

Hamburger Roll-Ups

Meat Filling:
- 1 medium chopped onion
- 1 pound ground beef
- 1 tablespoon oil
- ½ teaspoon salt
- Pinch of pepper

Sauce:
- 1 can mushroom soup
- ½ cup milk
- ⅓ cup chili sauce

Cook ingredients for meat filling together slowly until meat is cooked. Add 2 tablespoons flour and ½ cup milk. Cook a few minutes until thickened. Cool.

Mix biscuit dough from 2 cups baking mix following directions on package. Roll out dough about ½ inch thick. Cover with meat filling. Roll up like cinnamon roll. Cut in 1½-inch slices. Put on ungreased pans and bake 20-30 minutes at 375° or until done. Simmer sauce ingredients together several minutes and pour over top.

Easy Dressing for Turkey

- 1 loaf bread, cubed
- 2 chopped onions
- 1 cup water
- ¼ pound butter
- Salt, pepper, poultry seasoning, and parsley to taste

For each loaf of bread, boil 2 onions in 1 cup water for 5 minutes. Add ¼ pound (or less) butter. When butter is melted, pour liquid over chopped bread. Season to taste with salt, pepper, poultry seasoning, and parsley.

A large turkey will take 2 loaves of bread.

EASY GARDEN VEGETABLE PIE

- 2 cups sliced fresh broccoli or cauliflower
- ½ cup chopped onion
- ½ cup chopped green pepper
- 1 cup (about 4 ounces) shredded cheddar cheese
- 1½ cups milk
- 3 eggs
- ¾ cup baking mix
- 1 teaspoon salt
- ¼ teaspoon pepper

Heat oven to 400°. Lightly grease a 1½-inch deep 10-inch pie pan. Heat 1 inch salted water to a boil. Add broccoli. Cover and heat to boiling. Cook until almost tender (about 5 minutes). Drain thoroughly. Mix broccoli, onion, green pepper, and cheese in pie pan. Place milk, eggs, baking mix, and salt and pepper in blender container. Blend for 15 seconds and pour over vegetables. Bake 35-40 minutes or until golden brown. Test by inserting knife in center of quiche. It's done when knife comes out clean. Let stand for a few minutes before cutting. One package (10 ounces) frozen chopped broccoli or cauliflower, thawed and drained, can be substituted for the fresh vegetables.

Susana Siemens
Winnipeg, Manitoba

HAYSTACKS

- 3 pounds ground beef
- 1 large jar (28 ounces) Ragu spaghetti sauce
- Crushed soda crackers
- 2 cups cooked rice
- Shredded lettuce
- Cut-up tomatoes
- Chopped onion
- Crushed corn chips
- Sliced olives
- Chopped walnuts
- 2 cans (10¾ ounces each) cheddar cheese soup
- 1 cup milk

Brown ground beef and drain. Add Ragu sauce. Place crackers, rice, lettuce, tomatoes, onions, chips, olives, and walnuts in separate containers. Combine soup and milk. Heat. Allow diners to layer ingredients on their plates.

Serves 8.

Ann Goossen
Beatrice, Nebraska
Nebraska MCC Relief Sale, Aurora

Imam Bayildi (Stuffed Eggplant)

- 3 medium eggplants
- 6 medium onions, sliced thin
- Vegetable oil
- 1 pound lean ground beef
- 5 medium tomatoes
- 7 cloves garlic
- Salt
- Ketchup

Cut stems off eggplants. Slice in half lengthwise. Scoop out and save eggplant pulp. Leave 1-1½ inches of pulp attached to skin. Set aside. Sauté onions in a little oil until clear. Add beef. Chop and add 4 of the tomatoes. Add garlic. Season with salt. Simmer until most of the liquid has evaporated. Chop reserved eggplant pulp and add to sauce. Fill eggplant shells with sauce mixture. Slice remaining tomato and place on top of shells. Place stuffed eggplants in a baking dish containing 1 inch of water. Dilute ketchup with water and pour over each shell. Bake covered at 350° for 1 hour.

Helen Harmes
Aldergrove, British Columbia

Impossible Cheeseburger Pie

- 1 pound ground beef
- 1½ cups chopped onion
- ½ teaspoon salt
- ¼ teaspoon pepper
- 1½ cups milk
- ¾ cup baking mix
- 3 eggs
- 2 tomatoes, sliced
- 1 cup shredded cheddar cheese

Heat oven to 400°. Grease a 1½-inch deep 10-inch pie plate. Brown beef and onion. Drain. Stir in salt and pepper. Spread meat mixture in pie plate. Beat milk, baking mix, and eggs until smooth (15 seconds in blender on high or 1 minute with hand beater). Pour over meat mixture. Bake 25 minutes. Immediately top with tomatoes and sprinkle with cheese. Bake 5 minutes more.

Makes 6-8 servings.

Lynette P. Frey
Sterling, Illinois
Science Ridge Mennonite Church
Illinois MCC Relief Sale, Peoria

JUICY MEAT LOAF

- 1½ pounds ground beef
- ¼ pound ground pork
- ¼ cup finely cut onion
- 1 cup quick-cooking
  or regular rolled oats
- 2 teaspoons salt
- ¼ teaspoon pepper
- ½ teaspoon dry mustard or
  2½ teaspoons prepared mustard
- ¼ cup ketchup
- 1 beaten egg
- 1 cup water or milk

Mix all ingredients thoroughly. Pack into a 9x5-inch loaf pan. Bake at 375° for 1-1½ hours. Slice and serve garnished with parsley sprigs.

LAYERED MEAT LOAF

- 1½ pounds ground beef
- ¾ cup uncooked rolled oats
- 1 egg, beaten
- ¼ cup chopped onion
- 1½ teaspoons salt
- ¼ teaspoon pepper
- ¼ teaspoon oregano
- 2 teaspoons parsley flakes
- 1 cup tomato juice
- 1½ cups cooked sliced carrots
- 2 cups mashed potatoes
- 2 tablespoons grated cheese

Combine beef, oats, egg, onion, seasonings, and tomato juice. Pack into microwaveable 8-inch square pan. Bake in microwave about 10 minutes. Test to see that meat is set in center. Spread carrots over meat. Spread mashed potatoes evenly over carrots. Sprinkle with cheese. Return to microwave and bake 5 minutes more.

Lisa Kauffman
Pleasant View Mennonite Church
Goshen, Indiana

THE ONLY THING THAT KEEPS A MAN GOING IS ENERGY.
AND WHAT IS ENERGY BUT LIKING LIFE?

Ribbon Meat Loaf

Meatloaf:
- 1 pound hamburger
- 1 onion (or more), chopped
- Seasonings to taste
- 1-2 eggs

Dressing:
- 1½ cups bread crumbs
- Raisins and onions to taste
- Poultry seasoning and sage, if desired
- Beef or chicken stock to moisten
- Margarine or butter

Mix ingredients for meat loaf. Spread one layer in greased loaf pan. Mix together the dressing. Put a layer on top of the meat. Alternate layers until finished. Bake 1¼ hours at 350°. If desired, top with mashed potatoes in the last 30 minutes of cooking.

Serves 6-8.

Kraut Runza

Filling:
- 64 pounds lean ground beef
- 18 gallons sauerkraut
- 32 heads cabbage
- 64 onions
- 2 large or 4 small cooked hams, ground into crumbles
- 1 cup salt
- 1 cup pepper
- 1 cup garlic salt

Dough:
- 4 packages dry yeast
- ¾ cup sugar
- 4 teaspoons salt
- 25-pound sack of flour
- ¾ cup margarine

To prepare filling, crumble ground beef and brown. Drain off all liquid. Simmer sauerkraut and drain very well. Grind cabbages and onions in batches in a food processor. Sauté in a little margarine or butter until golden. Drain completely. Blend all ingredients and seasonings together. Cool overnight. Prepare 3 batches of the bread dough. Put ⅓ cup filling inside a round of flattened dough. Pinch shut. Bake at 350° for 15-20 minutes.

Country Auction and Relief Sale
Ritzville, Washington

LEBANON BOLOGNA

- 50 pounds beef
- 1 pound salt
- 3 tablespoons pepper
- 2 tablespoons nutmeg
- 1½ tablespoons potassium nitrate
- 2 ½ pounds sugar
- 1½ pounds salt
- 9 ounces peanut oil or ½ pound lard

Salt the meat with the salt and let stand for four days. Cut the meat to grind, then put it in a large container, making alternate layers of meat and a mixture of the remaining seasonings. Let stand a week or 10 days, turning the meat on top every day or so to prevent drying out. Grind to your desire, adding ½ pound melted lard to every 25 pounds of meat. Mix in wooden or enamel containers. Stuff and let hang 2-3 days to settle, then smoke. Do not overheat with smoke fire.

From Amish Cooking, *published by Pathway Publishers Corporation*

LEFTOVER TURKEY OR CHICKEN CROQUETTES

- Leftover turkey or chicken
- Turkey dressing
- Gravy
- Flour
- Beaten egg (1 or more)
- Bread crumbs
- Oil

Cut up leftover turkey or chicken and put it through a coarse chopper. Mix 2 parts turkey and 1 part dressing. Moisten with gravy. Form into patties and freeze. When ready to use, dip in flour, beaten egg, and bread crumbs and fry in oil.

PARTY BUNS

- 1 package cream cheese or 1 cup shredded cheddar cheese
- 1 can tuna or 1 cup chicken, turkey, or salmon
- 2-3 drops lemon juice
- ½ cup salad dressing
- 1-2 tablespoons chopped celery
- 1-2 tablespoons chopped onion
- 1-2 tablespoons chopped pepper
- 2 chopped hard-cooked eggs

Combine ingredients and pile into 8-10 buns (hamburger or southern type). Wrap in foil. Bake at 400° for 15 minutes or at 325° for 30 minutes.

PARTY SANDWICH LOAF

- 1 loaf French bread, sliced
- 1 pound Velveeta cheese
- 2 tablespoons butter
- Celery salt and paprika to taste

Soften and mix cheese, butter, celery salt, and paprika. Spread generously on bread slices. Pack all in order again. Wrap in foil. Bake at 325° for 1 hour. To prepare in advance, refrigerate 1-2 days, then bake at 350° for 1 hour.

PICKLED HEART AND TONGUE

- 1 beef tongue
- 1 beef heart
- 1½ cups vinegar
- ½ cup water
- Salt and pepper to taste

Scald tongue and remove outer skin. Trim fat off heart. Boil meat until tender. Cool. Slice meat into thin slices. Heat vinegar, water, salt, and pepper. Add meat and heat to boiling point. Put in jars and seal. Other seasonings can be used if desired. If desired, tongue may be placed in bowl, covered with vinegar, and cut into thin slices as needed to serve.

PLOU (CHICKEN AND RICE)

- 1 large chicken
- 3 quarts water
- 1 tablespoon salt
- 1½ teaspoons ground allspice
- 1 onion, diced
- 2 tablespoons shortening
- 2 cups uncooked rice
- 4 cups chicken broth
- 4 carrots, sliced
- ¼ teaspoon pepper

Put chicken in the water with the salt and allspice. Cook until tender. Remove chicken from bones and cut into small pieces. Sauté onion in the shortening. Add rice, chicken broth, carrots, and pepper. Simmer for 1½ hours. (Do not overcook. The rice should stay crumply.)

Serves 6-8.

Gretl Jantzen
Nebraska MCC Relief Sale, Aurora

PORCUPINES

- 1 pound hamburger
- 4 slices bread
- 1 egg
- 1 cup milk
- 1 onion
- ¼ cup uncooked rice
- 2 cups tomato juice

Crumble bread and soak in milk. Add beaten egg. Mix with other ingredients (except tomato juice). Shape into balls and place in casserole. Pour tomato juice over balls and bake 1½ hours at 350°.

PORK AND BEANS

- 5 pounds white beans, soaked overnight
- ½ teaspoon nutmeg
- ½ teaspoon pepper
- ½ teaspoon mustard
- 4 tablespoons molasses
- 2 tablespoons salt
- 2 pounds diced bacon or 1 ham bone

Combine ingredients and boil until beans are tender. Add ketchup to suit taste and simmer 10-15 minutes. If canning, steam pints 15 minutes and quarts 30 minutes. Instead of bacon, you can use 1 ham bone, which can be removed when beans are cooked.

PORK CHOPS

- 6 lean pork chops cut ¾ inch thick
- 1 tablespoon oil
- 4 cups sliced apples
- ¼ cup raisins
- ¼ teaspoon cinnamon
- 1 teaspoon grated lemon peel (optional)
- ¼ cup brown sugar
- ¼ cup water

Brown chops in oil in electric fry pan at 380°. Cover and cook at 200° until tender (about 30 minutes). Pour off fat. Add apples, raisins, cinnamon, lemon peel, sugar, and water. Cover and cook until apples are tender (15-20 minutes). Serve on warmed platter.

Serves 6.

Pork Chops and Rice Colonial

- 4 pork chops
- 1 cup uncooked rice
- ¼ cup chopped onion
- ½ teaspoon pepper
- ½ cup chopped green peppers or mushrooms
- 1 can consommé soup
- 1 cup water
- 2 teaspoons salt

Brown chops in fry pan. Place chops in casserole. Drain off excess fat in fry pan and lightly brown rice, onion, and peppers. Spoon rice mixture over chops in casserole. Add consommé, water, salt, and pepper. Cover and bake at 350° for 1 hour.

Stir-Fry Pork

- 1 can (14½ ounces) chicken broth
- ⅔ cup soy sauce
- 2 tablespoons sugar
- 3 tablespoons dry sherry
- 2 pounds lean pork, cut into thin strips
- ¼ cup salad oil
- 3 medium carrots, cut into thin strips
- 2 cups diagonally sliced green onions
- 2 cups diagonally sliced celery
- 1 cup broccoli, cut into thin strips
- 1 cup sliced fresh mushrooms
- 1 can sliced bamboo shoots, drained
- 1 can sliced water chestnuts, drained
- 3 tablespoons cornstarch
- 2 bags rice, cooked and drained

Combine broth, soy sauce, sugar, and sherry. Pour over pork and let marinate 1-2 hours. Heat oil in wok. Drain pork and reserve sauce. Add pork to wok and fry until cooked. Remove pork from wok. Add carrots, onions, celery, and broccoli stems. Cook a few minutes. Add broccoli tops, mushrooms, bamboo shoots, and water chestnuts. Return pork to wok. Cook until vegetables are tender-crisp. Mix cornstarch into reserved marinade. Add to wok. Cook until sauce boils and thickens slightly. Serve over cooked rice.

Alisa (Epp) Krehbiel
West Chester, Pennsylvania
Nebraska MCC Relief Sale, Aurora

QUICK ITALIAN BAKE

- ❖ 1 pound ground beef
  or Italian sausage
- ❖ 1 cup chopped tomato
- ❖ ¾ cup frozen peas
- ❖ ½ teaspoon Italian seasoning
- ❖ 1 cup baking mix
- ❖ 1 cup milk
- ❖ 2 eggs
- ❖ 1 cup shredded mozzarella cheese

Heat oven to 400°. Grease a 9-inch pie plate. Brown ground beef and drain. Stir in tomato, peas, and seasoning. Spread meat mixture in plate. Stir baking mix, milk, and eggs with a fork until blended. Pour over meat mixture. Bake 25 minutes or until knife comes out clean. Sprinkle with cheese. Bake 2-3 minutes longer or until cheese is melted. Serve with pizza sauce if desired.

Makes 6-8 servings.

Florence Blough
Hollsopple, Pennsylvania
MCC Quilt Auction and Relief Sale, Johnstown

ROAST PIG

- ❖ 1 pig, 200-220 pounds live weight
- ❖ 60 pounds of charcoal
- ❖ Enough sauerkraut or bread to fill
  the cavity of the pig (optional)

Use a regular pig roaster or 2 55-gallon barrels cut in half and welded together. Start charcoal and let it burn until it gets gray. Continue to add charcoal as needed to keep the temperature even. Roast pig 16-18 hours, or longer if necessary.

Makes 200-225 servings.

Gap Relief Sale, Pennsylvania

GIVE YOURSELF PLENTY OF TIME IF YOU DECIDE TO TRY THIS RECIPE.
IT CAN TAKE ALMOST 24 HOURS TO ROAST A 200-POUND PIG!

SALMON PATTIES

- 1 small onion, finely cut
- 2-3 tablespoons butter
- 2 cups salmon, flaked and boned
- ¾ cup coarse cracker crumbs
- 1 egg, slightly beaten
- ½ cup milk

Sauté onion in butter until golden yellow. Add to salmon, cracker crumbs, egg, and milk. Spoon into well buttered skillet and fry a golden brown. Turn and fry other side.

SAUERKRAUT AND PORK

- Fresh pork
- Water
- Sauerkraut

Cook fresh pork in lots of water. Add sauerkraut and simmer slowly for about 3 hours. Some people like to add dumplings at the end of the 3 hours and serve immediately after they have cooked (about 10-12 minutes).

SAMOSA

- 1 pound flour
- ½ pound butter
- 1 medium onion, chopped
- 1 pound minced meat
- ¼ pound green peas
- 1 teaspoon garlic powder
- ½ teaspoon salt
- 1 teaspoon ground black pepper
- ¼ teaspoon anardana
- 1 pound vegetable oil

Make a hard dough from the flour, 2 tablespoons of butter, and water. Pinch off small balls of dough and roll into 6-8 inch circles. Cut circles in half. Fry onion in a little of the remaining butter until brown. Mix in minced meat and fry over medium heat. Add peas and seasonings and cook until moisture is absorbed. Let filling cool. Place 1½ tablespoons of cooled filling onto each half-circle of dough. Close them up and use remaining butter to seal edges. Fry in hot vegetable oil.

Helen Harmes
Aldergrove, British Columbia

MAKE THIS RECIPE SPICIER BY ADDING ¼-1 TEASPOON OF
HOT CHILI PEPPER TO THE FILLING.

SLOPPY JOES

- 20 pounds ground beef
- 2 cans (7 pounds, 2 ounces each) ketchup
- 2 cans (8 ounces each) tomato sauce
- 1 cup mustard
- 1 pound brown sugar
- 5 ounces minced onion
- 5 ounces Worcestershire sauce
- 2 tablespoons salt
- 2 tablespoons pepper
- 3 tablespoons chili powder

Brown ground beef and drain well. Combine remaining ingredients in a large kettle. Warm over medium heat. Add browned beef and heat thoroughly. Serve two scoops per bun.

Marcella Powers
Missouri MCC Relief Sale, Harrisonville

SMOKY COUNTRY-STYLE RIBS

- 4 pounds country-style ribs
- Garlic salt
- Fresh ground pepper
- 1¼ cup ketchup
- ¾ cup firmly packed brown sugar
- ½ cup chili sauce
- 2 tablespoons vinegar
- 2 tablespoons liquid smoke seasoning
- 1 tablespoon lemon juice

Sprinkle ribs with garlic salt and pepper. Combine remaining ingredients in medium saucepan. Cook over medium heat for about 10 minutes, stirring occasionally. Keep warm. Place ribs, rib bones down, on a rack in a shallow roasting pan. Baste with sauce. Bake at 325° for 1½-2 hours, turning and basting with sauce every 30 minutes. Cut into serving portions. Heat remaining sauce and serve with ribs.

Serves 4-6.

Alisa (Epp) Krehbiel
West Chester, Pennsylvania
Nebraska MCC Relief Sale, Aurora

Spaghetti with Zucchini Sauce

- 1 large onion, chopped
- 1 tablespoon vegetable oil
- 6 cups sliced zucchini
- 3 cups fresh tomatoes, 1 jar tomato sauce, or whole canned tomatoes
- ½ teaspoon salt
- 1 bay leaf
- ¼ teaspoon pepper
- ¼ teaspoon basil
- ¼ teaspoon oregano

Sauté onion in oil. Add zucchini, tomatoes, and seasonings. Simmer covered for 15 minutes. Uncover and simmer 10 minutes. Discard bay leaf. Serve sauce over cooked spaghetti. Sprinkle with grated Parmesan cheese.

MCC Quilt Auction and Relief Sale, Johnstown

Spanish Veal

- 4 tablespoons shortening
- 1 pound cubed stewing veal
- 4 tablespoons chopped onion
- 4 tablespoons chopped celery
- 4 tablespoons chopped green pepper
- 4 tablespoons flour
- ½ teaspoon salt
- ¼ teaspoon paprika
- 1½ cups canned tomatoes

Brown veal, onion, celery, and pepper in hot fat in frying pan. Add flour and mix. Mix in the rest of ingredients in casserole or small roasting pan. Cover and bake at 300° for 1 hour, stirring occasionally. When doubling or tripling recipe, extend baking time to 2-3 hours.

Serves 3.

Spinach Pie

- 1 package spinach
- 6 raw potatoes
- 3 eggs
- 1 onion
- 4 tablespoons melted butter
- 1 teaspoon salt
- Pepper

Chop raw spinach very fine. Grate potatoes and add beaten eggs. Grate in onion. Add melted butter and seasonings. Place half of potato mixture into greased baking dish. Pack in spinach. Cover with remaining potato mixture. Bake at 350° for 30 minutes.

Serves 6.

STEAK ROULADIN

- 6 thin slices top round steak
- 2 pounds or 2 10-ounce cans mushrooms, sliced
- Garlic salt
- Salt and pepper
- 2 cups boiling water
- 2 beef bouillon cubes
- 2 tablespoons prepared mustard

Have butcher slice steak very thin. (Each slice makes 2 rolls.) Sprinkle each slice of meat with garlic salt and salt and pepper. Spread mushrooms generously on meat and roll each up like a jelly roll. Secure with toothpicks or string. Brown on all sides in a frying pan containing about 2 tablespoons butter. Remove to roast pan. Add the boiling water, beef bouillon cubes, and mustard to frying pan. Stir until all is blended. Pour over steak rolls. Bake at 325° for 2½ hours. Turn rolls once or twice during baking time. Onions can be substituted for sliced mushrooms and 2 cans of consommé can be used instead of bouillon cubes and boiling water.

Serves 6.

STEWED CHICKEN DINNER WITH BISCUITS

Chicken:
- 1 4-5 pound chicken, disjointed
- 2 teaspoons salt
- ½ cup chopped celery
- ½ teaspoon pepper
- ½ can cream of mushroom soup
- ½ can cream of celery soup
- Flour
- Water
- 1-1½ cups cooked peas and carrots

Biscuits:
- 2 cups flour (pastry and all-purpose combined)
- ½ teaspoon salt
- 4 teaspoons baking powder
- ½ teaspoon cream of tartar
- 2 teaspoons sugar
- ½ cup shortening or lard
- ½-⅔ cup milk

To prepare chicken, cover meat with water and add celery, salt, and pepper. Cook slowly until very tender. Remove meat from bones, cut into 1-inch pieces, and return to broth. Add both soups, undiluted. Thicken broth with a mixture of flour and water to desired thickness. To prepare biscuits, sift flour, salt, baking powder, cream of tartar, and sugar. Cut in shortening until mixture resembles coarse crumbs. Add milk all at once and stir until thoroughly mixed. Pat or roll ¾ inch thick and cut with biscuit cutter. Bake on ungreased cookie sheet at 450° for 10-12 minutes. Makes about 15 biscuits. When ready to serve, add peas and carrots to chicken. Serve over biscuits. Roasted turkey can be substituted for the chicken.

Super Eggs on Toast

- 2 tablespoons onion, finely minced
- 2 tablespoons butter
- 1 can cream of celery soup
- ⅓ cup milk
- 6 eggs
- 6 slices of bread
- 6 slices of cheese

Cook the onion in the butter. Add the cream of celery soup and milk. Heat, stirring, until combined. Meanwhile, poach the eggs and toast the bread. Place a slice of cheese on each slice of toast. When ready to serve, put under broiler until cheese is melted. Top with poached egg and sauce made with soup.

Sweet and Sour Chicken Wings

- 2 pounds chicken wings
- ⅔ cup brown sugar
- 2 tablespoons vinegar
- 2 tablespoons soy sauce
- Salt and pepper
- Garlic powder
- 1 cube of chicken bouillon

Split joints of chicken wings. Flour and brown in a little fat. Lay flat (the flatter the better) in a baking dish. Crumble ⅓ cup brown sugar over each pound of chicken. Sprinkle each pound of chicken with 2 tablespoons vinegar, 2 tablespoons soy sauce, a little garlic powder, and the crumbled cube of chicken bouillon. Add salt and pepper to taste. Put cover on dish and bake at 325° for 45 minutes. Serve with rice mixed with sautéed mushrooms and green pepper. Spareribs cut into 1-inch pieces can be substituted for chicken wings, but baking time must be increased to 1 hour.

Serves 4.

Sweet and Sour Meatballs

- 1½ pounds ground beef
- 2 eggs
- 3 tablespoons flour
- ¾ cup oil
- 1½ cups chicken bouillon
- 3 large green peppers, diced
- 6 slices pineapple, diced
- 2 tablespoons cornstarch
- 2 tablespoons soy sauce
- 1 tablespoon Accent
- ¾ cup vinegar
- ¾ cup pineapple juice
- ¾ cup sugar
- ½ teaspoon salt
- Pepper

Shape ground beef into 18 balls. Combine flour, eggs, salt, and pepper. Dip meatballs into mixture and brown. Keep hot. Pour out all but 1 tablespoon oil from skillet and add ½ cup bouillon, green pepper, and pineapple. Cover and cook over medium heat for 10 minutes. Mix in remaining ingredients. Cook, stirring constantly, until mixture comes to a boil and thickens. Add meatballs and simmer for 15 minutes. Serve with rice.

Saure Klops (Sour Meatballs)

Meatballs:
- 2 pounds ground beef
- 2 eggs
- 2 teaspoons salt
- ½ teaspoon pepper
- 1 cup cracker crumbs, rolled fine
- 1 scant cup water

Sauce:
- 5 cups water
- 12 whole allspice
- 4 bay leaves
- Salt
- Flour
- Cream
- 4 teaspoons vinegar
- 2 level teaspoons sugar

Mix all meatball ingredients together. Form into balls a little bigger than a golf ball. To make the sauces, bring the 5 cups water to a boil. Add the allspice, bay leaves, and salt. Put in meatballs. Boil 20 minutes. Combine flour and cream to make a thickening paste. Pour this into meatball cooking liquid to thicken it like gravy. Add vinegar and sugar. Stir well. Serve with potatoes or noodles.

Rogena (Friesen) Jantzen
Plymouth, Nebraska
Featured in the Nebraska MCC Relief
Sale Cookbook

Sweet and Sour Pigtails or Spareribs

- Pigtails or Spareribs

Sauce:
- ¼ cup brown sugar
- 3 tablespoons cornstarch
- ¼ teaspoon dry mustard
- ⅛ teaspoon ginger
- 1 teaspoon salt
- ¾ teaspoon chili powder
- 1 clove garlic
- 5 tablespoons vinegar
- 1 cup tomato juice
- 1 cup water
- 1 teaspoon soy sauce

Mix all ingredients and cook until thickened, stirring frequently. Pour over pigtails or ribs in roast pan. Bake in oven 1 hour. Add mushrooms, green pepper, and red pepper if desired and bake 1 more hour.

Swiss Steak

- 3 tablespoons fat
- 2 pounds round steak, 1 inch thick
- ½ cup flour
- 1½ teaspoons salt
- ¼ teaspoon pepper
- 1 can (10¾ ounces) cream of mushroom soup
- 1 soup can water

Melt fat in skillet. Cut steak into small pieces and roll/dredge in a mixture of the flour, salt, and pepper. Brown steak on both sides. Transfer meat to a baking dish or roaster. Combine mushroom soup and water. Pour over steak. Cover and bake at 350° for 1½ hours.

Serves 8.

Adella (Stutzman) Gingrich
Albany, Oregon

Verenike

Dough:
- ❖ 21 cups flour
- ❖ 12 eggs
- ❖ 2 tablespoons salt
- ❖ 2 cups cream
- ❖ 4 cups milk

Filling:
- ❖ 8 cups well-drained cottage cheese
- ❖ 2 eggs
- ❖ 2 teaspoons salt
- ❖ ½ teaspoon pepper

Prepare a soft dough from the ingredients listed. Roll out thin and cut in circles using a tin can 4 inches in diameter. Combine ingredients for cottage cheese filling. Place a spoonful of filling on each circle. Fold and seal edges well. Cook in boiling water until they float or fry in deep fat until golden brown. Top with cream gravy.

Serves about 190.

Bethesda Mennonite Church
Nebraska Relief Sale, Aurora

Verenike with Gravy

Dough:
- ❖ 12 cups milk
- ❖ 12 whole eggs
- ❖ 12 egg whites
- ❖ 2 tablespoons baking powder
- ❖ 2 tablespoons salt
- ❖ 1 pound margarine, melted
- ❖ 15 cups flour

Filling:
- ❖ 22 pounds cottage cheese
- ❖ 12 egg yolks
- ❖ 2 tablespoons salt
- ❖ 1 tablespoon pepper

Gravy:
- ❖ 1 pound margarine
- ❖ 1 scant cup flour
- ❖ 1 teaspoon pepper
- ❖ 2 teaspoons salt
- ❖ 6 cups water
- ❖ 5 cans evaporated milk
- ❖ ⅓ pail (ice cream size) sour cream

Prepare dough and filling. Add filling to sections of dough (size as desired). Cook in boiling water, bake, or fry. To prepare gravy, melt margarine and add salt, pepper, flour, and then water. Bring to a boil. Add evaporated milk. Bring to a boil. Remove from heat and add sour cream. Keep hot, but do not boil again or the gravy will curdle. Pour over verenike.

Louise Ens and Agnes Tschetter
Kelowna Relief Sale, British Columbia

Zucchini Quiche

- 3 cups grated zucchini
- 1 onion, chopped
- 1 cup baking mix
- 4 eggs, beaten
- ½ cup vegetable oil
- ½ cup grated Parmesan cheese
- 1 teaspoon parsley
- ¼ teaspoon salt

Mix all ingredients well. Pour into greased 9-inch pie pan. Bake for 30 minutes or until brown.

Grace Cable
Hollsopple, Pennsylvania
MCC Quilt Auction and Relief Sale, Johnstown

Verenike

Verenike, or Varenyki, is a type of stuffed dough similar to pierogies. Verenike can be stuffed with a variety of things, from potatoes, to meat, cheese, and even fruit. Venerike is probably Ukranian in origin, but similar dishes are found in Russia and Lithuania, and pierogies are of Polish descent. European Mennonites who lived in these countries likely brought the recipe with them when they emigrated to America to escape persecution.

EUROPEAN DISHES

Many Mennonites left their German-Prussian homelands to escape
persecution and build a new life in the Russian Ukraine from 1789-1797.
Empress Catherine II of Russia invited them, promising religious freedom.
They prospered and built churches, schools, and huge farms and businesses.
Rulers changed, however. Promises were broken, and the Mennonites were
oppressed and suffered with others in Russia.

Those wishing to emigrate were forced to leave homes, possessions,
and even family behind. Settling primarily in the west, they brought their
German-style cooking mixed with influences from the central European
countries in which they had sojourned. We share some of these unique
recipes in this section.

Apple Moos

- 3-4 cups peeled chopped apple
- 2 cups water
- 4 cups milk
- 2½ tablespoons cornstarch mixed in a little cold water
- ¼ cup sugar
- Few grains salt

Cook apples in water until soft. Bring milk and salt to boil over low heat. Add cornstarch mixture and cook for about 10 minutes until the taste of raw starch disappears. Add sugar (use more than ¼ cup if desired). Remove from heat and add the cooked apples, stirring constantly. Add more milk if mixture is too thick. Plums or dried fruits may be used in place of apples.

Apple Strudel

- 3 cups all-purpose flour
- ½ teaspoon salt
- 1 egg
- ½ cup warm water (or more if needed)
- 1 tablespoon salad oil
- 1 tablespoon melted shortening
- 8 apples
- ½ cup sugar
- Cinnamon to taste

Measure flour and salt into bowl. Beat egg, warm water, and salad oil. Work liquid into flour to make a soft dough that does not stick to board. Knead and roll well for at least 10 minutes. Cover with a bowl and allow to rest for 30 minutes. Spread clean cloth on card table. Flour. Roll dough as thin as possible, then stretch with hands until extremely thin. Stretch until dough is at least as large as the table and hanging over the sides. Brush with melted shortening. Sprinkle with peeled shredded apple, sugar, and cinnamon. Lift cloth and roll up as a jelly roll. Fry in electric fry pan in a little shortening until golden brown. You can also sprinkle apples with cottage cheese, roll up, and bake at 350°-375° for 1 hour.

Borscht

- 2 pounds beef with bone
- 1 large onion
- 1 carrot
- 1 red beet
- 3 potatoes
- ½ cabbage head, shredded
- Bunches of parsley and dill
- salt, hot red pepper,
  or peppercorns to taste
- 1 can tomatoes, chopped

Simmer meat in 2 quarts salted water until meat is done (about 2 hours). Add 1 can tomatoes. Tie onion, parsley, and dill in cheesecloth (include pepper if desired). Add shredded vegetables (carrot may be left whole and removed before serving). Simmer for 1 hour. If soup lacks body, a can of tomato soup may be added. Taste for seasoning. A spoon of sour cream may be added to each serving.

Bubbat (Sausage Square)

- 1 package yeast
- ½ cup warm water
- 1 teaspoon sugar
- ½ cup milk
- 3 tablespoons butter
- 2 eggs, beaten
- 1 teaspoon salt
- Flour to make soft dough
  (about 2½-3 cups)
- Bacon
- Smoked pork sausage

Combine yeast, warm water, and sugar. Let rise 10 minutes. Heat milk and butter slightly. Mix with eggs, salt, and yeast mixture. Add enough flour to make a soft dough that can barely be stirred with a spoon. Line a 9x9-inch pan with bacon strips. Spoon half of dough into pan. Arrange smoked pork sausage cut in 2-inch pieces over all. Put remaining dough on top. Let rise 1 hour. Bake at 375° for 45 minutes.

℃℧

CHRISTMAS COOKIES

Cream together:
- 3 cups white sugar
- 3 cups corn syrup
- 3 eggs
- ½ cup butter
- 20 drops oil of lemon (from drugstore)

Sift together:
- 1 teaspoon soda
- 1 teaspoon baking powder
- 2 teaspoons spices (cloves and cinnamon to taste)
- 1 teaspoon salt
- 4 cups flour (first amount)

Combine two mixtures and continue to add flour to make a dough that can be rolled (about 5 additional cups). Roll out and cut into rounds (a scalloped cutter may be used). Press ½ teaspoon jam on top and cover with another round. Press together. Bake at 375° for 12 minutes. Best if made several days before using. May be iced after they have been stored.

FASTNACHT DOUGHNUTS

- 1 cup milk
- 2 eggs, separated
- 1½ cups raisins
- ¼ cup butter
- 2 teaspoons salt
- 1 package dry yeast
- ¼ cup warm water
- 2 teaspoons sugar
- 1 teaspoon lemon rind
- 2½ cups flour

Dissolve sugar and yeast in warm water. Set aside for at least 10 minutes. Scald milk and add salt, butter, and egg yolks when it has cooled to lukewarm. Beat egg whites until stiff. Sift flour into bowl and make well in center. Add yeast mixture and milk mixture. Stir to mix. Stir in raisins and rind and fold in egg whites. Let rise for 1 hour. Heat fat in fryer to 425°. Drop batter in by teaspoonfuls. Sprinkle with sifted powdered sugar when cooled.

Fleisch Piroschky (Meat Buns)

Dough:
- ½ cup warm water
- 1 package dry yeast
- 1 tablespoon sugar
- 1 cup scalded milk
- ½ cup shortening
- 1½ teaspoons salt
- 3 cups flour

Meat Filling:
- 1 onion, chopped
- ½ pound ground leftover beef
- ½ teaspoon salt
- 1-2 hard-boiled eggs (optional)
- Leftover gravy or sour cream

To prepare dough, scald and cool milk. Add yeast dissolved in warm water and sugar. Add remaining ingredients to make soft dough as for rolls. Let rise. Pinch off pieces of dough and flatten into rounds with hands. Sauté onion for meat filling gently until yellow. Add to ground meat and eggs that have been put through food chopper. Add salt and enough gravy or sour cream to moisten. If desired, combine with a cup of mashed potato instead of gravy or sour cream (this makes the filling very light and fluffy). Place 1 tablespoon of meat filling on dough and form into an oblong bun. Place on well-greased cookie sheet and bake at 350° for 25-30 minutes or until golden brown.

Fruit Platz or Coffee Cake

- 3 tablespoons butter
- 3 tablespoons cream
- 1 egg
- ¼ cup sugar
- Dash of salt
- 1 cup all-purpose flour
- 2 teaspoons baking powder
- 1 teaspoon vanilla
- Fruit

Cream butter, cream, egg, sugar, and salt all together. Add flour, baking powder, and vanilla to make soft dough. Press into a greased 9x9x2-inch pan. Cover with sliced fruit (plums, cherries, apples, or apricots). Top with crumb mixture made of ½ cup flour, ½ cup sugar, and 3 tablespoons butter rubbed together. Bake at 375° for 30 minutes or until done. Serve plain or with whipped cream. Good hot or cold.

Glums Vareneki (Cottage Cheese Filled Noodles)

Noodles:
- 1 cup milk
- 2 eggs
- 2¾ cups flour
- 1 teaspoon salt

Cottage Cheese (Glums) Filling:
- 2 cups fine dry cottage cheese
- 1 teaspoon salt
- 2 egg yolks

Sift flour and salt for noodles. Add milk and eggs. Beat well to make a medium-soft dough. Roll out fairly thin. Cut in 4-inch squares or cut out with round cutter. Mix ingredients for filling well. Cook in boiling water for 5 minutes. Fill squares or rounds with glums filling and pinch edges well to seal. Serve with fried onions, cream gravy, or browned butter.

Hungarian Cheesecake

Dough:
- 4 tablespoons butter
- 2 egg yolks
- ⅛ teaspoon salt
- 2 tablespoons lemon juice
- 1½ cups sifted flour
- 1 teaspoon baking powder
- 2-3 tablespoons cold water

Filling:
- 1 cup dry cottage cheese
- 1 cup thick sour cream
- ⅓ cup sugar
- ½ teaspoon salt
- 3 eggs, well beaten
- 1 teaspoon grated lemon rind
- 1 cup crushed pineapple, drained
- ½ cup seedless raisins or cherries (whole or chopped)
- 1 egg white, slightly beaten

To make dough, cream butter. Beat in egg yolks, salt, and lemon juice. Add sifted dry ingredients and water to make a smooth dough. Pat out to ¼ inch thick in large pie plate or spring-form pan. To make filling, press cheese through sieve (or use very fine cheese) and measure. Add sour cream, sugar, salt, eggs, and lemon rind, beating well. Brush dough with egg white. Sprinkle evenly with pineapple and raisins or cherries. Add cottage cheese mixture. Add filling to uncooked pie crust. Bake at 450° for 10 minutes. Reduce heat to 350° and bake 20 minutes or until browned. Serve cold.

Kielke (Homemade Macaroni)

Noodles:
- ❖ 3 cups flour
- ❖ 2 teaspoons salt
- ❖ 3 eggs
- ❖ ½ cup milk

Cream Sauce:
- ❖ ½ cup cream
- ❖ 2 tablespoons melted butter

Mix all ingredients for noodles to make fairly hard dough. Knead well. Roll out very thin and flour both sides. Cut dough into 1-inch strips. Place 2 strips together and cut in fine pieces. Cook in boiling salt water for a few minutes. To prepare cream sauce, melt butter, browning slightly. Add cream and heat to boiling point. Pour over kielke. Serve with fried onions.

Krimmsche Schnittchen (Crimean Slices)

Dough:
- ❖ 1 package yeast dissolved in ½ cup water plus 1 teaspoon sugar
- ❖ 1 pound margarine (½ pound margarine combined with ½ pound butter may be used)
- ❖ 1 teaspoon salt
- ❖ 4 tablespoons sugar
- ❖ ¾ cup milk
- ❖ 3 eggs
- ❖ 6 cups flour

Nut Topping:
- ❖ ½ cup ground nuts
- ❖ ½ cup sugar
- ❖ 2 teaspoons cinnamon

Beat eggs well with sugar and salt. Add yeast mixture, milk, flour, and margarine by hand. Place in refrigerator overnight. Next day, roll out to ¼ inch thickness. Brush with an egg yolk mixed with about 2 tablespoons milk. Mix ingredients for nut topping and spread over dough. Let rise a bit and bake at 400° until golden brown. Can be served as a tea cake if desired.

NUSSKUCHEN

Cake:
- ½ cup butter
- ½ cup sugar
- 3 egg yolks
- 1½ cups all-purpose flour
- 2 teaspoons baking powder
- ½ teaspoon salt
- 2 tablespoons milk
- Rind of 1 lemon

Filbert Filling:
- 2 cups finely-ground filbert nuts
- 3 egg whites
- 1 cup sugar
- Few drops bitter almond oil

Mix all ingredients for cake and roll on floured board ¼ inch thick. Combine all ingredients for filling. Mix well. Spread filling on cake and roll as a jelly roll. Bake at 350° for 1 hour. Dust with powdered sugar. Should mellow for several days.

PASKA WITH CHEESE SPREAD (EASTER BREAD)

Paska:
- 3 packages yeast
- 4 cups sugar
- 16 eggs
- 1 cup butter
- 1 teaspoon salt
- 3 cups scalded milk
- 8 cups flour
- Juice and rind of 1 lemon

Cheese Spread:
- 4 cups cottage cheese
- Yolks of 9 hard-cooked eggs
- 1 cup cream
- 1 cup butter
- 1 cup sugar
- 1 teaspoon grated lemon rind
- 1 tablespoon lemon juice

To prepare paska, soften yeast in 1 cup warm water and 2 teaspoons sugar. Beat eggs well. Add remaining sugar gradually and beat until dissolved. Sift flour and salt. Make well in flour and add cooled scalded milk. Stir and add the egg mixture. Beat well. Add softened butter, fruit juice, and rind. Add yeast mixture and knead, adding more flour to make firm dough. Let rise in a warm place until double in bulk. Grease honey pails and fill each one-third full with dough. Let rise until light. Bake at 325° for 1 hour. To prepare cheese spread, press cheese and egg yolks through sieve (may be mixed in blender). Bring cream to a boil and cool. Cream butter and sugar with remaining ingredients. Mix well. (May be placed in a cheesecloth lined sieve and allowed to drain.) Spread over paska and serve.

Makes 12 paska.

Piramanie (Meat Pockets)

- 3 eggs
- 3 tablespoons water
- Flour
- Ground beef
- Onion, grated
- Salt and pepper

Combine eggs and water with enough flour to make a stiff dough. Roll dough fairly thin and cut into 2-inch squares. Fill with cooked ground beef seasoned with salt, pepper, and grated onion. Take two corners to make a triangle and press open edges together very firmly. Cook in boiling salted water or beef broth for 10 minutes. Drain. Pour browned butter over to serve.

Piroschky

- 2 cups flour
- 1 teaspoon baking powder
- 1 teaspoon salt
- 1 tablespoon lard
- ½ cup milk
- ½ cup cream
- 1 egg

Sift dry ingredients. Cut in lard. Add slightly beaten egg, milk, and cream. Add a little more flour if dough is too soft to handle. Roll out on floured board. Cut in squares and fill with apples, gooseberries, or any other fruit. Top with 1 tablespoon sugar (more if you like it sweeter). Fold opposite corners over and seal. Bake at 400° for 25 minutes.

ജ

RAISED PIROSCHKY

- ½ cup warm water
- 1 package yeast
- 1 cup scalded milk
- ½ cup sugar
- ½ cup shortening
- 1½ teaspoons salt
- 3 cups flour

Scald and cool milk. Add yeast dissolved in warm water and 1 teaspoon sugar. Add remaining ingredients to make a soft dough as for rolls. Let rise. Roll out to ¼ inch thick. Cut with round cutter into circles. Place dabs of fruit in the center of circles, fold dough over to form half circles, and seal edges. (Use either dried fruit, cooked and sweetened until consistency of jam, or fresh fruit.) Set on greased pan and bake at 350° for 25-30 minutes.

Use this dough as a base for fruit platz: Press into well-greased square pan. Let rise. Cover with halved pitted plums, other fresh fruit, or any well-drained canned fruit. Cover with "ruebel" crumbs made of ½ cup flour, ½ cup sugar, and 2-3 tablespoons melted shortening or salad oil.

PLUSKIE (SWEET BUNS)

- 2 packages yeast
- 1 cup warm water or potato water
- 1 tablespoon sugar
- 2 cups scalded milk
- 1½ cups fat (½ cup shortening, ½ cup margarine, and ½ cup butter)
- 2 cups white sugar
- 6 eggs
- 1 teaspoon salt
- 2 tablespoons vanilla
- All-purpose flour (about 8-10 cups)

Dissolve yeast in water with 1 tablespoon sugar. Let stand in warm place until spongy. Beat eggs and sugar until thick and light. Scald milk and cool to lukewarm. Add yeast mixture, egg mixture, fats, salt, and vanilla. Gradually add flour, first beating with spoon, then kneading until dough can be handled. Let rise in warm place until double in bulk. Pinch off small pieces of dough (the size of a golf ball) and place 1 inch apart on greased baking pan. Let rise again until double in bulk. Bake at 375° until golden brown.

Rollkuchen

- 4 cups flour
- 2 teaspoons baking powder
- 1 teaspoon salt
- 1 cup sour cream
- 1 cup milk
- 4 eggs

Sift dry ingredients and make well in the center. Add remaining ingredients. Mix well with hands. Roll out on floured board and cut into 2x4-inch strips. Fry in deep hot fat until golden brown on one side. Turn and fry on other side. If rolled thin, they will be very crisp. If a softer pastry is preferred, do not roll as thin.

Rosinen Stritzel (Raisin Bread)

- 3 cups scalded milk
- 3 cups flour
- ½ pound shortening
- ⅛ pound butter
- 1½ pounds raisins
- 1½ tablespoons salt
- 2 eggs, well beaten
- 2 packages dry yeast, dissolved as directed
- 7½ cups flour (more or less as needed)

When milk is cooled, add 3 cups flour, eggs, salt, and dissolved yeast. Work in shortening and butter by hand. Add raisins and 7½ cups flour to make a fairly stiff dough. Let rise until double in bulk. Shape into loaves and place in bread pans that have been well greased. Bake at 350° for 1 hour.

Schmoor Kohl (Stewed Cabbage with Fruit)

- 12 cups chopped white cabbage
- 2 cups chopped dried apples
- 15 prunes
- ¾ cup water
- ½ cup oil
- 2½ teaspoons salt
- ⅓ cup white sugar

Measure all ingredients into heavy saucepan. Cook several minutes, then cover and simmer 1½-2 hours. If fruit is very sour, add a little more sugar.

SCHNITTCHEN (FRUIT ROLLS)

- ❖ 2 cups flour
- ❖ 3 teaspoons baking powder
- ❖ 1 teaspoon salt
- ❖ 4 tablespoons shortening
- ❖ ⅔ cup milk

Sift dry ingredients and cut in shortening. Make a well and add milk. Mix well with a fork. Knead lightly on lightly floured board. Roll out to ¼ inch thick. Fold one edge of dough to make a 1-inch strip. Cut this double strip the length of the dough. Cut strip into 2-inch lengths. Repeat with remaining dough. Bake at 400° for 15 minutes or until golden brown.

Use this dough to make fruit rolls: Roll out dough and place thick preserves or jam in a long line at least 1 inch from edge. Roll dough over to cover fruit. Seal along edge with a little milk or egg yolk and cut from dough. Repeat until dough is used up. Place on greased baking sheet and brush rolls with milk or egg yolk. Bake same as schnittchen. Cut in diagonal pieces when cool.

ZWETSCHEN KNOEDEL

- ❖ 6 medium potatoes
- ❖ 1 tablespoon butter
- ❖ 1 egg, beaten
- ❖ 2 cups flour
- ❖ 1 teaspoon salt
- ❖ 40 fresh plums (German prune plums are best)

Cook potatoes. Peel and mash while warm. Add butter, salt, and egg. Mix well. Knead in enough flour to make a soft dough that can be rolled out. Cut off pieces large enough to cover one plum. Seal edges of dough around plum. When all knoedel are made, drop gently into boiling salted water, stirring gently so they will not stick to saucepan. Cook until fruit is done (about 10-15 minutes). Take out one at a time with slotted spoon and roll in fine bread crumbs and melted shortening. Serve with sugar and sour cream.

Zwieback

- 2 cups scalded milk
- 1 cup warm water
- 2 teaspoons salt
- 4 tablespoons sugar
- 1 package yeast
- 1 cup butter and shortening
- 8-10 cups flour

Scald milk. Add shortening, salt, and 2 tablespoons sugar. Put yeast in a small bowl. Add 2 teaspoons sugar and warm water. Set in a warm place until spongy. Add yeast mixture to warm milk. Mix well and stir in flour gradually. Knead dough until very soft and smooth. Cover and let rise in warm place until double in bulk. Pinch off small balls of dough the size of a small egg. Place 1 inch apart on greased pan. Put a smaller bun on top of each bun and press with thumb. Let rise again until double in bulk (1 hour). Bake at 400°-425° for 15-20 minutes.

Makes 4 dozen.

TRADITIONAL CLASSICS

There are a number of Mennonites whose faith calls them to forsake modern dress and conveniences in order to live a godly simple life. Depending on the group of which they are a part, this may include the use of a horse and buggy for transportation, living without electricity or telephones, and various dress codes.

Their recipes use products they produce on the farm. Foods are cooked and baked in their wood stoves. At mealtime, there is always a hot oven. Few homes have refrigeration or freezers, so the summer is busy with gardening, canning, and drying. Some of these recipes are shared in this section.

Of special interest to you will be the menus used for quilting bees, barn raisings, funerals, and weddings.

QUILTING BEES

Quilting bees are a common activity among many Mennonite women. Quilts are usually made as wedding gifts for family members or for some charitable benefit such as the relief sales.

Making a quilt is a time-consuming task. A quilt pattern is selected and fabric is chosen to cut into pieces to make up the quilted top. After stitching these small pieces together, the assembled top, along with the soft fiber batting and fabric backing, are pinned onto a large quilt frame. Skilled hands then stitch the quilt into a single piece.

The quilting bee holds true to the saying, "Many hands make light work." It is also an enjoyable social time of talk and fellowship.

See several examples below of food typically served by the hostess of a quilting bee.

TO REMOVE BLOOD CAUSED BY FINGER PRICKS FROM A QUILT, DAMPEN A SMALL WAD OF THE BATTING WITH WATER AND PLACE IT ON THE BLOOD STAIN FOR A HALF HOUR. USUALLY IT DRAWS OUT OF THE FABRIC.

AFTERNOON REFRESHMENTS FOR QUILTING LADIES

During an afternoon break, quilting ladies might enjoy homemade grape juice, poached eggs, and butterscotch popcorn.

QUILTING DINNER

A quilting dinner might consist of the following dishes: mashed potatoes, buttered corn, lima beans, farmers pork sausage, coleslaw, pickles, peaches, jam jams, tapioca fluff, and dried apple cake.

ℭℬ

Threshers' Dinner

Dinner for men threshing wheat during the day might consist of: bread, butter, preserves, mashed potatoes, baked home-cured ham, creamed dried corn, bean salad, pickled baby corn, plums, caramel pudding, large oatmeal cookies, hot mince pie, homemade ice cream, and coffee.

Threshers' Supper

Supper for men threshing wheat during the day might consist of: creamed potatoes, summer sausage, bread, butter, honey, cheese, corn on the cob, tomatoes, lettuce, mustard greens, pears, butterscotch sponge, and elderberry pie.

Barn Raising Dinner for 250 Men

When a fire destroys a barn in Amish and Mennonite communities, church members from near and far donate time, money, materials, and tools for the rebuilding. Plans are carefully made, enabling a crew of several hundred male volunteers to erect a large barn in a single day. The women volunteer food and time to prepare meals for the men. Although a barn raising is hard work, it is an enjoyable social event as well.

The following is a typical amount of food used to feed the workers: 24 loaves of bread; 5 pounds butter; 21 crocks potatoes, boiled and riced; 4 large roasters of gravy beef; 8 crocks carrots, boiled and buttered; 3 crocks carrot and cucumber pickle; 45 large jars applesauce; 12 crocks sweet apple schnitz and prunes; 350 Amish doughnuts; 5 gallons maple syrup; and 45 lemon drop pies.

There is usually enough left over to feed all of the women and children, usually numbering anywhere from 50-90.

Traditional Classics

FUNERAL DINNER FOR 200

Dinner for a funeral with 200 mourners might consist of: 13 crocks peeled potatoes, creamed; 50 pounds bologna; 50 pounds cheese; 3 boxes soda biscuits; 4 crocks sour red beets; 3 crocks raw cabbage pickle; 20 loaves of bread; 3 pounds butter; 12 cups honey; 9 crocks applesauce; 7 crocks prepared dried apples; 25 dozen plain buns; 4 batches oatmeal muffins; and 2 jars instant coffee.

Extra food is prepared intentionally so it can be served again at supper to the closest relatives who have stayed, then divided among the kind neighbors who helped with the work.

WEDDING DINNER FOR 100

Dinner for a wedding with 100 guests might consist of: 8 loaves of bread; 2 pounds butter; 3 roast pans scalloped potatoes; 150 pieces boneless dinner ham; 12 cans sliced pineapple to decorate ham; 3 quarts fruit relish; 10 orange gelatin molds; 14 quarts peas and corn, mixed; fruit salad; 3 batches shortbread; 1 double batch strawberry cookies; 6 dozen pink angel squares; wedding cake; and coffee.

PORK SAUSAGE

- ❖ 50 pounds meat
- ❖ 1 pound salt
- ❖ 5 tablespoons pepper

Mix salt and pepper with meat and put in casings with sausage stuffer (½ package casings for 75 pounds).

JAM JAMS

- ❖ 1 cup brown sugar
- ❖ 1 cup shortening
- ❖ 6 tablespoons corn syrup
- ❖ 1 teaspoon vanilla
- ❖ 2 eggs
- ❖ 1 ¾ teaspoons soda
- ❖ Flour

Combine all the ingredients with enough flour to make a stiff dough. Roll out and cut with cookie cutter. Bake and put together with apple butter or raspberry jam.

Tapioca Fluff

- 6 cups milk
- 6 tablespoons
  quick-cooking tapioca
- 1 cup sugar
- 4 eggs, separated
- ½ cup white sugar

Heat the milk, tapioca, sugar, and egg yolks. When boiling, cook and stir for 5 minutes. Remove from heat and add the egg whites, beaten stiff and sweetened with the white sugar. Stir together for 2 minutes. Pour into serving dishes.

Serves 12.

Dried Apple Cake

- 2 cups dried apples
- 2 cups molasses
- 1 cup butter
- 2 cups brown sugar
- 1 cup sour milk
- 2 eggs
- 2 teaspoons soda
- 4 cups flour
- Spices as desired

Soak the apples in water overnight. Drain and simmer for 1 hour with the molasses. Add the butter and cool. Add the brown sugar, milk, eggs, soda, flour, and desired spices (such as cinnamon or cloves). Bake in loaf pans.

'Poached Eggs' on Molasses Graham Bread

- ¼ cup sugar
- 2 cups flour
- 1½ teaspoons soda
- 1 teaspoon salt
- 1 teaspoon baking powder
- 1¾ cups graham flour
- ⅓ cup shortening
- 2 beaten eggs
- 1¾ cups sour milk (or buttermilk)
- ¾ cup molasses
- Whipped cream
- 1 can halved peaches

Sift together the sugar, flour, soda, salt, baking powder, and graham flour. Cut in the shortening. Blend eggs, sour milk (or buttermilk), and molasses. Pour into dry mixture. Stir just enough to blend together. Bake in 2 greased loaf pans at 350° for 40 minutes. Slice. Place 2 slices on dessert plate. Add a pile of sweetened whipped cream. Top with a canned peach half, round side up.

To Cure Ham

- 5 pounds salt
- 2 pounds brown sugar
- 2 ounces potassium nitrate
- 100 pounds of meat

Mix together salt, brown sugar, and potassium nitrate. Rub the meat once every three days with one-third of spice mixture. After the last rubbing, let meat sit in a wooden tub for 1 week to 10 days before smoking.

Creamed Dried Corn

- 2 cups dried corn
- 3 cups boiling water
- Salt to taste
- Flour
- ½ cup cream

To dry corn, cut kernels off corncobs. Spread thinly on cookie sheets and dry in 250° oven. Stir often. Leave oven door open slightly for steam to escape. Remove when kernels are hard and brown in color. Store in a tight container for as long as you wish. When ready to serve, combine the dried corn with the boiling water and salt. Boil until corn is soft, adding water as necessary. Make a paste of flour and water. Add and boil until thick. Add the cream.

Serves 4.

Yellow Bean Salad

Salad:
- 1 quart yellow (or green) beans, cooked
- ½ onion, chopped
- 2 hard-boiled eggs, chopped
- Salt and pepper to taste

Dressing:
- 1 teaspoon vinegar
- 1 teaspoon sugar
- ¾ cup sour cream

Combine the beans, onion, eggs, and salt and pepper. Combine the ingredients for the dressing and pour over bean mixture.

CREAMED POTATOES

❖ Potatoes
❖ Salt
❖ Water
❖ Rich cream
❖ Sweet marjoram or parsley

Slice potatoes thinly. Add salt and some water. Cook. Add rich cream and sprinkle with sweet marjoram or parsley.

SUMMER SAUSAGE

❖ Beef
❖ Pork
❖ 5½ ounces salt
❖ 4 ounces sugar (brown or white)
❖ 1 ounce pepper
❖ 2 tablespoons potassium nitrate
❖ Garlic (optional)

Use 2 parts beef and 1 part pork. Grind meat until it is very fine. For every 8 pounds meat, mix in 5½ ounces salt, 4 ounces sugar, 1 ounce pepper, 2 tablespoons potassium nitrate (saltpeter), and garlic to taste. Cover meat with spices. Put in factory cotton bags with sausage stuffer. Smoke 1 week.

HOMEMADE BREAD

❖ 2 packages yeast
❖ 2 large spoonfuls lard
❖ 1-2 handfuls salt
❖ 1 cup sugar
❖ Flour

Prepare the yeast as directed on package. Measure lard into a bowl. Add salt and sugar. Mix. Add yeast mixture and enough liquid for the right amount of bread. Mix flour with this to form a slush. Let stand 20 minutes, then work stiff. Let stand, then mold and let rise. Bake.

Makes 4-5 large loaves and 2 coffee cakes.

THE WORLD IS COMPOSED OF TAKERS AND GIVERS. THE TAKERS
MAY EAT BETTER, BUT THE GIVERS SLEEP BETTER.

Soda Cheese

- 4 gallons skim milk
- 2 eggs, well beaten
- 2 tablespoons soda
- Water
- ½ cup sweet cream
- 1 teaspoon caraway

Heat the milk to 98°. Put in large cheesecloth bag and squeeze out whey until dry. Put through food chopper to grind. Put in a crock and add the eggs. Dissolve the soda in 1 cup hot water and add to milk mixture. Add 1 cup cold water. Mix and let stand overnight. Next morning, cook in a double boiler, adding 3 cups water, the sweet cream, and the caraway.

Gravy Beef (Steak in Gravy)

- Beef roast
- Spices as desired
- Water
- Flour paste

Cut beef roast into serving pieces. Flavor to taste and roast until tender. Set pan with beef on top of stove. Cover with water and stir in flour paste. Boil until thick.

Egg or Easter Cheese

- 2 quarts milk
- 4-6 eggs
- 1 teaspoon salt
- 1 pint buttermilk

Use a buttered pot to heat milk on moderate heat (it scorches easily). Beat the eggs and mix with buttermilk and salt. Add to hot milk. Stir well. Continue heating, stirring occasionally. Reduce heat when curds start to form. When curds and whey are fully separated (2-3 minutes more), pour all through a cloth-lined colander or bag. Drain for 2 hours. Refrigerate. Serve with lots of fresh maple syrup.

DRIED APPLES

- ❖ Apples
- ❖ Water

Peel and core the apples and slice in eighths. Heat in oven at 200°, stirring often. Leave oven door open to let steam escape (will take 24 hours). Store in jars (do not have to be airtight). Before cooking, soak overnight in cold water. Good with prunes or raisins. If you want something special, add an orange, rind and all, that you have put through the meat chopper.

APPLE BUTTER

- ❖ 20 medium apples
- ❖ Water
- ❖ 1½ quarts apple cider
- ❖ 1 cup of sieved pumpkin or pears
- ❖ 1½ pounds white sugar
- ❖ 1 teaspoon ground cinnamon
- ❖ 1 teaspoon ground allspice
- ❖ 1 teaspoon ground cloves

Wash and cut apples into small pieces (remove stem and blossom). Cover with water and boil until soft. Put through sieve to remove skins and seeds. Bring the apple cider to boil. Add apples and remaining ingredients. Cook and stir until right thickness for spreading. Store in covered crocks in cool place.

DANDELION WINE

- ❖ 1 gallon dandelion flower heads
- ❖ 1 gallon boiling water
- ❖ 3 ½ pounds of sugar
- ❖ 1 orange, thinly sliced
- ❖ 1 lemon, thinly sliced
- ❖ Small pieces of ginger root
- ❖ 1 piece of toast
- ❖ ¼ ounce yeast

Place the dandelions in a granite kettle and cover with the boiling water. Cover and let stand 12 days, stirring every day. Strain off the liquid. Add the sugar, orange, lemon, and a few small pieces of ginger root. Boil gently for 20 minutes. When lukewarm, lay a piece of toast spread with the yeast on top. Cover. Let stand 2 days. Strain. Put in gallon glass jug with a cork stopper. Leave for 6 months or longer. Occasionally check stopper to make sure it is secure.

℘

Noodles

- 6 eggs
- 4 tablespoons cold water
- ½ teaspoon salt
- 4 cups all-purpose flour

Mix the eggs, cold water, and salt well. Add the flour and knead about 100 times. Roll thin and cut in strips of width desired. Allow to dry thoroughly and store in jars or plastic containers.

Rolly Polly

- Biscuit dough
- Apple butter

Make biscuit dough. Take half and roll out. Spread with apple butter. Roll up and place on baking sheet. Do likewise with other half. Bake. Cut in pieces and serve with warm milk.

SIDE DISHES AND VEGETABLES

BAKED BEANS

- 4 cans (No. 10 size) great northern beans, drained
- 5 cups brown sugar
- Half a can (No. 10 size) ketchup
- Half a can (46 ounces) tomato soup
- 1½ cups dried onion
- 2½ pounds bacon, fried and crumbled, or diced ham

Combine all ingredients in large pan or roaster. Mix well. Refrigerate overnight. Bake at 350° for 3-4 hours.

Makes 100-120 servings.

HEARTY BAKED BEANS

- 1 large can (2½ pounds) lima beans
- 1 medium onion, chopped
- Half a medium green pepper, chopped
- ½ cup brown sugar
- About ⅓ bottle ketchup
- 8 strips bacon

Place beans, onion, and green pepper in a casserole dish. Mix well. Blend brown sugar and ketchup. Stir into bean mixture. Fry bacon. Break into pieces and stir into beans. Bake at 300° for 1½-2 hours.

BAKED CORN

- 2 cups corn
- 2 tablespoons butter
- 1 tablespoon sugar
- 1 teaspoon salt
- ⅛ teaspoon pepper
- 2 eggs
- 1 cup milk
- 1½ tablespoons flour
- ½ cup bread crumbs (optional)

Combine all ingredients and mix in a blender or with a mixer. Put in a 2-quart greased casserole dish. Bake at 350° for 45 minutes or until center is done. Sprinkled bread crumbs over the top if desired.

Emma Lantz
Ronks, Pennsylvania

Barbecued Green Beans

- 2 strips bacon, diced
- 2 tablespoons chopped onion
- 1 can (14½ ounces) green beans, drained
- ¼ cup ketchup
- 2 tablespoons brown sugar
- 1½ teaspoons Worcestershire sauce

Brown bacon and onion in small skillet. Combine with beans in a casserole dish. Mix remaining ingredients and simmer 2 minutes. Pour over bean mixture. Bake at 350° for 20-30 minutes.

Betty Albrecht
Marion, South Dakota
Minn-Kota MCC Relief Sale
Sioux Falls, South Dakota

Barbecued Kraut

- 4 strips bacon, diced
- Half an onion, sliced
- ½ cup brown sugar
- 1 can (8 ounces) tomato sauce
- Dash each of A-1 steak sauce, Worcestershire sauce, and barbecue sauce
- 2 pounds sauerkraut, drained and rinsed

Brown diced bacon and drain grease. Combine bacon with remaining ingredients in mixing bowl. Mix well. Transfer to crock pot and simmer on high setting for 3 hours.

Corn on the Cob

Make buttering corn on the cob easy by melting butter in a microwave-safe dish that is large enough to hold an ear of corn. Roll the corn in the melted butter and salt to taste.

Broccoli Hot Dish

- 1 package frozen broccoli
- 1 can water chestnuts, sliced thin
- 1 large container (16 ounces) sour cream
- 1 package dried onion soup mix
- ¾ cup butter
- Crushed soda crackers

Cook broccoli in a little water just until thawed. Drain. Place in 9x9-inch baking dish. Add water chestnuts and mix well. Combine sour cream and onion soup mix. Mix well with vegetables. Melt butter in small skillet. Add crushed crackers and sauté until heated through. Spread over broccoli casserole. Bake at 350° for 30 minutes.

Serves 6-8.

Mrs. Kathy Graber
Freeman, South Dakota
Minn-Kota MCC Relief Sale
Sioux Falls, South Dakota

Sauce for Broccoli

- 1 cup water
- 1 teaspoon cornstarch
- 1 lump butter
- 1 tablespoon lemon juice
- 1 tablespoon onion juice

Combine some of the water with the cornstarch to make a smooth paste. Place remainder of the water in a saucepan. Add butter and lemon and onion juices. Bring to a boil. Stir in cornstarch paste gradually and simmer until moderately thickened (10-15 minutes). Serve over cooked broccoli.

Makes 1 cup.

Sally Ann Reddecliff
Johnstown, Pennsylvania
MCC Quilt Auction and Relief Sale, Johnstown

Carrot Casserole

- 1 pound carrots
- ½ cup chopped onion
- 1 cup diced celery
- 2 tablespoons margarine
- 8 cups cubed bread
- 1 teaspoon parsley flakes
- 1½ teaspoons salt
- ¾ cup melted margarine
- 2 eggs, well beaten

Peel and dice carrots. Cook in water until very soft. Drain and mash very fine. Sauté onion and celery in the 2 tablespoons margarine. Place bread cubes in a large bowl. Mix in sautéed onion-celery mixture, parsley, salt, and melted margarine. Stir in eggs and mashed carrots. Turn into 1½-quart casserole. Bake at 350° for 30 minutes or more.

Amy Cable
Hollsopple, Pennsylvania
MCC Quilt Auction and Relief Sale,
Johnstown, Pennsylvania

SIDE DISHES AND VEGETABLES

CARROT POTATO CHOWDER

* 2 cups scalded milk
* 1 onion, sliced
* 3 tablespoons butter or shortening
* 2 cups diced potatoes
* 1 cup diced carrots
* 2 cups boiling water
* 1 teaspoon salt
* ¼ teaspoon paprika
* 2 tablespoons flour

Brown onion in 1 tablespoon butter. Add potatoes, carrots, boiling water, salt, and paprika. Boil 15 minutes covered or until tender. Cream flour and remaining 2 tablespoons butter together in bowl. Add milk. Cook creamed mixture in double boiler, stirring until smooth. Combine sauce with vegetables.

Serves 4-6.

CORN CASSEROLE

* 1 can cream-style corn
* 1 can whole-kernel corn
* 1 stick (½ cup) margarine, melted
* 1 cup sour cream
* 1 box cornbread muffin mix
* 2 eggs, beaten

Thoroughly mix all ingredients. Pour into a 9x13-inch baking pan. Bake at 350° for 30 minutes.

Winifred Saner
Freeman, South Dakota
Minn-Kota MCC Relief Sale
Sioux Falls, South Dakota

CRISPY ONION RINGS

* 3 large onions, cut into rounds 1-2 inches thick
* 1 cup all-purpose flour
* ½ cup cornstarch
* 1 teaspoon baking soda
* ½ teaspoon salt
* 1½ cups ice water

Separate onions into rings. Soak in a bowl of ice water for 2 hours. Make batter by combining flour, cornstarch, baking soda, and salt in a large bowl. Add the 1½ cups ice water to the dry ingredients all at once. Whisk until batter is smooth. Refrigerate for at least 1 hour before using. Heat oil in fryer to 375°. Place drained onion rings in batter. Toss to coat each one well. Drop rings one by one into fryer. Fry, turning once, until golden brown (3-4 minutes). Drain well on paper towels. Sprinkle with a little salt or lemon pepper seasoning and serve hot. Serve as is or accompany with your favorite mustard, tomato ketchup, or salsa.

Sally Ann Reddecliff
Johnstown, Pennsylvania
MCC Quilt Auction and Relief Sale, Johnstown

Fresh Red Beets as a Vegetable

- 2 cups shredded beets
- 1 tablespoon butter
- ½ teaspoon salt

Melt butter in a heavy pan. Add beets and salt. Cook over medium heat, stirring occasionally. If beets are young, this takes only about 10 minutes after they are hot.

Serves 6.

Fried Cucumbers

- 1 egg
- 1 cup milk
- 2-3 cucumbers, peeled and sliced
- 2 cups cracker crumbs
- Butter or vegetable oil

Beat the egg and add milk. Dip the cucumber slices in the cracker crumbs. Lay out to dry a little, then dip in egg-milk mixture. Dip in cracker crumbs again and fry in butter or oil. Sprinkle with salt to taste.

From Amish Cooking, *published by Pathway Publishers Corporation*

Glazed Carrots

- 1 pound carrots, scraped and sliced on the diagonal
- ¼ cup butter
- ½ cup brown sugar

Cook carrots in a small amount of water until tender-crisp. Drain. Melt butter in a separate pot. Stir in sugar until well blended. Add carrots. Cook, stirring frequently, until syrup comes to a boil (about 10 minutes) and carrots are evenly coated/glazed. Carrots may also be put in a baking dish and baked at 300° for 30-45 minutes. Stir every 10 minutes to coat evenly.

Adella (Stutzman) Gingrich
Albany, Oregon

Green Beans Au Gratin

- 4 cups green beans
- 1 can (10¾ ounces) cheddar cheese soup
- 1 small can (2.8 ounces) french fried onions

Layer beans and soup (undiluted) in a buttered casserole dish. Arrange onions on top. Bake at 300° for 20 minutes.

Sally Ann Reddecliff
Johnstown, Pennsylvania
MCC Quilt Auction and Relief Sale, Johnstown

Hot Cabbage

- 1 quart cabbage
- 2 cups boiling water
- 1 teaspoon salt
- 1 tablespoon butter

Cook the cabbage in the boiling water and salt for 7 minutes. Drain. Add butter and serve.

Note: To make sweet and sour cabbage, add 2 tablespoons vinegar, 2 tablespoons sugar, and 3-4 tablespoons sweet or sour cream to hot cabbage.

Sweet-Sour Cabbage (Gadaemftes Kraut)

- 1 large onion, chopped
- 3 tablespoons shortening
- ⅓ cup sugar
- ⅓ cup white vinegar
- 1-2 teaspoons salt
- ⅓ cup water
- 8 cups shredded cabbage

Sauté onion in shortening in large frying pan until slightly golden. Add sugar, vinegar, salt, and water. Blend well. Slowly add cabbage. Cover and cook over medium heat until cabbage is tender (about 20-25 minutes).

Serves 8-12.

Lahae Waltner
Freeman, South Dakota
Minn-Kota MCC Relief Sale
Sioux Falls, South Dakota

Quick 'n Easy Sweet-Sour Cabbage

- 2 tablespoons shortening (lard)
- 1 large onion, chopped
- 2 tablespoons vinegar
- 2 tablespoons water
- 1 head cabbage, finely cut (3-4 cups)
- 1 teaspoon salt
- ½ teaspoon sugar
- Large dash pepper

Heat shortening. Add onion and sauté until clear. Add vinegar and water. Let cook 2-3 minutes. Add cabbage. Stir well to blend with onion mixture. Mix in salt, sugar, and pepper. Cook about 5 minutes, stirring constantly, until cabbage is hot, but still crunchy. Add more salt if desired.

Serves 3-4.

Bernice Stucky
Freeman, South Dakota
Minn-Kota MCC Relief Sale
Sioux Falls, South Dakota

SIDE DISHES AND VEGETABLES

KIELKE

Dough:
- ❖ 3 cups flour
- ❖ 2 tablespoons salt
- ❖ 3 eggs
- ❖ ½ cup milk

Onion Gravy:
- ❖ Chopped or sliced onions
- ❖ Lard or oil
- ❖ ½ cup cream
- ❖ 1 cup milk (use more or less as desired to change thickness of gravy)
- ❖ Salt and pepper to taste

Mix dough ingredients together. Use scissors to snip dough into small pieces. Put into boiling water and cook for a few minutes. Make gravy by browning onion in a little grease. Add cream and milk and season with salt and pepper. Bring to a boil. Pour over the hot kielke.

Irene Penner
Corn, Oklahoma
Oklahoma MCC Relief Sale, Fairview

AMISH POTATOES

- ❖ 3 tablespoons butter
- ❖ 8 potatoes, cooked and sliced
- ❖ 1½ cups half-and-half
- ❖ Salt and pepper

Melt butter in skillet. Add sliced potatoes and brown slightly. Add half-and-half and simmer until potatoes absorb the cream. Add salt and pepper to taste. You can also cook the potatoes and half-and-half in a crock pot.

Norma Thomas
Hollsopple, Pennsylvania
MCC Quilt Auction and Relief Sale, Johnstown

APRICOT SWEET POTATOES

- ❖ 1 cup brown sugar
- ❖ 1½ tablespoons cornstarch
- ❖ 1 teaspoon grated orange peel
- ❖ ¼ teaspoon salt
- ❖ ⅛ teaspoon cinnamon
- ❖ 1 can (5½ ounces) apricot nectar
- ❖ ⅓ cup water
- ❖ 2 tablespoons butter
- ❖ 1 can (18 ounces) sweet potatoes, drained
- ❖ 12 frozen (or 1 can) apricots
- ❖ ½ cup pecans (optional)

Mix sugar, cornstarch, orange peel, salt, and cinnamon in a heavy 1-quart saucepan. Stir in apricot nectar and water. Cook, stirring, on high heat until mixture comes to a full rolling boil. Stir in butter. Layer sweet potatoes and apricots in a greased casserole. Pour hot sauce over. Sprinkle with pecans if desired. Bake uncovered at 375° for 25 minutes or until hot and bubbly.

Serves 8.

Elizabeth M. Loewen
Mountain Lake, Minnesota
Minn-Kota MCC Relief Sale
Sioux Falls, South Dakota

Apricot-Glazed Sweet Potatoes

- 3 pounds sweet potatoes, cooked, peeled, and cut up
- 1 cup firmly packed brown sugar
- 5 teaspoons cornstarch
- ¼ teaspoon salt
- ⅛ teaspoon ground cinnamon
- 1 cup apricot nectar
- ½ cup hot water
- 2 teaspoons grated orange peel
- 2 teaspoons butter or margarine
- ½ cup chopped pecans

Place sweet potatoes in a 13x9x3-inch baking dish and set aside. Combine sugar, cornstarch, and cinnamon in a saucepan. Stir in apricot nectar, water, and orange peel. Bring to a boil, stirring constantly. Cook and stir 2 minutes more. Remove from heat. Stir in butter and nuts. Pour over sweet potatoes. Bake uncovered at 350° for 20-25 minutes or until heated through.

Serves 8-10.

Virginia Gindlesperger
Johnstown, Pennsylvania
MCC Quilt Auction and Relief Sale, Johnstown

Baked Potatoes with Choice of Topping

- 400 russet baking potatoes (about 175 pounds)

Broccoli, Cheese, and Ham Topping (for 200 potatoes):
- 22 pounds diced ham
- 2 gallons mild cheese sauce
- 4 pounds frozen California mixed vegetables
- 6 pounds frozen chopped broccoli
- 2 gallons white sauce, made in 1-gallon batches from:
- 1 gallon milk
- 1 pound butter
- 2 cups cornstarch
- 3 tablespoons salt and
- ½ teaspoon white pepper

Sour Cream and Bacon Topping (for 200 potatoes):
- 20 pounds bacon ends or commercial bacon bits
- 4 cartons (16 ounces each) sour cream

To prepare potatoes, wash, but do not prick. Wrap each one in aluminum foil. Bake 50 potatoes at 350° for 2 hours. (Or bake about 35 potatoes at a time in a roaster for 4 hours at 350°. Rotate potatoes and make sure there is water at the bottom of the roaster.)

To prepare broccoli, cheese, and ham topping, heat ham in roaster for 2 hours. In separate large double boilers, cook ingredients for 2 1-gallon batches of white sauce. Divide chopped frozen vegetables evenly between the roasters. Cook, covered, in a little water until tender. Add 1 gallon prepared white sauce and 1 gallon cheese sauce to each roaster. Stir well to mix. Keep hot in roasters. To serve, place 1 heaping tablespoon ham on each split potato. Cover with ½ cup cheese-broccoli sauce. Sprinkle with paprika.

To prepare sour cream and bacon topping, grind the bacon ends and fry until crisp. Drain. To serve, spoon sour cream over split potatoes and top with about 1 tablespoon crisp bacon bits.

Alma Wollman
Freeman, South Dakota
Minn-Kota MCC Relief Sale
Sioux Falls, South Dakota

Make-Ahead Potatoes

- 5 pounds potatoes
- 8 ounces cream cheese, softened
- 8 ounces sour cream
- 1 teaspoon onion flakes
- Milk
- ¼ cup melted margarine

Peel potatoes and boil in salted water. Drain. Add cream cheese, sour cream, and onion flakes. Mash or whip, adding enough milk for the desired consistency. Spread in a buttered 9x13-inch pan and refrigerate or freeze until needed. Drizzle melted margarine over top when ready to use. Bake at 350° for 1 hour.

Nancy Steele
Missouri MCC Relief Sale, Harrisonville

Mashed Potatoes

- 15 pounds potatoes
- 1½ quarts scalded milk
- ¼ cup salt
- ¼ cup butter or margarine

Pare potatoes. Wash and boil until tender. Mash until smooth. Add milk, salt, and butter. Beat until light and fluffy.

Serves 50.

Martha Tschetter
Freeman, South Dakota
Minn-Kota MCC Relief Sale
Sioux Falls, South Dakota

French Fried Mashed Potato Balls

- 1 cup mashed potatoes
- ½ cup flour
- 1 teaspoon salt
- 1 teaspoon baking powder
- 2 eggs, well beaten
- ½ cup freshly grated Parmesan cheese

Mix all ingredients together. Drop by tablespoon into a deep fryer. Fry until golden brown. Drain on absorbent paper.

Sally Ann Reddecliff
Johnstown, Pennsylvania
MCC Quilt Auction and Relief Sale, Johnstown

Let the other fellow talk occasionally—you can't learn much listening to yourself!

POTATO PATTIES

- 10 large potatoes
- 2 eggs, well beaten
- 1 heaping tablespoon flour
- ½ teaspoon salt
- Vegetable oil or shortening for frying
- Sour cream

Peel and grind potatoes. Stir in eggs, flour, and salt. Place by tablespoon into a heated skillet with a small amount of oil. Flatten each spoonful with the spoon as you add it to the skillet. Cook until brown on both sides. Serve with sour cream.

Vesta Schmidt
Mountain Lake, Minnesota
Minn-Kota MCC Relief Sale
Sioux Falls, South Dakota

HASH BROWN POTATOES

- 2 pounds frozen hash brown potatoes
- 1 pint half-and-half
- 1 cup shredded cheddar cheese
- ½ pound Velveeta processed cheese, shredded
- ¼ cup (half a stick) butter or margarine

Spread hash browns in a large casserole. Heat half-and-half and cheeses in a saucepan until cheeses melt. Pour mixture over hash browns. Let set 1 hour. Dot with butter and bake for 1 hour at 350°.

Iris Frank
East Peoria Mennonite Church
Illinois MCC Relief Sale, Peoria

HASHED BROWN POTATO CASSEROLE

Casserole:
- 2 pounds chunky frozen hashed brown potatoes, thawed
- 2 cups shredded cheddar cheese
- 1 stick (½ cup) butter, melted
- 1 pint sour cream
- 1 can (10¾ ounces) cream of chicken soup
- ⅔ cup chopped onion
- Salt and pepper

Topping:
- 3 cups cornflakes
- ¼ cup melted butter

Thoroughly mix all casserole ingredients in a large bowl. Season as desired with salt and pepper. Spread in a 9x13-inch buttered baking pan. Bake at 350° for 30 minutes. Mix cornflakes and melted butter for topping and spread over casserole. Return to oven and continue baking uncovered about 30 minutes more.

SCALLOPED POTATOES

- ❖ 1 cup butter
- ❖ ¾ cup flour
- ❖ 3 quarts milk
- ❖ 2 cans mushroom soup
- ❖ 20 pounds potatoes
- ❖ 1 onion, minced

Melt butter. Add flour and stir in milk to make a white sauce. Stir in soup and cook until heated through. Slice potatoes and onion. Layer in greased roaster. Pour hot sauce over potatoes. Bake at 350° for 1 hour, then reduce temperature to 250° to finish.

Serves 50.

CHEESY SCALLOPED POTATOES

- ❖ 6 potatoes
- ❖ ½ cup butter
- ❖ ½ cup chopped onion
- ❖ ½ teaspoon parsley flakes
- ❖ 1 teaspoon mustard
- ❖ 1 teaspoon salt
- ❖ ¼ teaspoon pepper
- ❖ ¼ cup milk
- ❖ ½ pound Velveeta cheese

Cook potatoes in skins. Peel when cooled and dice coarsely. Melt cheese in milk and add other ingredients. Stir in potatoes. Bake at 325° for 45 minutes or until bubbly.

R. Beiler
Quarryville, Pennsylvania

NEW IDEA IN SCALLOPED POTATOES

- ❖ 6 medium potatoes
- ❖ 1 cup grated cheese
- ❖ 1 cup diced ham
- ❖ 2 tablespoons flour
- ❖ 1½ teaspoons salt
- ❖ 1 tablespoon dried onion soup mix
- ❖ 2 cups hot milk
- ❖ 2 tablespoons ketchup
- ❖ ½ teaspoon Worcestershire sauce
- ❖ 2 tablespoons butter

Pare potatoes and cut into thin slices. Place half the potatoes in a buttered 2-quart casserole. Sprinkle with a third of the cheese, ham, and combined flour, salt, and onion soup mix. Top with remaining potatoes, then remaining cheese, ham, and seasoning mix. Combine milk, ketchup, and Worcestershire sauce and pour over potatoes. Dot with butter. Cover and bake 1 hour at 350°. Uncover during last 15 minutes of baking to brown top.

Serves 6-8.

Ardith Epp
Henderson, Nebraska
Nebraska MCC Relief Sale, Aurora

∞

Super Duper Potatoes

- 9 medium potatoes
- ¼ cup grated or finely diced onion
- 8 ounces shredded cheddar cheese
- 2 cups half-and-half
- ½ cup butter
- 1 teaspoon salt

Scrub potatoes and cook until tender. Cool. Peel and grate potatoes. Spread in buttered 9x13-inch baking pan. Mix in grated onion. Top with cheese. Heat half-and-half, butter, and salt until butter melts. Pour over potatoes. Bake at 350° for 1 hour.

Amy Hofer
Carpenter, South Dakota
Minn-Kota MCC Relief Sale
Sioux Falls, South Dakota

Vegetable Casserole

- 2 cups chopped celery
- 2 cups chopped green beans
- 1½ cups chopped carrots
- 2 cups chopped tomatoes
- ½ cup diced onion
- ¼ cup butter
- 2 scant tablespoons sugar
- 3 tablespoons tapioca pudding mix

Mix all ingredients thoroughly. Place in 2-quart casserole. Bake at 350° for 1½ hours.

Mianna Geissinger
Mountain Lake, Minnesota
Minn-Kota MCC Relief Sale
Sioux Falls, South Dakota

Vegetable Pizza Dough

- ¼ cup margarine
- ¼ cup boiling water
- 1 beaten egg
- 1 teaspoon salt
- 2 tablespoons sugar
- 1 package yeast dissolved in water
- 1½ cups bread flour

Roll out on a large cookie sheet. Bake at 350° until lightly brown.

R. Beiler
Quarryville, Pennsylvania

TWO THINGS ARE BAD FOR THE HEART—
RUNNING UP STAIRS, AND RUNNING DOWN PEOPLE.

BREADS

DUTCH HONEY BREAD

- ❖ 1 cup honey
- ❖ 1 cup brown sugar
- ❖ 1⅓ cups milk, scalded
- ❖ 4 cups pastry flour
- ❖ 1 teaspoon cinnamon
- ❖ 2 teaspoons baking soda
- ❖ ½ teaspoon cloves

Pour hot milk over honey and sugar and stir until dissolved. Sift together the pastry flour, cinnamon, baking soda, and cloves. Stir dry ingredients into liquid mixture. Do not overbeat. Pour into loaf pan lined with wax paper. Bake at 350° for 1 hour. Cool upside down on rack before removing wax paper.

GOD GIVES US THE INGREDIENTS FOR OUR DAILY BREAD, BUT HE EXPECTS US TO DO THE BAKING!

FARM BREAD

- ❖ 4 cups scalded milk, cooled
- ❖ 2 cups uncooked rolled oats
- ❖ 2½ tablespoons soft shortening
- ❖ 2 packages yeast
- ❖ 1 teaspoon sugar
- ❖ ¼ teaspoon ginger
- ❖ ½ cup warm water
- ❖ ⅔ cup molasses
- ❖ 1 tablespoon salt
- ❖ 2 cups whole wheat flour
- ❖ 7½ cups white flour
- ❖ 1 egg white

Place milk, oats, and shortening in a bowl. Mix and let stand 1 hour at room temperature. Dissolve yeast, sugar, and ginger in the warm water. Let stand 8 minutes or until bubbly. Stir yeast mixture, molasses, and salt into oat mixture. Stir in whole wheat flour and enough of the white flour to make a dough that is easy to handle. Knead dough 8 minutes. Let rise in greased bowl 1½ hours and punch down. Knead 10 minutes more. Return to bowl. Let rise 45 minutes or until double and punch down. Divide into thirds and shape into loaves. Let rise 45 minutes on greased baking sheet or in loaf pans. Brush tops of loaves with egg white and sprinkle with rolled oats. Bake at 325° for 45 minutes.

Makes 3 large loaves.

Minn-Kota Relief Sale
Sioux Falls, South Dakota

French Bread

- 4 tablespoons dry yeast
- 1 cup warm water
- 1 teaspoon sugar
- 4 tablespoons sugar
- 4 tablespoons shortening
- 4 teaspoons salt
- 4 cups hot water
- 14 cups flour
- 1 egg
- 2 tablespoons milk
- Sesame or poppy seeds (optional)

Dissolve yeast in the warm water with the 1 teaspoon sugar. Set aside. Combine the 4 tablespoons sugar with the shortening, salt, and hot water. Cool to lukewarm. Add yeast mixture. Stir in flour. Let rise until doubled. Divide dough into 4 parts. Roll each part to fit on a 20x24-inch cookie sheet. Slash each loaf 4-5 times diagonally across the top. Mix egg and milk and brush over top of each loaf. Sprinkle with sesame or poppy seed if desired. Let rise until double. Bake at 375° for 20 minutes.

Makes 4 loaves.

Alvin W. Goerzen
Newton, Kansas
Minn-Kota MCC Relief Sale
Sioux Falls, South Dakota

Mak Kuchen (Poppy Seed Rolls)

- 1¼ cups milk, scalded
- ¼ cup lard or shortening
- ¼ cup sugar
- 1 teaspoon salt
- 1 package yeast
- 3½-4 cups flour

Filling:

- 2¼ cups poppy seeds, ground
- 2¼ cups sugar
- ¾-1 cup water

Combine scalded milk, lard, sugar, and salt. Cool to lukewarm. Add yeast and flour. Knead well. Cover. Let rise and punch down 2-3 times. Make filling by mixing poppy seeds and sugar. Bring the water to a boil. Add poppy seed mixture. Bring back to a boil, stirring constantly. Add more water if needed. Cool. After last rising, divide dough into 3 equal parts. Let rise 10 minutes. Roll each ball of dough into a rectangle. Spread with one-third of the poppy seed filling. Roll up like a jelly roll and seal edges. Place in pans and let rise 10-15 minutes. Brush tops with beaten egg. Bake at 350° for 35 minutes.

Mid-Kansas MCC Relief Sale, Hutchinson

KRINGEL

- 2 cups milk
- 1½ packages dry yeast or
  1-inch square fresh yeast
- ⅓ cup warm water
- ½ teaspoon sugar
- ½ cup shortening
- 2 teaspoons salt
- 5-6 cups flour (enough to
  make a soft dough)
- ¾ pound butter, softened, or part
  butter, part margarine
- 2 cups raisins, washed and drained

Scald milk and let cool. Dissolve yeast in the warm water with the sugar. When milk is lukewarm, mix in mixing bowl with shortening, salt, and 2 cups of the flour. Beat. Add yeast mixture and enough of the remaining flour to make a soft dough. Beat. (Use electric mixer if desired.) Let rise. Roll out on a floured surface into a rectangle ½-¾ inch thick. Spread the butter over two-thirds of the dough. Fold dough into thirds, unbuttered third first. Then fold into thirds again in the opposite direction. Roll again. Cut into 4 strips. Place raisins (or almond paste filling) in center of each strip. Press edges of each strip together to make a long roll. Twist each roll. Place on cookie sheets and let rise. Mix some sugar with a little milk and brush on top of each kringel. Bake at 400° for 25-30 minutes or until browned.

Note: You can refrigerate the dough overnight after spreading it with the butter and folding it up. The dough is easier to work with when it's cold. Roll the dough for the second time and make the kringel the next day.

Makes 4 kringel.

Hildegard Jantzen
Beatrice, Nebraska
Nebraska MCC Relief Sale, Aurora

SOME MEN ARE SO BUSY EARNING BREAD FOR
THEIR CHILDREN, THEY FORGET THAT A CHILD
DOES NOT LIVE BY BREAD ALONE.

NO-KNEAD BREAD

- 2 packages yeast
- ½ cup warm water
- ⅔ cup sugar
- ⅔ cup dry milk
- ⅔ cup vegetable oil
- 2 eggs
- 1 teaspoon salt (less if desired)
- 2 cups hot water
- 4 cups whole wheat flour
- 3½ cups white flour

Dissolve yeast in the warm water in a small bowl and set aside. Mix sugar, dry milk, oil, eggs, and salt in a large bowl. Add the hot water and mix well. Stir in yeast mixture. Mix in the flours. Cover and let rise until double (about 1 hour). Stir down and let rise until double twice more for finer texture. Grease two 9x5-inch loaf pans. Divide dough between the pans. Let rise for 15 minutes. Bake at 350° for 30 minutes. Dough can be made into rolls by greasing hands and cookie sheets. Roll dough into small balls (about 2 inches round). Place 2 inches apart on sheets. Bake at 350° for 13 minutes, or until brown. Make dough into buns by rolling dough into slightly larger balls (about 3-4 inches round). Bake 15-20 minutes.

Makes 2 loaves.

Jane Roth
Pleasant View Mennonite Church
Michiana MCC Relief Sale, Goshen

OATMEAL ROLLS

- 2 packages dry yeast
- ¾ cup warm water
- ½ cup shortening
- ½ cup brown sugar
- 3 teaspoons salt
- 2 cups quick oatmeal
- 2 cups milk
- 2 eggs, beaten
- 6 cups all-purpose flour

Dissolve dry yeast in the warm water. Measure the shortening, brown sugar, salt, and oatmeal into a mixing bowl. Scald milk and pour over this mixture. Cool to lukewarm. Add the eggs and yeast mixture, then beat in 1 cup all-purpose flour. Let stand about 15 minutes until bubbly and light, then work in about 5 more cups flour. Knead until a soft dough. Place in greased bowl and let rise until double. Punch down and let rise again. Work into rolls. Let rise again and bake at 400° for 10 minutes.

ORANGE BUTTER ROLLS

- 1 package yeast
- ¼ cup warm water
- ¼ cup sugar
- 1 teaspoon salt
- 2 eggs
- ½ cup sour cream
- 6 tablespoons softened margarine
- 2¾-3 cups flour

Filling:
- ¾ cup sugar
- ¾ cup coconut
- 2 tablespoons orange rind

Glaze/Topping:
- ¾ cup sugar
- 2 tablespoons orange rind
- ½ cup sour cream
- ¼ cup margarine
- ¼ cup coconut

Soften yeast in the warm water. Combine yeast mixture with sugar, salt, eggs, sour cream, and softened margarine in large bowl. Stir until blended. Gradually add flour, mixing well. Let dough rise in a greased bowl in a warm area. While dough rises, prepare filling by mixing the sugar, coconut, and orange rind well. Set aside. Divide dough in half. Roll each half into a circle about 12 inches in diameter. Spread each circle first with some softened margarine and then with half the filling mixture. Cut in pie-shaped wedges and roll up crescent-style (wide end first). Place point-end down in a well-greased 13x9-inch pan. Let rolls rise again. Bake at 325° for 20-25 minutes or until brown. Meanwhile, prepare glaze by combining sugar, orange rind, sour cream, and margarine in a heavy saucepan. Bring to a boil, stirring constantly. Boil for 3 minutes. Spread on rolls while warm. Sprinkle the ¼ cup coconut over the glaze.

Brenda Oyer
Gridley, Illinois
Salem Evangelical Mennonite Church, Gridley
Illinois MCC Relief Sale, Peoria

PLUCKETTS

- 1 package yeast
- ½ cup lukewarm water
- 1 teaspoon sugar
- ⅓ cup scalded milk
- 2 tablespoons white sugar
- 1 tablespoon shortening
- 1 teaspoon salt
- 2¼ cups flour
- ½ cup white sugar
- 1¼ teaspoon cinnamon
- ½ cup nuts, finely chopped
- ⅓ cup butter

Dissolve 1 teaspoon sugar in water. Sprinkle with yeast. Let stand 10 minutes. Mix together milk, 2 tablespoons white sugar, shortening, and salt. Add ¼ cup flour to milk mixture, then egg. Add another ¼ cup flour, then beat in yeast mixture. Add 1¾ cups flour and knead until elastic (8-10 minutes). Let rise until double (about 2 hours). Combine ½ cup white sugar, cinnamon, and nuts. Melt butter. Punch down dough and cut into 24 pieces. Roll each piece in hand, then in butter, then in sugar mixture. Put in well-greased 9-inch square pan or a tube cake pan. Layer the pieces if necessary. Let rise until double (1½-2 hours). Bake at 350° until done. Serve warm. Can be reheated before serving.

Pilgrims' Bread

- ½ cup yellow cornmeal
- ½ cup brown sugar
- 1 tablespoon salt
- 2 cups boiling water
- ¼ cup vegetable oil
- 2 packages dry yeast
- ½ cup warm water
- ¾ cup whole wheat flour
- ½ cup rye flour
- 4¼-4½ cups unbleached white flour

Combine cornmeal, sugar, and salt in a small bowl. Gradually stir cornmeal mixture into the boiling water. Add oil. Cool to lukewarm. Dissolve yeast in the warm water. Add to cornmeal mixture. Beat in whole wheat and rye flours. Stir in white flour by hand. Turn dough onto lightly floured surface. Knead until smooth and elastic. Place in a lightly greased bowl. Turn once to grease surface. Cover and let rise in a warm place until double. Punch dough down and turn onto lightly floured surface. Divide in half and knead a second time for 3 minutes. Shape dough into 2 loaves and place in greased pans. Cover and let rise again in warm place until double in bulk. Bake at 350° for 35-40 minutes.

Makes 2 loaves.

Contributed by Alvin W. Goerzen
Newton, Kansas
Minn-Kota Relief Sale
Sioux Falls, South Dakota

Quick Water Bread

- 1 package dry yeast
- 1 cup lukewarm water
- 1 tablespoon white sugar
- 4 cups all-purpose flour
- 2 teaspoons salt

Dissolve sugar in water and sprinkle with yeast. Let stand 10 minutes. Stir. Sift flour and salt into separate bowl. Add yeast mixture. Add just enough water to make a soft dough (about ⅓ cup). Stir well. Let rise until double in bulk. Divide dough in half and place in 2 buttered casseroles. Let rise again. Bake at 400° for 40 minutes.

REFRIGERATOR ROLLS

- ❖ ¾ cup lard
- ❖ 1 cup boiling water
- ❖ 1 cup cold water
- ❖ 1 tablespoon salt
- ❖ 2 packages yeast
- ❖ 1 cup warm water
- ❖ ½ cup white sugar
- ❖ 2 eggs, beaten
- ❖ 7 cups all-purpose flour

Part 1:
Pour boiling water over lard to melt it. After lard has melted, add cold water and salt.

Part 2:
Dissolve yeast in warm water. Combine with white sugar and eggs. Let stand 10 minutes.

Mix parts 1 and 2 and add flour (more if needed). Set in refrigerator until needed. Put in pans and let rise 3 hours. Bake. Dough keeps a week in refrigerator.

Missouri MCC Relief Sale, Harrisonville

REFRIGERATOR ROLLS

- ❖ 1½ cups milk
- ❖ 1 cup butter or margarine
- ❖ ½ cup sugar
- ❖ 1 teaspoon salt
- ❖ 3 eggs
- ❖ 1 package dry yeast
- ❖ 2 teaspoons sugar
- ❖ ⅛ cup lukewarm water
- ❖ 5-5½ cups flour
- ❖ Softened butter

Scald milk. Stir in the 1 cup butter, the ½ cup sugar, and the salt. Cool. Add eggs one at a time to milk mixture. Dissolve yeast and the 2 teaspoons sugar in the lukewarm water. Add yeast mixture, then flour, to milk mixture. Beat well. Let rise until double. Punch down and place in refrigerator overnight. The next day, divide dough into 3 parts. Roll each part into a round, as for pie crust. Spread with a little softened butter. Cut each round into 16 wedges. Roll up each wedge from wide end to pointed end. Let rolls rise on a greased pan until light (1½ hours). Bake at 375° for 10-15 minutes.

Makes 48 rolls.

Rolled Oat Bread

- 2 cups milk
- 1 cup rolled oats
- 2 tablespoons white sugar
- 2 teaspoons salt
- 3 tablespoons lard
- 2 tablespoons refined molasses
- ½ cup lukewarm water
- 1 teaspoon white sugar
- 1 envelope dry yeast
- 3¾-4 cups all-purpose flour

Scald milk. Add oatmeal, 2 tablespoons sugar, salt, lard, and molasses. Cool to lukewarm. Dissolve 1 teaspoon white sugar in ½ cup warm water and sprinkle with yeast. Let stand 10 minutes. Add yeast to milk and oatmeal mixture. Add 1 cup flour and beat well until smooth and elastic. Work in remaining flour until a smooth soft dough. Let rise to double in bulk. Punch down and form into 2 equal portions. Let rest 10 minutes, then shape into loaves. Let rise again to double in bulk. Bake at 350° for 1 hour.

Makes 2 good-sized loaves.

Semmel (German Crusty Rolls)

- 1 package yeast
- ¼ cup water
- 2 cups warm water
- 4 cups flour
- ½ teaspoon salt to taste

Dissolve yeast in the ¼ cup water to which a little sugar has been added. Measure the warm water into a mixing bowl. Beat in 2½ cups of the flour. After yeast starts action, beat it into the flour mixture. Add salt and remaining flour. Cover tightly and let rise until double. Stir down and refrigerate for a few hours or overnight. Dip a tablespoon into water for easier handling. Use coated tablespoon to drop dough by the spoonful onto well-greased baking sheets. Do not place too close together. Bake at 450°-500° until brown.

Makes about 14-16 semmel.

Contributed by Elizabeth Reimer
Beatrice, Nebraska

Sesame Multigrain Bread

- 6 cups warm water
- 1 cup honey
- 3 heaping tablespoons yeast
- 2 cups rye flour
- 1 cup oatmeal
- 1 cup milk powder
- 3-4 cups whole wheat flour
- 3 tablespoons salt
- 1 scant cup vegetable oil
- 1 cup sesame seeds
- ½-¾ cup sunflower seeds
- ½ cup millet (optional)
- Unbleached white flour

Combine warm water, honey, and yeast in a large mixing bowl. Let set. When frothy, add rye flour, oatmeal, milk powder, and enough of the whole wheat flour to make a batter. Cover with plastic wrap and let rise until it reaches top of bowl (about 20-30 minutes). Stir down and add salt, oil, sesame and sunflower seeds, and millet. Stir or work in enough unbleached white flour to make a dough. Knead for 5-10 minutes or until dough is of a good texture. Let dough rise and punch down. Let it rise again and punch down. Form into loaves to fit four 9½x5-inch pans plus four 6x3-inch pans. Bake at 350°-375° (mini-loaves for 25-30 minutes, large loaves for 30-35 minutes).

Makes 4 large and 4 small loaves.

Lola Hershberger
Denver, Colorado
Rocky Mountain Mennonite Relief Sale

White Bread

- 2 cups milk
- 4 tablespoons sugar
- 2 tablespoons salt
- 4 tablespoons shortening
- 1 cup lukewarm water
- 1 teaspoon sugar
- 1 package yeast
- 2 eggs, beaten
- 2 cups cold potato water
- 14 cups all-purpose flour

Scald the milk. Add the 4 tablespoons of sugar, salt, and shortening. Stir until all is dissolved. In a separate bowl, combine the warm water and the teaspoon of sugar. Stir to dissolve. Sprinkle with the yeast and let stand 10 minutes. Beat with a fork and add to first milk mixture. Add the eggs and potato water. Stir in 4 cups of the flour and beat well. Work in the remaining flour and knead 200 times. Let rise in warm place until double. Work down and let rise again. Shape into loaves and let rise again. Bake at 275° for 1 hour. Brush hot loaves with melted butter.

WHOLE WHEAT BREAD

- 1½ cups milk
- ½ cup brown sugar or molasses
- 2 tablespoons salt
- ½ cup shortening
- 2 ¼ cups water
- 2 teaspoons sugar
- 1 cup lukewarm water (100°)
- 2 envelopes (or 2 tablespoons) active dry yeast
- 6 cups whole wheat flour
- 6-6½ cups all-purpose flour

Scald the milk. Pour into a large bowl and add the brown sugar or molasses, salt, and shortening. Stir until shortening melts. Add the 2¼ cups water. Cool to lukewarm. Dissolve the sugar in the lukewarm water. Sprinkle with yeast. Let stand 10 minutes. Stir briskly with a fork. Add softened yeast to lukewarm milk mixture. Stir. Beat in the whole wheat flour. Beat vigorously by hand or with electric mixer, then gradually beat in the all-purpose flour with spoon. Work in last of flour with a rotating motion of hand. Turn dough on floured surface and knead 9-10 minutes. Shape into smooth ball and place in greased bowl, rotating dough to grease surface. Cover with a damp cloth and let rise until doubled (about 1¼ hours). Keep in a warm place. Punch down and shape into 4 loaves. Place in greased 8½x4½-inch loaf pans and let rise again until doubled (about 1 hour). Bake at 375° for 35 minutes.

WHAT IS POTATO WATER?

Potato water refers to water in which potatoes have been boiled. After boiling, some of the starch from the potatoes is left behind in the water. This water is often called for in bread recipes (such as the White Bread recipe on page 148), because it makes the bread incredibly moist. It can also replace milk in a bread recipe. Make potato water by boiling several peeled and cubed potatoes for 20 minutes. Let the water temperature come down before you use it.

Honey Whole Wheat Bread

- 2 packages active dry yeast
- ½ cup warm water (105°-115°)
- ⅓ cup honey
- ¼ cup shortening
- 1 tablespoon salt
- 1¾ cups warm water
- 3 cups whole wheat flour
- 3-4 cups white flour

Dissolve yeast in the ½ cup warm water in a large mixing bowl. Stir in honey, shortening, salt, the 1¾ cups warm water, and the whole wheat flour. Beat until smooth. Mix in enough white flour to make a dough that's easy to handle. Turn dough onto lightly floured surface. Knead about 10 minutes. Place in greased bowl. Cover and let rise in warm place until double (about 1 hour). Punch down and divide dough in half. Form into 2 loaves and place in greased baking pans. Let rise until double (about 1 hour). Bake at 375° for 40-45 minutes or until loaves are golden brown and sound hollow when tapped. Remove from pans and cool.

Makes 2 loaves.

Judy Buller
Beatrice, Nebraska
Nebraska Mennonite Relief Sale, Aurora

Zwiebach

- 2 cups milk
- 1 tablespoon sugar
- 2 tablespoons yeast
- 1 tablespoon salt
- ½ cup vegetable oil
- Flour

Combine milk and sugar. Warm slightly. Add yeast. Let set a short while until yeast is dissolved. Add remaining ingredients, plus a small amount of flour. Mix. Add a little more flour and mix. Continue adding flour and mixing until dough is smooth and soft. Knead well (or use a dough mixer). Cover with a towel and let rise until double in bulk. Punch down. Take a good-sized lump of dough with well-greased hands. Pinch off little pieces of dough (about the size of an egg) with thumb and forefinger. Set on a greased baking sheet. Pinch off smaller pieces, setting one firmly on top of each larger piece. Let rise again until double. Bake at 350° for 15-20 minutes.

Irene Penner
Corn, Oklahoma
Oklahoma MCC Relief Sale, Fairview

BASIC SWEET DOUGH

- 1½ cups milk
- ¼ cup white sugar
- 2¼ teaspoons salt
- ¾ cup shortening
- ¾ cup lukewarm water
- 1 tablespoon white sugar
- 3 envelopes yeast (3 tablespoons)
- 3 well-beaten eggs.
- 7 cups all-purpose flour

Scald the milk. Add the ¼ cup white sugar, salt, and shortening. Stir to dissolve and cool to lukewarm. Measure the lukewarm water and tablespoon of white sugar into a large bowl. Stir until dissolved. Sprinkle with yeast. Let stand 10 minutes. Beat with fork. Stir yeast mixture into milk mixture. Add eggs. Stir in 4 cups all-purpose flour and beat until smooth and elastic. Work in about 3 more cups flour. Turn on slightly floured board and knead lightly until smooth (about 5 minutes). Place in a greased bowl and lightly grease top of dough. Let rise in warm place free from draft until double in bulk (about 1½ hours).

Use this Basic Sweet Dough recipe to make the following 6 recipes.

CINNAMON ROLLS

- ¼ Basic Sweet Dough (above)
- Melted butter
- ½ cup of brown sugar
- 2 teaspoons cinnamon

Take one-quarter of Basic Sweet Dough (above) and roll into 9x12-inch rectangle. Brush with melted butter. Sprinkle with brown sugar and cinnamon. Roll up tightly, beginning at wide side. Seal edge well. Cut into 12 slices and place in well-greased rectangle pan. Let rise until double. Bake at 350° for 30 minutes.

BREADS

CHELSEA BUNS

- ❖ ½ cup raisins
- ❖ ⅓ cup melted butter
- ❖ ½ cup brown sugar
- ❖ Pecans or walnuts

Follow instructions for Cinnamon Rolls (page 151), but also sprinkle the dough with the raisins before rolling it up. Cut into 9 slices. Put the melted butter in an 8-inch square pan and sprinkle with the brown sugar and pecans or walnuts as desired. Arrange the 9 slices in pan with butter. Let rise until double and bake at 350° for 30 minutes. Turn upside down on a wire rack for 5 minutes to allow syrup to run over buns.

JAM RING

- ❖ Basic Sweet Dough (page 151)
- ❖ ⅓ cup nuts
- ❖ White icing

Roll out a portion of Basic Sweet Dough (page 151) into a 16x8-inch rectangle. Spread with the nuts. Roll up loosely. Twist dough from end to end and form into a ring on greased pan. Let rise until double and bake at 325° for 25-30 minutes. Spread hot ring with white icing and decorate top.

SWEDISH TEA RING

Tea Ring:
- ❖ ¼ Basic Sweet Dough (page 151)
- ❖ Melted butter
- ❖ ⅓ cup brown sugar
- ❖ ⅓ cup blanched almonds (or raisins)
- ❖ 1-2 tablespoons mixed cut citrus peel

Icing:
- ❖ 1 cup powdered sugar
- ❖ 2 tablespoons milk
- ❖ ½ teaspoon vanilla
- ❖ Chopped nuts or maraschino cherries

Roll one-quarter of Basic Sweet Dough (page 151) into 14x9-inch rectangle. Spread with melted butter. Sprinkle with brown sugar, almonds (or raisins), and citrus peel. Roll up lengthwise like a jelly roll. Shape into a circle, seam side down, on greased baking sheet. With scissors, make cuts two-thirds of the way through the ring from the outside edge (cuts should be about 1 inch apart). Turn slices partly to one side so they overlap each other. Cover and let rise until doubled. Bake at 375° for 25 minutes. Combine ingredients for icing. When tea ring is cool, drizzle icing over top and garnish with chopped nuts or maraschino cherries.

Applesauce Nut Bread

- 1½ cups flour
- 1 teaspoon baking powder
- 1 teaspoon soda
- 1 teaspoon salt
- 1 teaspoon cinnamon
- ½ teaspoon nutmeg
- 1 cup oatmeal
- 1 cup chopped walnuts
- ½ cup raisins
- ⅓ cup shortening
- ½ cup brown sugar
- 2 eggs
- 1 cup unsweetened applesauce
- ½ cup milk

Sift together the flour, baking powder, soda, salt, cinnamon, and nutmeg into a mixing bowl. Stir in the oatmeal, walnuts, and raisins. Cream the shortening and brown sugar together. Add the eggs and beat until light and fluffy. Blend in the applesauce and milk. Add this creamed mixture to the dry ingredients and beat 30 seconds. (Do not overbeat or batter can become lumpy.) Bake at 350° for 50-60 minutes.

CHOP NUTS THE EASY WAY—PUT BETWEEN LAYERS
OF WAX PAPER AND ROLL WITH A ROLLING PIN.

Banana Nut Bread

- ⅔ cup shortening
- 2½ cups sifted cake flour
- 1⅔ cups sugar
- 1¼ teaspoons baking powder
- 1 teaspoon soda
- 1 teaspoon salt
- 1¼ cups mashed very ripe bananas (about 3)
- ⅔ cup buttermilk
- 2 eggs
- ⅔ cup chopped walnuts

Stir shortening to soften. Sift dry ingredients into same bowl. Add bananas and half of buttermilk. Mix until all flour is dampened. Beat vigorously for 2 minutes. Add remaining buttermilk and eggs and beat 2 minutes longer. Fold in slightly floured nuts. Bake in 2 wax-paper-lined lightly greased loaf pans. Bake at 350° for 35 minutes. Can also be baked in 8-inch square cake pan or as cupcakes.

Berliner Pfannkuchen (Prune-Filled Doughnuts)

- 1 pint milk
- ¾ pound soft butter
- ½ cup sugar
- 2 packages dry yeast
- 8 egg yolks
- 4 whole eggs
- About 8 cups flour
- 2 large packages medium pitted prunes, cooked about 5 minutes to soften

Scald milk. Add butter and sugar. Let cool slightly. Dissolve yeast in ½ cup hot water (105°-115°). Add 1-2 cups flour to the milk mixture and beat well. Add dissolved yeast and beat well. Beat in egg yolks, then whole eggs one at a time (beat well after each egg is added). Add remaining flour. Beat until smooth and shiny. Let rise until double. Have ready enough cold water to dip your teaspoon into so the dough will not stick to it and a small bowl of flour to drop your dough into so you can work with it (the dough is soft and sticky). Take a teaspoon of dough with the wet spoon and drop it into the flour. Work the dough around a prune, being sure the dough covers the prune well. By the time you've made all the berliners, the first ones will be ready to fry. Fry in hot oil or fat (375°) until brown. Roll in sugar before serving.

Makes about 125.

Mrs. Gerald (Rogena Friesen) Jantzen
Plymouth, Nebraska
Nebraska MCC Relief Sale, Aurora

Carrot Bread

- ½ cup salad oil
- 1 cup sugar
- 2 eggs, beaten
- 1 cup shredded carrots
- 1½ cups sifted all-purpose flour
- 1 teaspoon soda
- 1 teaspoon baking powder
- ¼ teaspoon salt
- 1 teaspoon cinnamon
- ½ cup milk
- ½ cup chopped walnuts (optional)

Mix sugar and salad oil. Add beaten eggs. Stir in shredded carrots. Sift flour, baking powder, soda, salt, and cinnamon. Add small amounts to sugar mixture alternately with milk. Stir in walnuts. Bake in a 9x5x3-inch well-greased loaf pan for 55 minutes at 350°.

Cheese Biscuits

- 2 cups flour
- 4 teaspoons baking powder
- 2 tablespoons white sugar
- ¾ teaspoon salt
- 1 cup grated sharp cheese
- ¼ cup chopped green tops of onions (chives)
- ⅓ cup vegetable oil
- ¾ cup milk

Measure flour, baking powder, sugar, and salt together. Add cheese and onions. Stir. Add oil and milk. Stir to form a soft ball of dough (add more milk if needed). Turn dough out onto lightly floured board and knead 8-10 times. Roll or pat to a thickness of ¾-1 inch. Cut with biscuit cutter. Place biscuits close together on a greased pan for moist sides. Bake at 425° for 15 minutes.

Anne Neufeld
Coaldale Alberta
MCC Relief Sale, Coaldale

Cherry Tea Bread

- ¼ cup margarine or butter
- ¾ cup white sugar
- ⅛ teaspoon almond flavoring
- ½ cup well drained red maraschino cherries, halved
- 1 egg, well beaten
- 2 cups sifted all-purpose flour
- 2½ teaspoons baking powder
- ½ teaspoon salt
- ¾ cup milk

Cream margarine, sugar, and flavoring. When smooth, add egg and cherries. Mix well. Add sifted dry ingredients alternately with milk. Do not overheat. Pour batter into well-greased loaf pan. Bake at 325° for 1 hour. While still hot, brush top of loaf with margarine or butter to prevent cracking. Loaf slices better after 24 hours.

Christmas Braid

- 5½ cups plus 2 tablespoons flour
- 1 package yeast
- 2 cups milk
- ½ cup sugar
- 6 tablespoons butter or margarine
- 1 teaspoon salt (optional)
- 1 egg
- 1 cup raisins
- 1 cup finely-chopped mixed candied fruit
- ½ cup chopped nuts
- 1 egg yolk
- 1 tablespoon water

Combine 3 cups of the flour with the yeast in a large bowl. Measure milk, sugar, butter, and salt into a saucepan. Heat to 120°-130°. Add to flour mixture. Add egg. Beat on low speed with an electric mixer for 30 seconds. Increase speed to medium and continue beating for 3 minutes. Stir in raisins, candied fruit, nuts, and enough of the remaining flour to form a stiff dough. Turn out onto a floured surface and knead until smooth and elastic (8-10 minutes). Place in a greased bowl and turn once to grease top. Cover and let rise until doubled (about 1½ hours). Divide dough into thirds, then divide into thirds again. Roll each piece into a 15-inch rope. Place 3 ropes 1 inch apart on a greased baking sheet. Begin braiding loosely in the middle and work toward the ends. Pinch ends together and tuck under. Repeat with remaining ropes to make two more loaves. Cover and let rise until doubled (30-40 minutes). Combine egg yolk and water and brush over braids. Bake at 350° for 20-25 minutes or until browned.

Makes 3 loaves.

Mrs. Paul (Mary Helen) Wade
Sterling, Illinois
Science Ridge Mennonite Church
Illinois MCC Relief Sale, Peoria

CINNAMON BREAD

- 2-3 packages yeast
- 1 tablespoon sugar
- 1 cup warm water
- 1 stick (½ cup) margarine
- ⅔ cup sugar
- 1⅓ cup powdered milk
- 2 teaspoons salt
- 4 cups hot water
- 12 cups flour
- 1 cup sugar
- 4 teaspoons cinnamon

Dissolve yeast and the 1 tablespoon sugar in the warm water. Stir and set aside. Measure the margarine, the ⅔ cup sugar, powdered milk, and salt into a Tupperware Fix-n-Mix bowl. Add the hot water, stirring until margarine is melted. Stir in 6 cups of the flour. Add the yeast mixture. Gradually add at least 6 cups more flour to make a dough that is easy to knead. Turn dough onto floured board and knead at least 100 times. Put into bowl and seal. Set aside in warm place for about 1½ hours until doubled in bulk. Punch down and divide into 4 parts. Let rest 10 minutes. Mix the 1 cup sugar with the cinnamon. Roll each portion of dough into a 7x15-inch rectangle. Brush lightly with water. Sprinkle ¼ cup of the cinnamon-sugar mixture over the dough. Roll up as for a jelly roll. Moisten edge and seal. Place in a well-greased pan. Repeat with the other three portions. Let rise in a warm place until loaves reach just above top of pans. Bake at 350° for 35-40 minutes.

Makes 4 loaves.

Frances E. Bumgardner
Morton, Illinois
First Mennonite Church of Morton
Illinois Mennonite Relief Sale

EASY SCONES

- 2 cups flour
- 4 teaspoons baking powder
- 2 teaspoons sugar
- ⅓ cup milk or cream
- ½ teaspoon salt
- 4 tablespoons butter or margarine
- 2 eggs

Sift dry ingredients. Work in butter with pastry mixer or fork. Add milk and well-beaten eggs (reserve a small amount of unbeaten egg white). Toss on floured board. Pat and roll ¾ inch thick. Cut in squares, diamonds, or triangles. Brush with reserved egg white diluted with 1 teaspoon water. Sprinkle with sugar and bake for 15 minutes at 450°.

Makes 12 scones.

German Buns

Dough:
- 4 cups sifted all-purpose flour
- 1 teaspoon salt
- 1 cup white sugar
- 1 teaspoon soda
- 2 teaspoons cream of tartar
- 1 egg, well beaten
- ½ cup lard
- ½ cup butter
- ¼ cup milk
- ¼ cup water

Filling Spread:
- 1 egg, beaten
- 1 cup brown sugar
- ½ cup flour

To make dough, sift dry ingredients together into mixing bowl. Add egg, lard, and butter. Mix to a soft dough with milk and water. Roll to ½ inch thickness. Combine ingredients for filling and spread on dough. Roll up like a jelly roll and cut in slices. Place in greased pan (not too close, as they spread). Bake at 375° for 8-10 minutes.

Hot Cross Buns

- 5 cups flour
- ½ cup sugar
- 1¼ teaspoons salt
- 1 tablespoon grated lemon rind
- 2 packages dry yeast
- ½ cup milk
- ½ cup potato water
- ½ cup butter
- 2 eggs
- ¾ cup lukewarm mashed potatoes
- ¾ cup raisins
- 1 egg yolk beaten with 2 tablespoons water
- Powdered sugar
- Egg white

In a large bowl, stir together 1½ cups of the flour with the sugar, salt, lemon rind, and yeast. In a small saucepan, combine milk, potato water, and butter. Heat. Gradually add warm liquid to dry ingredients. Beat 2 minutes at medium speed. Add eggs, mashed potatoes, and ½ cup more flour. Beat at high speed for 2 minutes. Add enough of the remaining flour to make a stiff dough. Turn out onto a floured board and knead 8-10 minutes. Place in a greased bowl. Cover and let rise until doubled in bulk (about 1 hour). Punch down. Knead in raisins. Shape into balls. Brush tops with the egg yolk/water mixture. Let rise 1 hour. Bake at 375° for 25 minutes. While warm, frost with a mixture of egg white and powdered sugar.

Makes 24 buns.

Lynette Preheim
Marion, South Dakota
Minn-Kota MCC Relief Sale
Sioux Falls, South Dakota

Johnny Cake

- 1 teaspoon soda
- 1 cup cream (sweet or sour)
- 1 egg
- 1 cup sugar
- 1½ cup cornmeal
- 1 cup flour
- 1 teaspoon salt

Dissolve the soda in the cream. Add the egg and sugar. Add the cornmeal, flour, and salt. Bake in 9x9-inch pan at 350° for 40 minutes. Can also be baked in muffin tins.

Lazy Daisy Duff

- ¼ cup butter
- 1 cup flour
- ½ cup sugar
- 1 tablespoon baking powder
- Pinch salt
- ⅔ cup milk
- 2 cups berries or chopped fruit

Melt butter in an 8-inch ovenproof frying pan or casserole dish. Set aside. In a small bowl, mix flour, sugar, baking powder, and salt. Quickly stir in the milk to form a batter. Spoon batter over melted butter in pan. Top with the fruit. Do not stir. Bake at 350° for about 35 minutes.

Lemon Tea Bread

Bread:
- ⅓ cup shortening
- 1 cup white sugar
- 2 eggs, well beaten
- ½ cup milk
- 1 teaspoon baking powder
- ⅛ teaspoon salt
- 2 cups flour
- ½ cup walnuts
- 2 teaspoons lemon juice
- 1 teaspoon lemon rind

Icing:
- 2 teaspoons sugar
- 2 teaspoons lemon rind
- 1 teaspoon lemon juice

Cream shortening and sugar well. Add beaten eggs. Sift 1 cup of the flour, baking powder, and salt. Add to creamed mixture. Blend in milk, lemon rind, juice, and nuts. Sift the remaining cup of flour and blend into creamed mixture. Pour into greased loaf pan and bake at 300° for 90 minutes. Combine ingredients for icing and spread over bread while still hot.

☙

Pumpkin Bread

- 3½ cups flour
- ½ teaspoon baking soda
- 2 teaspoons baking powder
- 1½ teaspoons salt
- 1 teaspoon cinnamon
- ½ teaspoon cloves
- 4 eggs, beaten
- 2⅔ cups sugar
- 2 cups cooked pumpkin
- ⅔ cup water
- ½ cup vegetable oil
- ⅔ cup raisins
- ⅔ cup chopped walnuts or other nuts (optional)

Sift together first 6 (dry) ingredients. Add sugar, pumpkin, water, and oil to beaten eggs. Mix well. Add liquid ingredients to dry ingredients. Mix until dry ingredients are well moistened. Fold in raisins and nuts. Pour batter into 2 greased 9x5-inch loaf pans. Bake at 350° for 1 hour or until tester inserted in loaves comes out clean. Wrap and store loaves for 24 hours before serving.

Makes 2 loaves.

Pumpkin Bread

- 1¾ cups flour
- 1½ cups sugar
- 1 teaspoon soda
- ¾ teaspoon salt
- ½ teaspoon cloves
- ½ teaspoon cinnamon
- ½ teaspoon nutmeg
- ½ cup salad oil
- ⅓ cup water
- 1 cup pumpkin
- 2 eggs, beaten
- ½ cup chopped nuts
- ½ cup raisins

Sift flour, sugar, soda, salt, cinnamon, and nutmeg into mixing bowl. Add cloves. Add salad oil, water, pumpkin, eggs, nuts, and raisins. Put in greased loaf pan or soup or vegetable tins (only fill tins halfway). Bake at 350° for 35-40 minutes.

Arnaud Christian
Fellowship Cookbook
(contributed by Elly Kathler)
Ben Sawatzky
Winnipeg, Manitoba
MCC Manitoba Relief Sale

RAISIN BREAD

- 2 packages yeast
- 1 cup water
- 2 teaspoons sugar
- 1 cup milk
- ½ cup butter
- ½ cup sugar
- 2 teaspoons salt
- 3 eggs
- 6½ cups flour
- 2½ cups raisins

Dissolve yeast in the water with the 2 teaspoons sugar. Scald milk. Add butter, sugar, salt, eggs, flour, and raisins. Let rise until double in bulk (at least 1 hour). Divide dough in fourths and place in 4 loaf pans. Let loaves rise until double in bulk. Bake at 375° for 30-40 minutes.

Makes 4 loaves.

Alice Klassen
Coaldale, Alberta
Alberta MCC Relief Sale, Coaldale

RHUBARB BREAD

- 1½ cups white sugar
- ⅔ cup vegetable oil
- 1 egg
- 1 cup buttermilk
- 1 teaspoon vanilla
- 2½ cups flour
- 1 teaspoon baking soda
- 1 teaspoon salt
- 1½ cups diced rhubarb
- ½ cup chopped nuts or 1 cup washed and drained raisins
- ½ cup sugar mixed with a dash of cinnamon
- 1 tablespoon butter, melted

Combine the 1½ cups sugar, oil, egg, buttermilk, and vanilla in a mixing bowl. Mix well. Sift together flour, soda, and salt. Add to liquid mixture. Stir in rhubarb and nuts or raisins. Pour batter into 2 greased loaf pans. Sprinkle with the sugar-cinnamon mixture. Drizzle with melted butter. Bake at 325° for 1 hour. Remove loaves from pans and brush with butter. Sprinkle with a mixture of sugar and cinnamon.

Makes 2 loaves.

Tillie Janzen
Mountain Lake, Minnesota
Minn-Kota MCC Relief Sale
Sioux Falls, South Dakota

Zucchini Orange Coconut Bread

- 1 cup vegetable oil
- 1¾ cups sugar
- 3 eggs
- 2 teaspoons almond extract
- 3 cups flour
- 1 teaspoon baking soda
- 1 teaspoon baking powder
- 1 teaspoon salt
- ¾ cup orange juice
- 1½ cups coconut
- 2 cups grated zucchini

Mix together all ingredients. Divide batter evenly between 2 bread pans. Bake at 350° for 50-55 minutes.

Makes 2 loaves.

Lena Sala
Hollsopple, Pennsylvania
MCC Quilt Auction and Relief Sale, Johnstown

Fruity Coffee Cake

- 4 cups sliced fresh fruit
- 1 cup water
- 2 tablespoons lemon juice
- ½-1 cup sugar
- 6 tablespoons cornstarch
- 1 cup butter or margarine
- 1½ cups sugar
- 4 eggs
- 1 teaspoon vanilla
- 3 cups flour
- 1½ teaspoons baking powder

Glaze:
- 1 cup powdered sugar
- ½ teaspoon vanilla
- 2 tablespoons melted butter or margarine
- Warm milk

Cook fruit in the water until tender. Stir in lemon juice. Mix together the sugar (to taste) and the cornstarch. Add cinnamon if desired. Stir into hot fruit. Cook, stirring, until thick. Cool. Mix butter, the 1½ cups sugar, eggs, and vanilla until smooth. Add flour and baking powder. Mix until smooth. Spread two-thirds of the batter in a greased jelly roll pan. Spread cooked fruit over. Spoon remaining batter over fruit. Bake at 375° for 30 minutes. While cake is baking, mix together glaze ingredients with enough warm milk to make a thick liquid. Pour glaze over cake while still warm. Serve warm or cold.

Makes 18 or more servings.

Donna Wharton
Marion, South Dakota
Minn-Kota MCC Relief Sale
Sioux Falls, South Dakota

BREADS

Quick Coffee Cake

- 1 cup sugar
- 1 tablespoon oil
- 1 egg
- 1 teaspoon vanilla
- 1 cup milk
- 2 cups flour
- 1 tablespoon baking powder
- ½ teaspoon salt

Topping:
- 1 cup brown sugar
- 1 teaspoon cinnamon
- ¼ cup melted margarine
- 1 cup chopped pecans

Combine all cake ingredients. Beat by hand until smooth. Pour into a greased 9x13-inch pan. Mix together topping ingredients. Sprinkle over batter. Bake at 350° for 35 minutes.

Debby Ross
Missouri MCC Relief Sale, Harrisonville

CLEAN COFFEE PERCOLATOR BY PERKING BAKING
SODA IN WATER. RINSE THOROUGHLY.

Sour Cream Coffee Cake

Topping:
- 1 cup chopped pecans or walnuts
- ½ cup butter, melted
- ¼ cup white sugar
- ⅓ cup brown sugar
- 1 teaspoon cinnamon

Batter:
- ½ cup shortening
- 1 cup sugar
- 2 eggs
- 1 teaspoon vanilla
- 2 cups flour
- 1 teaspoon baking powder
- 1 teaspoon soda
- ½ teaspoon salt
- 1 cup sour cream

Mix ingredients for topping and set aside. Cream shortening and sugar. Beat in eggs and vanilla. Mix dry ingredients and alternately add the batter (half at a time) with 1 cup sour cream (half at a time). Put half the topping in a greased tube pan. Add half the batter. Repeat. Bake at 350° for 45 minutes or until done. Let cool for 5 minutes before turning out on a rack.

SOUR CREAM TWISTS

- 3½ cups flour
- 1 cup shortening
- 1 package yeast
- ½ cup warm water
- 2 teaspoons sugar
- 1 cup sour cream
- 1 egg plus 1 egg yolk
- 1 teaspoon vanilla
- ¾ teaspoons salt
- 1 cup white sugar

Mix flour and shortening as for pastry. Dissolve yeast in the warm water with the 2 teaspoons sugar. Add to flour-shortening mixture along with sour cream, egg and yolk, vanilla, and salt. Mix well. Dough will be quite soft. Put in refrigerator for 1 hour to rise. Pat out half the dough to ¼ inch thick (use sugar if dough sticks to board). Spread dough with ½ cup of the white sugar, working it in with a finger. Fold dough into thirds and flatten again to ¼ inch thick. Cut into 1x3-inch strips. Twist into desired shapes and bake at once at 375° for about 20-25 minutes. Repeat same procedure with remaining half of dough.

Herta Janzen
Coaldale, Alberta
Alberta MCC Relief Sale, Coaldale

TEABALLS

- 3 eggs
- 1 cup sugar
- 1 cup milk
- 2 tablespoons melted fat
- ½ teaspoon vanilla
- ½ teaspoon nutmeg
- ½ teaspoon salt
- 2 teaspoons baking powder
- 2 cups flour

Beat eggs. Add sugar, vanilla, and milk. Add sifted dry ingredients. Beat well and add warm fat. Drop by spoonfuls into hot fat (350°-365°).

TEA BISCUITS

- 2 eggs
- 1 cup sweet cream
- ½ teaspoon salt
- 2 teaspoons baking powder
- 1¾ cups all-purpose flour.

Put unbeaten eggs in mixing bowl. Add cream and salt. Sift flour with baking powder and add to egg mixture. Stir well and drop on greased cookie sheet or bake in square 8x8-inch pan. (For shortcake bake in pie plate.) Bake at 375° for 20 minutes.

DATE NUT MUFFINS

- 2 cups whole wheat flour
- ⅔ cup all-purpose flour
- 2 teaspoons soda
- 1 teaspoon salt
- 1⅓ cups white sugar
- 2 eggs
- 1 cup salad oil
- 1½ cups milk
- 1 teaspoon maple flavoring
  (or ⅓ teaspoon cinnamon)
- 3 ounces applesauce
- ⅓ cup chopped dates
- 1 cup chopped walnuts

Sift first 5 ingredients together into mixing bowl. Mix all wet ingredients in another bowl, then combine both mixtures. Add nuts and dates. Stir until blended and smooth. Put in greased muffin tins and bake at 400° for 20 minutes.

Makes 2 dozen muffins.

HEATHER'S CORN MUFFINS

- 2 cups cornmeal
- ½ cup all-purpose flour
- 2 teaspoons baking powder
- ½ teaspoon baking soda
- ½ teaspoon salt
- 1 tablespoon sugar
- ¼ cup vegetable oil
- 1½ cups buttermilk
- 2 eggs

Preheat oven to 350°. Mix all ingredients together and beat vigorously. Pour into greased muffin pan. Bake for 20 minutes. Makes 12 muffins.

Morning Glory Muffins

- ❖ 2 cups flour
- ❖ 1¼ cups white sugar
- ❖ 2 teaspoons baking soda
- ❖ 2 teaspoons cinnamon
- ❖ ½ teaspoon salt
- ❖ 3 eggs, beaten
- ❖ 1 cup vegetable oil
- ❖ 2 teaspoons vanilla
- ❖ 2 cups grated carrots
- ❖ ½ cup raisins
- ❖ ½ cup coconut
- ❖ ½ cup chopped nuts
- ❖ 1 apple, shredded

Combine flour, sugar, baking soda, cinnamon, and salt. Mix thoroughly. Beat together eggs, oil, and vanilla. Blend into flour mixture. Fold in carrots, raisins, coconut, nuts, and shredded apple. Bake at 350° for 20 minutes or until tester comes out clean.

Makes 14 large muffins.

Susana Siemens
Winnipeg, Manitoba
MCC Manitoba Relief Sale

Oatmeal Muffins

- ❖ 1 cup flour
- ❖ ¼ cup white sugar
- ❖ 3 teaspoons baking powder
- ❖ ½ teaspoon salt
- ❖ 3 tablespoons shortening
- ❖ 1 cup quick oats
- ❖ ½ cup chopped dates or raisins
- ❖ 1 egg, well beaten
- ❖ 1 cup milk

Sift flour, sugar, baking powder, and salt. Cut in shortening. Add oatmeal and dates and blend well. Add milk and beaten egg. Mix lightly. Fill greased muffin tins two-thirds full and bake at 425° until done.

Makes 1 dozen muffins.

Pumpkin Spice Muffins

- 2 eggs
- ½ cup sugar
- ¾ cup canned pumpkin
- ¼ cup vegetable oil
- 1½ cups flour
- 1 teaspoon baking powder
- ½ teaspoon baking soda
- ½ teaspoon salt
- ¼ teaspoon cinnamon
- ¼ teaspoon cloves
- ¼ teaspoon nutmeg
- ¾ cup raisins
- ½ cup chopped nuts (optional)

Preheat oven to 400°. Beat together eggs, sugar, pumpkin, and oil. Stir in remaining ingredients. Mix until blended. Spoon batter into muffin tins (fill cups two-thirds full). Bake 18-20 minutes.

Phyllis Garber
Goshen, Indiana
Yellow Creek Mennonite Church
Indiana MCC Relief Sale, Goshen

THE DISCOVERY OF A NEW DISH MAKES MORE FOR THE HAPPINESS OF MAN THAN THE DISCOVERY OF A STAR.

Apple Fritters

- 2 cups all-purpose flour
- 2 tablespoons sugar
- 1 teaspoon salt
- 3 teaspoons baking powder
- 2 eggs
- Milk
- Apples, sliced into rings

Sift together the flour, sugar, salt, and baking powder. Beat the eggs slightly in a 2-cup measuring cup. Add milk to the 2-cup level. Beat together with the dry ingredients using beater (blender works too). Dip apple rings in batter. Fry in deep fat at 375° (electric fry pan works well).

Froese-Fritz Apple Fritters

- 8 cups flour
- ¼ cup baking powder
- 4 teaspoons salt
- 1⅓ cups dry milk powder
- 1¼ cups sugar
- 8 eggs
- 8 cups water
- Apple rings

Mix all ingredients (except apples) with a whisk. Dip apple rings in batter. Drop into hot oil (375°) to fry.

Ann Froese Fritz
Rocky Mountain Mennonite Relief Sale,
Rocky Ford

Oppel Kuchen (Apple Fritters)

- 1 egg
- ½ cup milk
- ½ teaspoon baking powder
- ¼ teaspoon salt
- 1 cup flour
- Apples, cut into small chunks

Mix all ingredients (except apples) together. Add as many cut apples as the batter will hold. Drop by spoonfuls into deep fat. Fry on both sides. Drain on absorbent paper. Sprinkle with sugar and eat. Fresh cherries may be used in place of the apples.

Nebraska MCC Relief Sale, Aurora

Funnel Cakes

- 4 eggs
- 3 cups milk
- ¼ cup sugar
- 4 cups flour
- 4 teaspoons baking powder
- 2 teaspoons salt
- Vegetable oil for frying
- Powdered sugar

Beat eggs. Add milk and sugar. Sift dry ingredients together. Add to egg-milk mixture. Beat with a wire whisk until smooth. Heat oil to 375°. Pour ½ cup batter through funnel into heated oil. Fry a couple of minutes on each side. Drain on paper towels and sprinkle with confectioner's sugar before serving.

Ardith Epp
Nebraska MCC Relief Sale, Aurora

Hungarian Walnut Strudel

Dough:
- ½ cup lukewarm milk
- 1 package yeast
- 1 tablespoon sugar
- 1½ cups all-purpose flour
- ½ cup butter
- 3 egg yolks
- Juice from half a lemon
- 2 tablespoons sour cream

Walnut Filling:
- ½ pound walnuts
- 3 egg whites
- ¾ cup sugar
- 2 tablespoons fine dry bread crumbs
- Pinch salt

To prepare dough, sift flour and cut in butter. Dissolve sugar in lukewarm milk and sprinkle with yeast. Let stand 10 minutes. Make a well in flour mixture and add egg yolks, lemon juice, sour cream, and yeast mixture. Mix by hand, adding more flour to make a dough that doesn't stick to the fingers. Knead on lightly floured board, rolling and folding until shiny. To prepare filling, beat egg whites with salt until stiff. Add sugar gradually, beating. Fold in ground walnuts and bread crumbs. Roll out half of the dough to ½ inch thickness and spread with walnut filling. Roll up and place, edge down, on well-greased pan. Let rise for 1 hour. Brush with egg yolk. Bake at 375° for 30 minutes. Turn oven off and let stand 15 minutes longer.

ɔʒ

KIRSCHEN PFLINZEN

Pflinzen:
* 1½ cups flour
* 1 tablespoon granulated sugar
* ½ teaspoon salt
* 2 cups milk
* 3 eggs, slightly beaten

Kirschen:
* 2-3 cups canned (or frozen and thawed) red sour cherries and their juice
* ¾ cup granulated sugar
* 2 heaping tablespoons cornstarch
* 2 tablespoons cool water
* Red food coloring

Make pflinzen batter by combining flour, sugar, and salt. Gradually add milk and eggs. Beat well until batter is very smooth. Batter should be very thin. Prepare kirschen by adding enough water to the cherries and their juice to make 4-4½ cups cherries and liquid. Heat to boiling. Make a smooth paste of the sugar, cornstarch, and cool water. Add paste to hot cherries. Cook, stirring, until clear. Stir in several drops red food coloring. Keep cherries hot (but not boiling) while frying the pflinzen. Heat and lightly grease an 8-inch frying pan. Pour in just enough batter to cover bottom of pan. Tilt pan so batter runs over entire surface. Fry (over medium heat) until edges are golden brown. Turn and fry other side. As pflinzen are fried, stack immediately in a clear glass bowl with kirschen. Start with 2 pflinzen, then a layer of kirschen, then 2 more pflinzen, and so on, ending with cherries. To serve, cut stack into pie-shaped wedges. Serve warm or cool.

Claassen Family
Albany, Oregon
Oregon MCC Fall Festival, Albany

KNIE BLATZA (NOTHINGS)

* 1 dozen eggs
* 1 teaspoon salt
* 1½ cups sweet or sour cream
* 1 teaspoon cream of tartar or ½ teaspoon baking soda if sour cream is used
* 8-12 cups flour

Mix first 4 ingredients with beater. Beat in some of the flour. When dough gets too thick to beat, knead in rest of flour. Shape into balls the size of walnuts. Cover with waxed paper and damp towel. Let rest 20 minutes. Roll flat and round. Place over knee and stretch thin. Fry in deep fat. Sprinkle with sugar.

Makes 85-90.

Mrs. Amos Amstutz
Ohio Mennonite Relief Sale, Kidron

Kuchli (Nothings)

- 1 dozen large eggs
- 1 tablespoon salt
- 1 scant teaspoon baking soda
- 1 pint slightly sour cream
- Flour

Beat eggs and salt in a large bowl. Dissolve baking soda in cream. Add enough flour to make a rather heavy dough. Knead dough on floured board until it no longer sticks to board. Take a sharp knife and make slits through the lump. If dough is sticky, add more flour and keep kneading (about 30 minutes). Make dough into balls the size of walnuts. Put between plastic to keep from getting crusty. Roll as thin as possible. Stretch and fry in hot oil. Sugar the nothings as soon as they are fried.

Makes 85-90.

Mrs. Metta Nussbaum
Ohio Mennonite Relief Sale, Kidro

Noni Snicki or Nolles Nicki (Crepe Suzettes)

Filling:
- 2 cups cottage cheese
- 2 teaspoons sugar
- 2 tablespoons flour
- 2 eggs
- 1 teaspoon cinnamon

Pancakes:
- 1 cup flour
- 1½-2 cups milk
- 2-3 eggs, beaten
- 1-2 tablespoons vegetable oil
- ½ teaspoon salt

Mix all filling ingredients well. Set aside while making pancakes. Prepare pancake batter by mixing flour and milk until smooth. Add remaining ingredients and mix until smooth. Pour enough batter over bottom of large skillet to make a big, but very thin, pancake. When brown on first side, flip to brown other side. After making all the pancakes (or as you make each one), spread some filling on the brownest side and roll up pancake. Place in cake pan and bake at 350° for about 30 minutes. These pancakes can also be filled with cooked rhubarb or with applesauce. They can also be sprinkled with sugar and served with sour cream.

Gertie Graber
Freeman, South Dakota
Minn-Kota MCC Relief Sale
Sioux Falls, South Dakota

℃ℬ

RULL KUCHEN

- 3 eggs
- ¾ cup sweet cream
- ¼ cup sweet milk
- 1 teaspoon salt
- ½ teaspoon baking powder
- About 4 cups flour
  (enough to make a soft dough)

Put all ingredients (except flour) into a large bowl. Stir in enough flour to form a soft dough. Knead on a lightly floured surface. Roll out dough. For crisp crullers, roll very thin. For puffy ones, roll about ¼ inch thick. Cut dough into squares or oblong pieces. Fry in hot oil (375°) until brown.

Nebraska MCC Relief Sale, Aurora

ROLLKUCHEN

- 4 cups flour
- 2 teaspoons baking powder
- 1 teaspoon salt
- 1 cup sour cream
- 1 cup milk
- 4 eggs

Sift dry ingredients and make well in the center. Add remaining ingredients. Mix well with hands. Roll out on floured board and cut in 2x4-inch strips. Fry in deep hot fat until golden brown on one side. Turn and fry on other side. If rolled thin, they will be very crisp. If a softer pastry is preferred, do not roll as thin.

Nebraska MCC Relief Sale, Aurora

Relief Sale Doughnuts

- 1 package yeast dissolved in 1 cup warm water
- 1 cup mashed potatoes
- 1 cup lard
- 1 cup scalded milk
- ½ cup sugar
- 2 eggs
- Flour

Mix in order given, adding enough flour so dough will not stick to fingers. Let rise until double in bulk. Roll out and cut. Put on trays sprinkled with flour. Let rise again, fry, and drain. Dry and dip in syrup made of 1 pound powdered sugar and ½ cup water. Dip while still hot.

Ruth Ellen Doughnuts

- 2 cups milk
- 1 cup sugar
- ¾ cup shortening or vegetable oil
- 2 teaspoons salt
- 1 package yeast
- 1 cup warm water
- 2 eggs
- 10-11 cups bread flour (enough to make a soft dough)

Scald milk. Stir in sugar, shortening, and salt. Set aside to cool. Dissolve yeast in the warm water. Set aside. Beat eggs. When milk mixture is cool, mix in eggs and yeast. Stir in enough flour to make a soft dough. Let dough rise until double in size. Roll out and cut into doughnuts. Let rise again until light. Fry in hot lard (365°). Sugar or glaze according to your taste.

Makes about 65 average-size doughnuts.

Ruth Ellen Riehl
Contributed by Mildred Weaver
Bath, New York
Southern Tier Mennonite Relief Sale, Bath

BREADS

CB

Soft Pretzels

- ❖ 1 envelope yeast
- ❖ 1 teaspoon sugar
- ❖ 2 teaspoons salt
- ❖ 4-5 cups flour
- ❖ Butter as needed
- ❖ 4 teaspoons baking soda
- ❖ Coarse salt for sprinkling

Dissolve yeast in ¼ cup warm water. Stir in an additional cup of warm water and the sugar. Pour yeast mixture into a bowl. Add salt. Beat in flour to make a stiff dough. Knead for 10 minutes (or until dough is elastic). Place in bowl and spread with butter. Cover. Let rise 45 minutes or until double. Shape in sticks or twists, making the sticks half the thickness of desired pretzel. Bring 4 cups water to a boil with baking soda. Drop 3 pretzels in at a time. Boil 1 minute or until they float. Remove and drain. Place on buttered cookie sheets. Sprinkle with coarse salt. Bake at 475° for 12 minutes or until golden brown. To make pretzels crisp, lay them on a cookie sheet and place them in a warm oven set at 200° for 2 hours.

From Amish Cooking, *published by Pathway Publishers Corporation*

APPLE PANCAKES

- 3 tablespoons flour
- 1 egg
- Pinch of salt
- Enough sweet milk to make batter a little thicker than cream (¼-⅓ cup)

Chop 2 apples. Fry in a covered pan to cook. Combine all other ingredients (except flour) to create a thin batter that will spread over the entire pan. Cut in flour and turn as best you can.

Serves 2.

BUCKWHEAT PANCAKES

- 1 cup white flour
- ½ cup whole wheat flour
- 1 cup buckwheat flour
- 5 heaping tablespoons sugar
- 2 teaspoons salt
- 1 package dry yeast
- 2 cups warm water
- ⅓ cup baking soda dissolved in a bit of warm water

Mix flours, sugar, and salt in a large bowl. Mix the yeast with the warm water. Mix into the dry ingredients. Let batter rise, covered, for 2 hours. Mix the soda water into the batter just before frying.

Corinne Hanna Diller
Houston, Texas
Houston Mennonite Church
Texas MCC Relief Sale, Houston

BUTTERMILK PANCAKES

- 2 cups buttermilk
- 2 cups flour
- 3 tablespoons butter
- 1 teaspoon baking powder
- ½ teaspoon salt
- 1 teaspoon soda
- 2 teaspoons sugar
- 2 eggs

Sift dry ingredients. Add buttermilk and beat until smooth. Add egg yolks and melted butter. Fold in beaten egg whites. Bake on hot slightly greased griddle until golden brown.

Griddle Cakes

- ❖ 1 egg
- ❖ 1 cup milk
- ❖ ½ teaspoon salt
- ❖ 1 cup bread flour
- ❖ 2 teaspoons baking powder
- ❖ 1½ tablespoons melted shortening

Beat egg and add milk. Sift flour with baking powder and salt. Beat into mixture. Add shortening. Drop by tablespoon on hot griddle and brown on both sides. Serve with maple syrup.

Pflinzen

- ❖ 1 cup flour
- ❖ ½ teaspoon salt
- ❖ ¾ cup milk
- ❖ ¾ cup water
- ❖ 1 egg

Place flour and salt in a bowl. Gradually add liquids and egg. Beat until batter is smooth (batter will be thin). Pour about ¼ cup batter into a hot greased frying pan. Allow it to run over entire surface, forming a thin layer. When edges begin to brown, turn pancake and fry on other side.

Makes 6-8 pancakes.

Frances Von Riesen
Beatrice, Nebraska
Nebraska MCC Relief Sale, Aurora

BREADS

RUSSIAN PANCAKES

- ❖ 5 eggs
- ❖ 1 tablespoon sugar
- ❖ 2 teaspoons salt
- ❖ 1 stick (½ cup) margarine, melted
- ❖ 6 cups milk
- ❖ 4 cups flour

Beat eggs. Add sugar, salt, and margarine. Mix. Add two-thirds of the milk and half the flour. Mix well. Add remaining milk and flour. Mix again. Pour batter into hot greased pan. Lift and tilt pan so that batter covers bottom. Brown pancake lightly on first side. Flip to other side and brown.

Vernon Wiebe
Hillsboro, Kansas
Mid-Kansas Relief Sale, Hutchinson

RUSSIAN PANCAKES

These pancakes were a favorite of Germans living in Russia who later emigrated to the United States. Traditionally, a filling was added to the pancakes, which were then rolled up and eaten with a fork.

WHOLE WHEAT PANCAKES

- ❖ 2 eggs
- ❖ 1 cup brown sugar
- ❖ 1 tablespoon butter
- ❖ ½ teaspoon salt
- ❖ 2 teaspoons baking powder
- ❖ 1 cup milk
- ❖ 2 cups whole wheat flour

Beat eggs. Add sugar and milk. Sift dry ingredients and add to liquid. Add melted shortening and blend together. Bake on hot lightly greased griddle or pan.

Makes 8-10 pancakes.

CHEESEMAKING

General Directions for Cheesemaking

Let milk set in cool place overnight to ripen (a commercial starter may be added to hasten ripening). Add about 1 cup to 1 gallon of milk.

The next morning, warm the milk slowly to 86°.

Dissolve cheese color tablets in ¼ cup water and add to milk (use ¾ tablet for 10 gallons milk). Never mix the cheese coloring with the rennet tablet solution.

Dissolve the cheese rennet tablet in ¼ cup cold water. Mix with the milk at 86°. (Ice cream junket tablets may also be used instead of the rennet.)

Remove the milk from the stove. Stir gently, but thoroughly, with a wooden spoon for 2 minutes.

Cover container and let stand by a warm stove for 1 hour or until thick enough. To test, put finger into milk and bring up like a hook. If the curd breaks clean across finger like jelly, it is thick enough.

Cut curds into cubes using a long-blade knife that extends to the bottom of the kettle. Cut ½-inch squares, then cut diagonally. (A wire bent in a U-shape may be used to cut the curds horizontally, using two ends as handles.) Cutting should give a clear whey. A milky whey signifies loss of casein and fat.

Let stand 5 minutes. Return curds to stove, then stir slowly and gently to keep pieces from sticking together while the temperature is slowly raised to 100°-102° and kept there. Then, only stir occasionally so pieces won't stick together. Instead of returning the curds to the stove, some of the whey may be taken from the top, strained into a dipper, then brought to a boil. Slowly pour the hot whey back into the curds, stirring the curds all the time. Continue this process until the temperature has risen to 100°-102°.

The curds are ready when a handful, squeezed firmly, does not squirt out between the fingers, but almost falls apart when hand is opened. Takes about 1 hour.

Pour heated curds into a colander which has been lined with cheesecloth, organdy, or a gauze diaper cloth. Catch whey. The whey is a healthy drink, may be used in recipes calling for water, and is also a good tonic for flowers.

Gently work salt into the curds (about 1 tablespoon to 2 gallons of milk or according to taste).

☙

Leave the curds in cloth, having only 1 thickness over the top. Place in the prepared press (lard press, bucket, or cans). Do not use an aluminum container. Place the lid on top of the cheese. Weigh down with 2 bricks or the equivalent in weight. In the evening, turn the cheese and double the weight. The next morning, remove the cheese from the press. Keep it in a warm room for 36-48 hours. Lay it in the sun by a window for half a day to hasten the aging process.

Seal the cheese by brushing it with smoking hot paraffin. Take heed, for hot paraffin catches fire like oil. If cheese is not solid, do not seal. Instead of paraffin, vegetable or mineral oil may be rubbed into the cheese to keep from molding. Another method to prevent molding is to mix only half of the salt into the cheese, then rub salt over it every few days. If mold appears, wash the cheese in warm salt water and salt again. Turn every few days.

Place cheese in room (cellar) with temperature about 60° and turn every day for 3-6 weeks. If kept longer, turn twice a week. Cheese may be kept several months. The longer it is cured, the sharper it becomes.

One gallon of curds produces approximately 1 pound of cheese.
To make hard dry cheese, press with 25-30 pound weights.

If mold forms on cheese that's being used, trim off the mold and use the rest.

To keep cheese longer, place it in a large container. Set a cup with vinegar beside it. Cover container tightly and set in a cool place. Do not set vinegar with cheese while cheese is in the aging process.

Rennet tablets and coloring may be bought at a drug or grocery store.

From Amish Cooking, *published by Pathway Publishers Corporation*

CREAM CHEESE

- ❖ 1 quart light cream of good flavor
- ❖ ¼ cup fresh sour milk

Mix well in top of double boiler or stainless bowl. Cover and let stand at room temperature until thick. Skim thin layer off top if necessary. Cut in squares. Heat over warm water to 110°. Make a few strokes across bottom while warming. Handle carefully so cream doesn't get thin and drain off with the whey. Pour into cloth bag. After 15 minutes, place bag on rack in freezer with bowl underneath to catch whey. Drain about 10 hours. Press curd with weight on top of bag until curd is pasty. Turn into bowl. With fork or mixer, work in salt to taste (about ¾ teaspoon). Mix thoroughly. Good with crushed pineapple and served on drained pear chunks.

From Amish Cooking, *published by Pathway Publishers Corporation*

TAKE ALL YOU WANT, EAT ALL YOU TAKE.

Soft Cheese

- Rich milk
- Skim milk or a commercial starter
- Dissolved rennet (2 ounces for each 10 pounds of milk)
- Salt

Select a quantity of very rich milk. Mix with clean well-soured skim milk or a commercial starter measuring 3-5 percent of the rich milk's bulk. Add dissolved rennet and set the mixture at 80°. When well thickened, cool down to 60° by placing in a refrigerator or by letting cold water run around the container. Care should be taken not to break the curd. After it has cooled for 24 hours, turn it into a cheesecloth sack and allow to drain for another 24 hours. Add salt to taste. (The presence of fat makes a smooth, soft cheese.) This cheese can be molded into balls or printed in a butter printer and wrapped in oil paper or tinfoil.

From Amish Cooking, *published by Pathway Publishers Corporation*

Smear Kase

- Dry cheese, drained
- Salt and pepper
- Milk or cream

Take the cheese and add salt, pepper, and milk or cream. Mix until smooth, then spread on bread. May be topped with molasses or apple butter.

From Amish Cooking, *published by Pathway Publishers Corporation*

CHEESEMAKING

Pickles, Relishes, and Sauces

BREAD AND BUTTER PICKLES

- ❖ 8 cups cucumbers, thinly sliced
- ❖ 2 sliced onions

Syrup:
- ❖ 2 cups sugar
- ❖ 2 teaspoons salt
- ❖ 2 teaspoons dry mustard
- ❖ 2 teaspoons turmeric
- ❖ 1 cup water
- ❖ 1 cup vinegar

Soak cucumbers and onions in cold water for 3 hours and drain. Combine syrup ingredients. Cook pickles in the syrup for several minutes. Place in jars and process in boiling water for 5 minutes.

R. Beiler
Quarryville, Pennsylvania

BREAD-AND-BUTTER PICKLES

- ❖ 30 medium-sized cucumbers (1 gallon sliced)
- ❖ 8 medium-sized onions
- ❖ ½ cup pickling salt

Pickling Syrup:
- ❖ 5 cups sugar
- ❖ 5 cups vinegar
- ❖ 2 tablespoons mustard seed
- ❖ 1 teaspoon turmeric
- ❖ 1 teaspoon celery seed

Slice cucumbers and onions into thin rings. Dissolve salt in ice water and pour over sliced vegetables. Let stand 3 hours. Drain. Combine syrup ingredients and bring to a boil. Add well-drained vegetables. Heat to boiling point, but do not boil. Pack into hot sterilized jars. Seal.

COMPANY BEST PICKLES

- ❖ 10 medium cucumbers
- ❖ Water
- ❖ 8 cups white sugar
- ❖ 4 cups vinegar
- ❖ 2 tablespoons pickling spices
- ❖ 5 teaspoons salt
- ❖ Few drops green food coloring

Scrub and cover the cucumbers with boiling water. Let stand 24 hours and drain. Repeat 3 times (4 days in all). On fifth day, drain and cut into serving pieces. Combine the sugar, vinegar, pickling spices, salt, 2 cups water, and the food coloring. Bring above mixture to boil and pour over drained and sliced cucumbers. Let stand 48 hours, then bring to a boil and seal in sterile jars.

COPPER PICKLES

- 1 gallon (30) cucumbers
- 6-8 onions
- ½ cup pickling salt
- Ice water
- 2 cups vinegar
- 2 cups sugar
- 2 teaspoons mustard seed
- 2 teaspoons celery seed
- 1 teaspoon turmeric
- 1 teaspoon whole cloves

Slice the cucumbers into thin slices and the onions into thin rings. Add the pickling salt to ice water and cover the cucumber and onion slices. Let stand at least 3 hours or overnight. Drain well. Boil the vinegar, sugar, mustard seed, celery seed, turmeric, and cloves. Mix well and bring to boil. Add slices and bring again to boiling point. Seal in sterile jars.

CRISP PICKLE SLICES

- 1 gallon medium cucumbers, sliced quite thin
- ¾ cup pickling salt dissolved in boiling water

Cooking Brine:
- 6 cups water
- 2 cups vinegar
- 1 tablespoon alum
- 1 tablespoon turmeric

Pickling Syrup:
- 1½ cups vinegar
- 1½ cups water
- 6 cups sugar
- 1½ teaspoons dill seed
- 1 tablespoon pickling spice
- 1 tablespoon mustard seed

Cover cucumbers with the boiling water/salt solution. Let stand overnight. Drain and wash the next morning. Combine ingredients for cooking brine. Add cucumbers and simmer 30 minutes. Drain and rinse. Bring pickling syrup ingredients to a boil. Pack cucumber slices in jars. Pour boiling syrup over slices and seal immediately.

Mildred Hauder
Milford, Nebraska
Nebraska MCC Relief Sale, Aurora

Dill Pickle Spears

- 4-5 quarts cucumbers, cut into spears
- Ice water
- Onion slices
- Fresh dill heads or dried dill seed

Pickling Syrup:
- 3 cups sugar
- 3 cups water
- 1½ cups vinegar
- 1 tablespoon salt

Soak cucumber spears in ice water for 2 hours and drain. Pack spears into jars. Add a few onion slices and 1 head fresh dill or 1-1½ teaspoons dill seed to each jar. Bring syrup ingredients to a boil. Pour boiling syrup over cucumbers in jars and seal. Process in boiling water bath for 10 minutes.

Stella Roth
Milford, Nebraska
Nebraska MCC Relief Sale, Aurora

Dill Pickles

- Several large cucumbers
- 2 tablespoons salt
- ½ cup vinegar
- 1 clove garlic
- 2 sprigs dill
- Water

Prick large cucumbers in several places and fill quart jars. Add 2 tablespoons salt, ½ cup vinegar, 1 clove garlic, and 2 sprigs dill (1 in center, 1 on top) to each jar. Fill jars with cold water. Seal and shake. This recipe does not require cooking.

Favorite Sweet Pickles

- 7 pounds medium cucumbers
- Boiling water to cover
- 1 quart vinegar
- 8 cups sugar
- 2 tablespoons pickling salt
- 2 tablespoons mixed pickling spice

On the first day, wash cucumbers in the morning. Cover them with boiling water. Let stand 8-12 hours. Drain. Drain again in the evening, then cover with fresh boiling water. Repeat the steps from the first day on the second day. On the third day, cut cucumbers into rings ¼ inch thick. Combine vinegar, sugar, salt, and spices. Bring to a boil. Pour over sliced cucumbers. Let stand 24 hours. On the fourth day, drain syrup. Bring to a boil. Pour over cucumbers. Repeat the steps from the fourth day on the fifth day. On the sixth day, drain syrup. Bring to a boil. Add cucumber slices and bring to the boiling point. Pack into hot sterilized jars. Seal.

Grandma Hannah's Ready-to-Eat Pickles

- 7 cups thinly sliced cucumbers
- 1 tablespoon celery seed
- 1 tablespoon salt
- 1 cup sliced onions
- 1 cup sliced red or
  green pepper (optional)
- 2 cups sugar
- 1 cup vinegar

Sprinkle cucumber slices with celery seed and salt. Let set 30 minutes and drain. Add onions and peppers. Mix together sugar and vinegar. Stir until sugar is dissolved (do not heat). Pour over drained vegetables. Pickles can be eaten immediately or stored in the refrigerator.

Carole Giagnocavo
Lancaster, Pennsylvania

'Heinz' Pickles

- 7 pounds cucumbers
- Alum (size of a walnut)

Pickling Liquid:
- 2½ pints vinegar
- 2½ pounds sugar
- 1 ounce cassia buds
- 1 ounce celery seed
- 1 ounce whole allspice

Soak cucumbers 3 days in salt brine strong enough to bear an egg. Then, soak 3 days in clear water, changing the water each of the 3 mornings. Pour boiling water over alum and cucumbers. Simmer 3 hours. Do not boil. (You may cut simmering time to 1½ hours instead of 3.) Pour simmering liquid right off. Combine ingredients for pickling liquid and bring to a boil. Split cucumbers and pour boiling liquid over top. Leave in open jar for at least 5 weeks or until used. You may also store cucumbers in quart jars.

Bernice Schroll
Contributed by N. Elizabeth Graber
Wayland, Iowa
Iowa MCC Relief Sale, Iowa City

Lime Pickles

- 7 pounds cucumbers
- 2 cups hydrated lime
- 2 gallons water
- 9 cups sugar
- 1 teaspoon celery seed
- 1 teaspoon mixed pickling spices
- 1 tablespoon or less pickling salt
- 2 quarts vinegar

Wash cucumbers well. Slice ¼ inch thick. Mix lime and water and pour over slices. Let stand 24 hours. Stir occasionally very carefully with hands. Drain. Wash cucumbers to remove lime residue and soak in clear water for 3-6 hours. Mix together sugar, celery seed, pickling spice, pickling salt, and vinegar. Drain cucumber slices and pour cold vinegar mixture over them. Let stand 12 hours. Boil cucumbers in the vinegar mixture for 35 minutes or until cucumbers begin to appear clear. Put in jars and seal.

LIME STICK PICKLES

* 4 pounds large green cucumbers
* 1 gallon water
* 1 cup hydrated lime

Pickling Syrup:
* 1 quart vinegar
* 5 cups sugar
* 1 tablespoon pickling salt
* 1 tablespoon celery seed
* 1 tablespoon mixed pickling spice

Peel cucumbers, remove seeds, and cut into sticks. Soak overnight in a solution of the water and lime. Drain cucumbers and wash well the next morning. Cover with fresh water and soak for 3 hours. Combine syrup ingredients (do not heat). Drain cucumbers and pour cold syrup over them. Let stand overnight. The next day, simmer pickles in syrup for 30 minutes. Put in jars and seal.

Marcia Roth
Wayland, Iowa

MOTHER'S FAVORITE PICKLE

* 1 quart raw cabbage, chopped fine
* 1 quart dark red beets, boiled, skinned, and chopped fine
* 2 cups white sugar (more if desired)
* 1 tablespoon salt
* 1 teaspoon pepper
* 1 cup horseradish
* 1 teaspoon mustard
* 1 teaspoon ginger (optional)

Cover all ingredients with vinegar that has been diluted with the juice in which beets were boiled. Heat just to boiling point. (Do not allow to boil, as boiling fades color of beets.) Although recipe calls for equal quantities of cabbage and beets, this relish looks much nicer if more beets than cabbage are used.

MUSTARD BEAN PICKLES

* 1 peck (2 gallons) beans, cut in pieces
* Salt water
* Vinegar
* 4 cups brown sugar
* ½ cup dry mustard
* ½ cup flour
* 3 tablespoons turmeric
* 1 teaspoon celery seed
* ½ cup water

Cook the beans for 30 minutes in weak saltwater liquid and drain. Bring 3 parts vinegar and the brown sugar to a boil. Make a paste of the mustard, flour, turmeric, celery seed, and water. Add to vinegar and water and cook until thickened. Add beans and cook 5 minutes longer. Seal in sterile jars.

RED CINNAMON PICKLES

- 2 gallons cucumber chunks
- 2 cups lime
- 2 gallons water

Cooking Brine:
- 1 cup vinegar
- 1 small bottle red food coloring
- 1 tablespoon alum
- Water to cover

Pickling Syrup:
- 4 cups vinegar
- 15 cups sugar
- 2 packages Red Hot cinnamon candies
- 8 sticks cinnamon
- 4 cups water

Cover cucumber chunks with a solution of the lime and 2 gallons water. Soak for 24 hours. Drain and rinse well. Soak in cold water for 3 hours and drain. Place cucumbers in a large kettle. Add brine ingredients. Simmer 2 hours. Drain and rinse thoroughly. Mix together syrup ingredients and bring to a boil (be sure candy is dissolved). Pour syrup over drained cucumbers. Let stand overnight. Drain and heat 3 mornings. On the third morning, pack in jars and seal. Put one cinnamon stick in each jar.

Nina Stutzman
Milford, Nebraska
Nebraska MCC Relief Sale, Aurora

FOR THIS RECIPE, USE LARGE CUCUMBERS THAT HAVE A YELLOWISH COLOR. THE LIGHTER-COLORED FLESH WILL PRODUCE A BETTER RED COLOR.

REFRIGERATOR CUCUMBERS

- 4 cups vinegar
- 4 cups sugar
- 1½ cups water
- ¼ teaspoon salt
- 1½ teaspoons turmeric
- 1½ teaspoons mustard seed
- 1 tablespoon celery seed
- 1 chopped onion (optional)

Slice cucumbers thinly. Place in a glass gallon jar. Mix well with other ingredients, refrigerate, and serve.

Anna M. Kauffman
Morgantown, Pennsylvania

REFRIGERATOR PICKLES

- 16 cups thinly sliced cucumbers
- 2 cups sliced onions
- 3 tablespoons salt
- 2 cups vinegar
- 4 cups sugar
- 1 teaspoon turmeric
- 1 teaspoon celery seed
- ½ teaspoon powdered alum

Mix together cucumbers, onions, and salt. Let stand 3 hours. Drain liquid from vegetables, squeezing to remove as much as possible. Mix together remaining ingredients and pour over cucumbers. Mix well. Spoon pickles into jars. Keep in refrigerator.

Amy Cable
Hollsopple, Pennsylvania
MCC Quilt Auction and Relief Sale
Johnstown, Pennsylvania

SWEET PICKLE STICKS

Syrup:
- 4 cups vinegar
- 5 cups sugar
- 1 tablespoon salt
- 1 teaspoon ground cloves
- 2 tablespoons mixed pickling spice (tied in cloth bag)
- 1 teaspoon ground cinnamon

Peel and remove center seeds from 12-15 large cucumbers. Cut in sticks 3-4 inches long. Cover with boiling water. Let cool and drain. Boil syrup for 5 minutes. Add cucumber sticks and cook 5 minutes longer. Seal in sterile jars.

SWEET-SOUR DILL PICKLES

- Medium-sized cucumbers
- 12-16 onion slices
- 2 stalks celery, quartered
- 8 heads fresh dill
- 4 cups sugar
- ½ cup pickling salt
- 1 quart vinegar
- 2 cups water

Wash freshly picked cucumbers. Cut into chunks or slices ¼ inch thick (enough to fill 4 clean quart jars). Add 3-4 onion slices, 2 pieces celery, and 2 heads dill to each jar. Dissolve sugar and salt in vinegar and water. Bring to a boil. Pour boiling liquid over cucumbers in jars. Seal at once. Do not use for 30 days.

Anna Mae Roth
Milford, Nebraska
Nebraska MCC Relief Sale, Aurora

SWEET GHERKINS

- 5 quarts (about 7 pounds) small cucumbers (1½-3 inches long)
- ½ cup salt
- 8 cups sugar
- 6 cups vinegar
- ¾ teaspoon turmeric
- 2 teaspoons celery seed
- 2 teaspoons whole mixed pickling spice
- 8 1-inch pieces stick cinnamon
- ½ teaspoon fennel (optional)
- 2 teaspoons vanilla (optional)

Wash cucumbers thoroughly (stem end may be left on if desired).

First day:
In the morning, cover cucumbers with boiling water. Let sit for 6-8 hours. In the afternoon, drain cucumbers and cover with fresh boiling water.

Second day:
In the morning, drain cucumbers and cover with fresh boiling water. In the afternoon, drain cucumbers and add salt. Cover with fresh boiling water.

Third day:
In the morning, drain cucumbers. Prick each cucumber in several places with a table fork. (You may want to slice thicker ones in half.) Make a syrup of 3 cups of the sugar and 3 cups of the vinegar. Add turmeric and spices (except vanilla). Heat to boiling and pour over cucumbers. (Syrup will only partially cover cucumbers.) In the afternoon, drain syrup into pan. Add 2 cups sugar and 2 cups vinegar and heat. Pour over pickles.

Fourth day:
In the morning, drain syrup into pan. Add 2 cups sugar and 1 cup vinegar and heat. Pour over pickles. In the afternoon, drain syrup into pan. Add remaining 1 cup sugar and the vanilla. Heat-pack pickles into pint jars and cover with syrup. Adjust lids. Process for 5 minutes in boiling water bath. Start to count processing time as soon as water returns to boiling.

Makes 7-8 pints.

Ann Roth
Milford, Nebraska
Nebraska MCC Relief Sale, Aurora

PICKLED BABY CORN

- ❖ 6 quarts of small corncobs
- ❖ Salt water
- ❖ 5 cups vinegar
- ❖ 4 cups white sugar
- ❖ 2 tablespoons pickling spices

The corn for this recipe must be picked just as the tassels are starting to form and the small cobs are no more than 2 inches long. Field corn is usually used. Husk and remove the silk from cobs. Boil cobs 7 minutes in salt water. Boil syrup made of the vinegar, white sugar, and pickling spices (tied in cloth bag) for 5 minutes. Remove spice bag. Pack hot corncobs in sterile jars. Cover with boiling syrup and seal immediately.

PICKLED BEETS

Syrup:
- ❖ 4 cups vinegar
- ❖ 1 cup water
- ❖ 3 cups white sugar
- ❖ ½ teaspoon pepper
- ❖ 1½ teaspoons salt
- ❖ ½ teaspoon cloves or pickling spice

Boil 6-quart basket beets until tender. Peel. Place in sterile jars (if beets are too large, cut into pieces). Bring syrup ingredients to boil. Fill jars and seal. These beets will keep in refrigerator for some time.

SPICED PICKLED BEETS

- ❖ 10-15 beets (depending on size)
- ❖ 2 cups sugar
- ❖ 2 cups vinegar
- ❖ 2 cups water
- ❖ 1 teaspoon ground cloves
- ❖ 1 teaspoon ground cinnamon

Trim beet tops down to 1 inch. (Do not cut into beets or color will bleed during cooking.) Wash beets well. Cook in boiling water until tender. Drain and cover with cold water. Slip skins off and trim off tops and roots. Cut beets into quarters or eighths depending on size. (Beets may also be sliced.) Combine remaining ingredients. Bring to a boil. Add beets to syrup and boil 10 minutes. Pack into sterilized jars and seal.

Anna Mae Roth
Milford, Nebraska
Nebraska MCC Relief Sale, Aurora

PICKLES, RELISHES, AND SAUCES

Pickled Eggs

- 2 cups vinegar
- 1 cup water
- ½ cup white sugar
- Salt and pepper
- 2 bay leaves
- Hard-boiled eggs

Boil until sugar is dissolved. Cool and add cold peeled hard-boiled eggs. Best after standing about 2 days.

Pickled Watermelon Rind

- 9 cups watermelon rind
- 3 tablespoons salt
- 4 cups water
- 4 cups white sugar
- 2 cups white vinegar
- 2 cups water
- 6 cinnamon sticks
- 2 tablespoons whole cloves
- 2 tablespoons whole allspice

To prepare the rind, trim off outer green skin and most of pink flesh, leaving only a bit of pink on white rind. Cut rind into 1½x1¾-inch pieces. Soak prepared rind overnight in a brine made of the salt and 4 cups water. In the morning, drain, cover with fresh water, and cook until tender. Heat the sugar, vinegar, and 2 cups water to boiling point. Tie the cinnamon sticks, cloves, and allspice in cloth bag and add. Add cooked rind and simmer until rind is transparent (about 45 minutes). Pack hot rind in sterile jars. Remove spice bag from syrup and bring to boil again. Pour boiling syrup over rind, making sure syrup completely covers rind. Seal jars.

Spiced Crab Apples

- 4 pounds crab apples
- 2 cups vinegar
- 2 cups water
- 2 cups sugar
- 1 tablespoon whole cloves
- 3 cinnamon sticks
- 1 teaspoon whole ginger
  tied in cheesecloth bag

Wash crab apples and remove blossom ends. Boil the vinegar, water, and sugar together. Add the cloves, cinnamon sticks, and ginger. Add the crab apples. Simmer until tender. Seal in sterile jars.

COUNTRY-STYLE HOT DOG RELISH

- 4 cups sliced cucumbers, not pared, but with seeds removed
- 3 cups roughly chopped onions
- 3 cups roughly chopped cabbage
- 2 cups roughly chopped green tomatoes
- 3 red peppers, cut in chunks
- 3 green peppers, cut in chunks
- ½ cup pickling salt
- 2 tablespoons mustard seed
- 1 tablespoon celery seed
- 1 tablespoon turmeric
- 5 cups sugar
- 4 cups vinegar
- 2 cups cold water

Grind all vegetables using a coarse blade. Drain. Sprinkle with salt and let stand overnight. Drain and rinse well. Combine remaining ingredients and pour over vegetables. Heat to a full boil. Boil 7-10 minutes. Place in hot jars and seal.

Berniece Beckler
Milford, Nebraska
Nebraska MCC Relief Sale, Aurora

GREEN HOT DOG RELISH

- 4 quarts cucumbers
- 1 quart onions
- 2 bunches celery
- 4 red sweet peppers
- 4 green sweet peppers
- ¼ cup salt
- 5 cups white sugar
- 1 quart vinegar
- 5 drops oil of cinnamon (or 1 teaspoon ground cinnamon)
- 5 drops oil of cloves (or ½ teaspoon ground cloves)

Put the first 5 ingredients through a meat chopper. Add the salt and let stand in crock overnight. Add the sugar and vinegar. Boil slowly for 1 hour. When cold, add the oil of cinnamon and oil of cloves. Let stand 2 days at room temperature, stirring occasionally. Heat to boiling point and put in sterile jars.

Cucumber Relish

- 12 cups cucumbers, finely chopped
- 1 quart onions, finely chopped
- 1 large head cauliflower, chopped
- 4 red sweet peppers, chopped
- ¼ cup salt
- 8 cups white sugar
- 3 cups cider vinegar
- 1½ tablespoons mustard
- 2 tablespoons turmeric
- 1½ tablespoons celery seed
- ⅔ cup flour mixed with 1 cup water

Add the salt to the cucumbers, onions, cauliflower, and peppers. Let stand overnight. Next morning, drain well and add the sugar, vinegar, mustard, turmeric, and celery seed. Bring to boil and add the flour, mixed with the 1 cup water. Boil 30 minutes and seal in sterile jars.

Fruit and Tomato Relish

- 6-quart basket peeled tomatoes
- 6 large pears
- 6 large apples
- 6 large peaches
- 4 onions
- 4 cups granulated sugar
- 2 tablespoons salt
- ½ cup pickling spices
- 1 pint vinegar

Chop fruits and vegetables finely. Add the sugar, salt, pickling spices (tied loosely in a bag), and vinegar. Simmer in large pot for 1 hour, stirring often. Remove spice bag and seal in hot sterile jars. Chopped red and green sweet pepper may also be added.

Pickles, Relishes, and Sauces

Queen of Pickles

- 1 quart small pickling onions, peeled
- 1 quart small cucumbers
- 3 sweet red peppers, chopped
- 3 sweet green peppers, chopped
- ½ cup coarse salt
- Water
- 1 large head cauliflower
- 1 quart very small carrots
- 1 quart chopped onions
- 1 quart chopped cucumbers
- 1 quart vinegar
- 7 cups white sugar
- 1 tablespoon mustard seed
- 1 tablespoon celery seed
- ⅔ cup all-purpose flour
- ¼ cup dry mustard
- 2 tablespoons turmeric
- ¼ cup vinegar

At night, cut the quart of small cucumbers into ½-inch-long pieces. Combine with the pickling onions, red peppers, and green peppers. Cover with a brine made of the salt and enough boiling water to cover. Break the cauliflower into florets. Cover with boiling water and let stand overnight. Next morning, cook cauliflower and the carrots until nearly tender. Drain. Drain brine from first mixture and rinse well. Mix together and add 1 quart of chopped onions, 1 quart chopped cucumbers, the vinegar, sugar, mustard seed, and celery seed. Boil 5 minutes. Make paste of the all-purpose flour, dry mustard, turmeric, and ¼ cup vinegar. Add to hot pickle mixture. Boil thoroughly to cook flour. Seal in hot sterile jars.

Chili Sauce

- 7-8 quarts ripe tomatoes
- 2 green peppers, chopped
- 2 red peppers, chopped
- 2 stalks celery, diced
- 3 medium onions, diced
- 1 cup sugar
- 1 cup vinegar
- 2 tablespoons salt
- 2 tablespoons paprika
- 1½ teaspoons each of ground cloves, gound allspice, black pepper, and cinnamon
- ½ teaspoon dry mustard

Cover tomatoes with boiling water to make it easy to slip off skins. Quarter or chop tomatoes and place in a large pot. Add remaining ingredients and cook until thick, stirring occasionally. Pour into hot sterilized jars and seal.

Makes 8 pints.

Anna Mae Roth
Milford, Nebraska
Nebraska MCC Relief Sale, Aurora

Gooseberry Ketchup

- 4 pounds gooseberries
- 2 pounds white sugar
- ½ pint vinegar
- 1 tablespoon cinnamon
- 1 tablespoon cloves
- 1 teaspoon black pepper
- 1 teaspoon salt

Boil all ingredients together for 30 minutes or until thick. Stir frequently to prevent sticking.

To clean brass, rub ketchup on a soft cloth and polish. Rinse.

Homemade Ketchup

- 12½ cups seeded tomatoes
- 2½ cups celery
- 2½ cups onions
- 2 cups cider vinegar
- 4 cups sugar
- 2 tablespoons pickling salt
- 1 tablespoon pickling spice, tied in a cheesecloth bag

Purée the tomatoes in a blender. Purée the celery in a blender with 1 cup of the vinegar. Purée the onion in a blender with the remaining vinegar. Cook the puréed tomatoes, celery, and onion to a "boiled down" consistency. Add the sugar, pickling salt, and pickling spice. Cook to the desired thickness. Put in jars. Seal and process in a water bath for 15 minutes.

Anna Mae Roth
Milford, Nebraska

Hot Sauce

- 1 pound fresh tomatoes, peeled, or use peeled canned tomatoes
- ¼-½ pound serrano chilies
- 10 cloves garlic
- Salt to taste

Boil tomatoes and chilies together until the chilies turn light green. Put mixture in blender with garlic and salt. Blend until smooth.

Amalia Martinez
Orange Cove Mennonite Brethren Church,
El Buen Paster (The Good Shepherd)
West Coast Mennonite Sale and Auction
for World Relief

Ikra

- 4-6 sweet green peppers (enough to make 2 cups chopped)
- 10 cups grated carrots
- 6 cups stewed tomatoes or peeled chopped fresh tomatoes in season
- 2 tablespoons chopped fresh parsley
- 4 teaspoons salt
- 6 cups chopped onion (about 4 large)
- ⅓ cup vegetable oil (half olive oil)
- Sugar to taste

Quarter green peppers and remove seeds and stems. Place in a saucepan. Pour boiling water over top and parboil for about 5 minutes. Chop to make 2 cups when cool enough to handle. Place raw grated carrot, tomatoes, parsley, and salt in a large heavy pot. Use half of the oil to sauté chopped onions in a large frying pan until transparent and add to other vegetables. Sauté peppers with remaining oil and add to vegetables. Simmer slowly for 1 hour or more until vegetables are tender, but not mushy. Add sugar to taste. If you wish to store the relish on the shelf, put it in preserving jars, adjust lids, and process in a canner in a boiling water bath for 15 minutes to seal jars. To store in the refrigerator without processing, pour very hot relish into hot sterilized jars and cap jars firmly using new rubber rings.

Marlene Neustaedter
Winnipeg, Manitoba
MCC Manitoba Relief Sale

Salsa

- 10 cups cut-up skinned tomatoes
- 4 cups chopped onions
- 4 cups chopped green bell peppers
- 1 cup chopped yellow banana peppers
- Half a jar jalapeno peppers or fresh peppers
- 10 whole garlic cloves, pierced
- 3½ teaspoons pickling salt
- ⅓ cup vinegar
- 2 cans (12 ounces each) tomato paste

Combine all ingredients except tomato paste. Cook until vegetables are tender. Stir in tomato paste. Cook 15 minutes. Remove garlic cloves. Pack salsa in hot sterilized jars. Process in boiling water bath for 15 minutes.

Vada Roth
Milford, Nebraska
Nebraska MCC Relief Sale, Aurora

SANDWICH SPREAD

- ❖ Green tomatoes
- ❖ 2 red peppers
- ❖ 2 green peppers
- ❖ 1 teaspoon salt
- ❖ ½ cup water
- ❖ 6 sweet pickles, ground
- ❖ 1 cup sugar
- ❖ ½ cup vinegar
- ❖ 2 rounded tablespoons flour
- ❖ 1 cup sour cream
- ❖ 2 tablespoons prepared mustard
- ❖ 3 well-beaten eggs

Grind enough green tomatoes to measure 1 pint after juice is squeezed out. Grind red and green peppers. Add to green tomatoes and sprinkle salt over all. Let stand 1 hour. Drain. Add the ½ cup water to the ground vegetables and cook until tender. Mix in the ground sweet pickles. Combine remaining ingredients and cook until consistency of dressing. Stir in ground vegetables. Put up in sterilized jars while hot.

Iowa MCC Relief Sale, Iowa City

TOMATO BUTTER

- ❖ 12 medium tomatoes
- ❖ 1½ cups white sugar
- ❖ 2 cups white vinegar
- ❖ 1 teaspoon salt
- ❖ 1 teaspoon whole cinnamon
- ❖ 1 teaspoon cloves

Peel the tomatoes and cut them into small pieces. Add the sugar and boil 1 hour, stirring often to prevent sticking. Add the vinegar, salt, cinnamon, and cloves (tied in bag). Boil until thick.

PICKLES, RELISHES, AND SAUCES

JAMS, JELLIES, AND FRUIT BUTTERS

BLACK CURRANT PRESERVES

- 2 cups black currants
- 4 cups cold water
- 6 cups sugar

Boil the black currants in 2 cups water for 10 minutes. Mash thoroughly. Add 2 more cups water and the sugar. Boil 20 minutes. Seal in sterile jars. Serve on ice cream or with cream.

BLUEBERRY RHUBARB JAM

- 5 cups diced rhubarb
- 1 cup water
- 5 cups sugar
- 1 can blueberry pie filling
- 1 package (6 ounces) raspberry-flavored gelatin
- Half a package unflavored gelatin

Cook rhubarb in the water until tender (10 minutes). Add sugar and cook 3 minutes longer, stirring constantly. Add pie filling and cook 8 minutes. Remove from heat. Soften both flavored gelatin and unflavored gelatin in a bit of cold water and add to rhubarb mixture. Stir until gelatin is completely dissolved. Pour into jars and seal.

Mrs. Helen Schmidt
Marion, South Dakota
Minn-Kota MCC Relief Sale
Sioux Falls, South Dakota

CIDER APPLE BUTTER

- 4 gallons (about 20 pounds) Jonathan apples
- 4 pounds sugar (1 pound per gallon of apples)
- 2 cans (12 ounces each) frozen apple juice per gallon
- 1 teaspoon cinnamon per gallon

Wash the apples well. Core, but do not peel. Slice into eighths. Add 4 pounds sugar (1 pound per gallon of apples). Let sit overnight (8-12 hours) until juice forms. Put apples and juice into a pressure cooker. Cook 30 minutes at 10 pounds pressure. Put mixture through a food mill. Stir in 2 cans (12 ounces each) frozen apple juice and 1 teaspoon cinnamon per gallon of mixture. Put on stove and cook over low heat. Can in pints or quarts.

Mary Wenger
Missouri MCC Relief Sale, Harrisonville

Heavenly Jam

- 7 cups rhubarb, chopped
- 6 cups sugar
- 1 20-ounce can pineapple
- 3 ounces cherry gelatin powder
- 3 ounces pineapple gelatin powder

Combine the rhubarb, sugar, and pineapple. Boil for 20 minutes. Add the gelatin powders. Stir until dissolved and put into jars. Store in refrigerator.

Peach Conserve

- 3 pounds (6 cups) ground or chopped peaches
- 6 cups white sugar
- ½ dozen small oranges, ground
- ⅔ cup brown sugar
- ⅔ cup corn syrup

Combine all ingredients and boil together until thick (about 20 minutes). Seal in sterile jars.

Rhubarb Jam

- 4 cups finely chopped rhubarb
- 4 cups sugar
- 1 cup strawberries
- 1 package strawberry-flavored gelatin

Stir rhubarb, sugar, and strawberries in a heavy saucepan until thoroughly mixed. Place on heat, bring to a boil, and boil 15 minutes. Remove from heat. Add gelatin, stirring until dissolved. Seal in sterilized jars. Substitute 1 cup crushed pineapple and 1 package pineapple-flavored gelatin for the strawberries and strawberry-flavored gelatin to vary recipe. You can also increase the rhubarb to 5 cups and use 1 package of any flavor gelatin.

Marie Harder
Mountain Lake, Minnesota
Minn-Kota MCC Relief Sale
Sioux Falls, South Dakota

STRAWBERRY RHUBARB JAM

- ❖ 5 cups rhubarb
- ❖ 4 cups sugar
- ❖ 1 6-ounce package
  strawberry gelatin

Mix the strawberry gelatin and let stand overnight. In the morning, boil 5 minutes. Add strawberry gelatin. Seal into sterile jars. Store in refrigerator or cool place.

A MAN WHO GIVES HIS CHILDREN HABITS OF INDUSTRY PROVIDES
FOR THEM BETTER THAN BY GIVING THEM A FORTUNE.

TOMATO MARMALADE

- ❖ 4 cups tomatoes,
  peeled and cut fine
- ❖ 4 cups brown sugar
- ❖ 1 orange and 1 lemon,
  shredded very finely

Combine all ingredients and cook until thick (about 20 minutes), stirring frequently.

TURTLE BRAND DANDELION JELLY

- 1 quart dandelion flowers (best picked in the morning)
- 2 quarts water
- Lemon juice
- Several packages (1¾ ounces each) powdered fruit pectin
- 5½ cups sugar

Rinse the dandelion flowers in cold water and remove stems. Bring flowers to a boil in the 2 quarts water. Boil 3 minutes. Cool and strain, pressing petals with the fingers to extract all the juice. You may have to strain the juice several times to remove all small specks. Measure the liquid. Add 2 tablespoons lemon juice and 1 package (1¾ ounces) powdered fruit pectin to every 3 cups of dandelion liquid. Bring to a boil. Add the sugar. Continue stirring. Bring to a boil and boil hard for 2½ minutes. Pour into jars and seal.

J. Wayne Beachy
Midlothian, Virginia
Virginia Relief Sale, Fisherville

ZUCCHINI JAM

- 6 cups peeled and chopped zucchini
- 6 cups sugar
- ¼ cup lemon juice
- 1 cup crushed pineapple
- 1 package (6 ounces) flavored gelatin (orange, apricot, strawberry, or flavor of choice)

Mix together zucchini and sugar in a large heavy saucepan. Boil 15 minutes. Add lemon juice and pineapple. Boil 8 minutes. Remove from heat and mix in flavored gelatin. Stir well. Put into jars. Seal with wax, process, or freeze.

Makes about 3 pints.

Mrs. Silas (Verlyn) Waltner
Marion, South Dakota
Minn-Kota MCC Relief Sale
Sioux Falls, South Dakota

Desserts and Sweets

CANDIED GRAPEFRUIT

- ❖ 2 silver grapefruits
- ❖ Water
- ❖ Salt
- ❖ 1 cup white sugar
- ❖ Green food coloring
- ❖ Granulated sugar

Cut the rind from the grapefruit and cut the flesh into pieces. Cover with water. Add a dash of salt. Boil for 5 minutes and drain. Repeat twice more. Boil the sugar with 2 cups water. Add the rinds and boil until syrup is well soaked in. Add green color if desired. Roll in granulated sugar and store.

CANDY CRUNCH

- ❖ 1½ cups Cap'n Crunch peanut butter crunch cereal
- ❖ 1½ cups Rice Krispies
- ❖ 1½ cups unsalted peanuts
- ❖ 1½ cups thin stick pretzels, broken into small pieces
- ❖ 1-pound block white chocolate

Combine cereals, peanuts, and pretzels. Melt chocolate, pour over dry ingredients, and mix thoroughly. Spread candy on foil-covered cookie sheets. Refrigerate. To serve, break sheet of candy into pieces.

Lena Sola
Hollsopple, Pennsylvania
MCC Quilt Auction and Relief Sale
Johnstown, Pennsylvania

CARAMEL CORN

- ❖ 7 quarts popped corn
- ❖ 2 cups brown sugar
- ❖ 1 cup butter
- ❖ Vanilla
- ❖ ½ cup corn syrup
- ❖ 1 teaspoon salt
- ❖ ½ teaspoon soda

Boil sugar, butter, and corn syrup for 4 minutes. Remove from stove and add salt, soda, and vanilla. (This will foam when soda is added.) Pour over popped corn. Stir carefully. Put into a large pan. Bake at 250° for 1 hour. Carefully stir every 10 minutes. If pan is big enough, shake popcorn so it doesn't crumble as much.

NO DREAM COMES TRUE UNTIL YOU WAKE UP AND GO TO WORK.

Molasses Caramel Corn

- 2 cups brown sugar
- 1 cup margarine
- ½ cup white corn syrup
- 2 teaspoons molasses
- 1 teaspoon salt
- ½ teaspoon baking soda
- 8 quarts popped corn

Combine sugar, margarine, corn syrup, molasses, and salt in a heavy saucepan. Bring to a boil and cook 5 minutes. Remove from heat and carefully stir in baking soda (mixture may foam up). Pour syrup over corn. Stir well to mix. Bake on cookie sheets at 250° for 1 hour. Stir every 15 minutes during baking. Store in airtight container.

Children's Favorite Maple Cream

- 4 cups brown sugar
- 2 tablespoons flour
- 2 teaspoons baking powder
- 1 cup thin cream
- 4 tablespoons butter
- Pinch of salt

Mix ingredients well. Cook, stirring constantly, until mixture forms a soft ball when tried in cold water. Add chopped pecans or walnuts if desired. Spread into buttered shallow pan.

Chocolate Fudge

- 22 cups white sugar
- ⅔ cup evaporated milk
- Few grains salt
- ¼ cup butter
- Vanilla
- 2 cups miniature marshmallows
- 1 package (6 ounces) chocolate chips
- ½ cup chopped walnuts

Boil the first 4 ingredients for 5 minutes, stirring constantly. (Start timing when it boils at the edges.) Add the vanilla, marshmallows, chocolate chips, and walnuts. Beat until mixture starts to set. Drop each piece and press a pecan on top or pour into pan and cut.

Peanut Butter Fudge

- 2 cups white sugar
- ½ cup sweet milk
- 2 large tablespoons peanut butter

Mix well and boil exactly 5 minutes. Beat until thick. Put into buttered pans to cool.

 C3

CREAMY WHITE FUDGE

- 2 tablespoons butter
- 3 cups sugar
- 1¼ cups milk
- 1 cup black walnut meats
- 1½ teaspoons vanilla
- ½ cup maraschino cherries

In a heavy 3-quart saucepan, combine butter, sugar, and milk. Cook over medium heat until candy reaches the soft ball stage, stirring all the time. Remove pan from heat and let stand at room temperature until cooled to warm. Stir in walnuts, vanilla, and cherries. Beat until creamy. Pour into buttered 9x5x3-inch bread pan. Let stand at room temperature until cool. Wrap pan in foil and let stand overnight or until ready to use.

Bernice Schroll
Contributed by N. Elizabeth Graber
Wayland, Iowa
Iowa MCC Relief Sale, Iowa City

CANDY STAGES

Recipes in this section might refer to candy syrup that has reached the soft ball stage or the hard ball stage. Syrup that has reached the soft ball stage has a temperature of about 235°. If you drop a spoonful of syrup at this temperature into cold water, it will form a ball that is soft and malleable to the touch. You will be able to flatten it a few moments after removing it from the water. Syrup that has reached the hard ball stage has reached a temperature between 250° and 265°. When syrup at this temperature is dropped into cold water, it will form a hard ball that won't flatten, although you should still be able to change its shape slightly by squeezing it.

CHOCOLATE NUT CARAMELS

- 2 cups white sugar
- ½ cup corn syrup
- 2 cups cream
- ½ cup butter or margarine
- 6 tablespoons cocoa
- 1 cup walnuts
- 2 teaspoons vanilla

Boil together sugar, corn syrup, cocoa, butter, and 1 cup of the cream. Boil until it threads. Slowly add the other cup of cream. Boil until mixture reaches the firm ball stage when tested in cold water. Add vanilla and nuts. Beat until creamy.

CRACKER-JACK

- 1 small box puffed rice
- ½ pound blanched peanuts
- 1 cup corn syrup
- 1 cup molasses
- 2 cups brown sugar
- 1 tablespoon butter
- 2 tablespoons vinegar
- ½ teaspoon soda

Boil all ingredients (except puffed rice and peanuts) until a small amount will form a ball in cold water. Pour mixture over puffed rice and peanuts. Stir until mixed. Form into balls with buttered hands and drop on buttered pans.

EASY CARAMELS

- 3 cups white sugar
- 1 cup corn syrup
- 1 cup heavy cream
- 1 cup milk
- 2 tablespoons cornstarch
- 4 tablespoons butter
- ½ teaspoon salt
- 1 teaspoon vanilla
- 1 cup nutmeats (optional)

Thoroughly mix cornstarch, sugar, corn syrup, milk, cream, butter, and salt. Stir mixture over low heat until sugar is dissolved. Cook until mixture is 248° or until a few drops are as hard as caramels should be when finished. Stir only occasionally so mixture will not stick to bottom of pan. Remove from heat and let cool a few minutes before adding nuts and vanilla. Pour into buttered pan. When cold, cut and wrap in waxed paper.

Note: Be sure to use a heavy saucepan.

HARD TACK CANDY

- ¾ pound white sugar
- 1 cup water
- 1 cup light corn syrup
- Flavoring of choice

Cook all together until 280°, then add coloring. Leave on stove until it reaches 290°. Remove and add chosen flavor (⅛ ounce peppermint, spearmint, wintergreen, thyme, anise, cinnamon, etc., flavoring.). Make each flavor a different color. Pour at once on greased cookie sheet or marble slab. As soon as it is cool enough to work with, cut with scissors into strips and various-sized pieces. You can begin cutting on edges almost immediately. Flavoring can be bought at drug store.

From Amish Cooking, *published by Pathway Publishers Corporation*

HOREHOUND CANDY

- ¾ cup brewed horehound tea
- ¼ cup vinegar
- 2 cups white sugar

Combine ingredients, but do not stir. Boil until syrup cracks in cold water. Pour into small narrow pan until hardened. The candy will become as clear as glass. You will not be able to cut it, but should break it into pieces.

LITTLE TWISTER FLAVORED PRETZELS

- 2 bags (1 pound, 2 ounces each) pretzels
- 1 cup salad oil
- 1 package Hidden Valley Ranch salad dressing mix

Spread pretzels on cookie sheets. Combine oil and dressing mix. Pour over pretzels. Mix well to coat. Bake at 200° for 1 hour. Stir and lift pretzels during baking every 15 minutes with a spatula so that oil is well distributed over entire batch.

A Brief History of the Pretzel

It has been recorded that monks in the regions near southern France and northern Italy used scraps of dough as a reward for children who did well in their studies and who said their prayers. The pieces of dough were folded in such a way that they resembled a child's arms folded in prayer. The three holes left in the dough were meant to represent the Christian Holy Trinity. The snacks were known as pretiola, or "little reward." The pretzel would later grow to be a symbol of luck and prosperity, and its form was sometimes incorporated into the architectural details of buildings.

Marshmallows

- 2 envelopes unflavored gelatin
- ½ cup cold water
- ½ teaspoon salt
- 2 cups sugar
- 1 teaspoon vanilla
- ¾ cup boiling water

Boil sugar and water together until a thread forms when syrup drops from spoon. Remove from heat. Soften gelatin in cold water. Add to hot syrup and stir until dissolved. Let stand until partly cool, then add salt and flavoring. Beat until mixture becomes thick, fluffy, and soft. Pour into an 8x4-inch pan thickly covered with powdered sugar. Have the mixture 1 inch in depth. Let stand in refrigerator until thoroughly chilled. With a sharp wet knife, loosen around edges of pan. Turn out on a board and lightly flour with powdered sugar. Cut in squares and roll in powdered sugar, chopped nuts, or coconut.

From Amish Cooking, *published by Pathway Publishers Corporation*

MUNCH MIX

- ❖ 6 cups Cheerios
- ❖ ½ cup sugar
- ❖ ¼ cup margarine
- ❖ 2 tablespoons corn syrup
- ❖ ¼ teaspoon baking soda
- ❖ 8 ounces M&Ms

Place Cheerios in a 2-quart glass casserole. Set aside. Combine sugar, margarine, and syrup in a 1-quart glass bowl. Microwave on full power for 2 minutes, stirring once. Microwave again on low (30%) for 3 minutes. Stir in soda. Pour syrup over cereal and toss to coat. Microwave on half-power (50%) for 4 minutes. Spread on waxed paper to cool. Add M&Ms.

PEANUT BRITTLE

- ❖ 2 cups white sugar
- ❖ 1 cup corn syrup
- ❖ ½ cup water
- ❖ 3 cups salted peanuts
- ❖ 1 teaspoon butter, melted
- ❖ 1 teaspoon soda
- ❖ 1 teaspoon vanilla

Combine sugar, syrup, and water. Cook until it reaches the hard ball stage. Add peanuts and melted butter. Continue cooking until syrup is a golden brown. Stir during cooking. Remove from heat and add soda and vanilla. Beat until soda is mixed through syrup. Pour into buttered pans and break into pieces when cold.

Shanty Candy

- 2 cups granulated sugar
- ¾ cup molasses
- ¼ cup water
- 2 egg whites
- Vanilla
- ½ cup chopped English walnuts
- ½ cup dates

Bring sugar, molasses, and water to a boil. Boil until it reaches hard ball stage on a candy thermometer (or until it is crisp when a small amount is dropped into cold water). While syrup is cooking, beat egg whites until very stiff. When syrup is ready, pour it slowly into beaten whites. Beat candy until too stiff to work, mixing in vanilla, walnuts, and dates just before it stiffens up. Pour into buttered pan. Cut into squares before it hardens.

Mrs. Aaron Kauffman
Cochranville, Pennsylvania
Gap Relief Sale, Pennsylvania

Taffy

- 1 quart white sugar
- 1 pint cream
- 1 tablespoon gelatin dissolved in ¼ cup cold water
- 1 tablespoon paraffin
- 1 pint light corn syrup

Combine all ingredients and boil until it forms a hard ball in cold water when dropped from a tablespoon (250° on candy thermometer). Pour onto a well-greased cookie sheet. When cool enough to handle, start pulling. When an ivory color is obtained, pull into a long thin rope and cut with kitchen scissors.

From Amish Cooking, *published by Pathway Publishers Corporation*

APPLE BLOSSOM COOKIES

Cookie Dough:
- ½ cup shortening
- 1 cup sugar
- 2 eggs
- 2 tablespoons cream
- 1 teaspoon vanilla
- 2 cups all-purpose flour
- 1 teaspoon baking powder
- ½ teaspoon salt
- Raspberry jelly
- Coconut

Marshmallow Icing:
- 1 3-ounce package of raspberry gelatin powder
- ½ cup boiling water
- 2 egg whites
- 1½ cups sugar
- 5 tablespoons water
- 1 tablespoon corn syrup
- Pinch of salt

To make cookie dough, cream together the shortening, sugar, eggs, cream, and vanilla. Sift together the all-purpose flour, baking powder, and salt. Sift into the creamed mix, ending by mixing with hands. Chill. Roll to ⅛ inch thickness and cut into rounds 1½-2 inches thick. Bake at 350° for 10 minutes. Add the boiling water to the raspberry gelatin powder and set aside in a warm place to use later. Measure out the remaining ingredients for the marshmallow mix into the top of a double boiler. Beat with a rotary beater for about 7 minutes until icing forms sharp peaks. Stir in the gelatin mix and beat well again. Cool, stirring occasionally, until icing has a marshmallow texture. Drop a small spoonful of raspberry jelly on each cookie, then add a spoonful of marshmallow icing on top of that. The edge of the cookie should show evenly. Turn each cookie upside down and dip into coconut while the mixture is still moist.

Makes 5 dozen.

BEST EVER CHOCOLATE CHIP COOKIES

- ½ cup solid vegetable shortening
- ½ cup margarine
- 1 cup brown sugar
- ½ cup white sugar
- 2 eggs
- 1 teaspoon vanilla
- 2 cups flour
- 1 teaspoon baking soda
- ¼ teaspoon salt
- 2 cups chocolate chips

Cream shortenings and sugars. Beat in eggs, then vanilla. Add dry ingredients, which have been sifted together. Stir in chips. Drop by teaspoons onto greased cookie sheets. Bake at 350° for 10-11 minutes.

Arlene Preheim
Freeman, South Dakota
Minn-Kota MCC Relief Sale
Sioux Falls, South Dakota

BUTTER CRUNCH COOKIES

- 1 cup all-purpose flour
- ¼ teaspoon baking powder
- ½ teaspoon baking soda
- ⅔ cup soft butter
- 1 cup brown sugar
- 1 egg
- 1 teaspoon vanilla
- ¾ cup oatmeal
- 1 cup flaked coconut
- 1 cup corn flakes

Sift flour, baking powder, and baking soda. Cream butter, brown sugar, egg, and vanilla in order given. Fold in dry ingredients, then add oatmeal, coconut, and corn flakes. Drop in small balls on ungreased cookie sheet. (They spread as they bake.) Bake at 350° for 10-12 minutes.

Makes 3½ dozen.

BUTTER NUT CHEWS

- ½ cup brown sugar, packed
- ¼ cup shortening mixed with ¼ cup butter
- 1 cup sifted all-purpose flour
- 2 eggs, well beaten
- ½ cup brown sugar
- ½ cup corn syrup
- 1 teaspoon vanilla
- 1 tablespoon flour
- ½ teaspoon salt
- ½ teaspoon baking powder
- 1 cup coconut
- 1 cup walnuts or pecans

Mix first three ingredients to form crumbs and press into an ungreased 9x9x2-inch pan. Bake at 350° for 10 minutes. Mix remaining ingredients in order given. Spread over crumbs, return to oven, and bake for 25 minutes or until golden brown.

Makes 24 bars.

BUTTERSCOTCH SQUARES

- ¼ cup butter
- 1 cup brown sugar
- 1 egg
- 1 cup flour
- 1 teaspoon baking powder
- ¼ teaspoon salt
- ½ cup chopped nuts
- 1 teaspoon vanilla

Melt butter and add to sugar. Add egg and mix well. Sift dry ingredients and mix with first mixture. Add nuts and vanilla. Spread into greased 8x8-inch pan. Bake at 350° for 30 minutes. Cut into squares or bars while warm.

CB

CHERRY SURPRISES

- ½ cup soft butter
- 1¾ cups sifted powdered sugar
- 1 tablespoon orange juice
- 1½ cups desiccated coconut
- 1½ dozen maraschino cherries
- Graham cracker crumbs

Beat together the butter, sugar, orange juice, and coconut to form a batter. Make the cookies by putting batter around a cherry, then rolling in the graham cracker crumbs.

CHERRY WINKS

- ¾ cup shortening
- 1 cup sugar
- 2 eggs
- 1 teaspoon vanilla
- 2¼ cups all-purpose flour
- 1 teaspoon baking powder
- ½ teaspoon soda
- ½ teaspoon salt
- 1 cup chopped pecans
- 1 cup chopped dates
- 2½ cups corn flakes
- Maraschino cherries, halved

Cream the shortening, sugar, eggs, and vanilla. Sift the flour, baking powder, soda, and salt. Mix the creamed mixture with the sifted ingredients. Add the pecans and dates. Shape dough into balls. Roll in the corn flakes and press half a maraschino cherry into each. Bake at 350°-375° for 10-12 minutes.

CHOCOLATE COOKIES

- 2 cups sugar
- 1 package (7 ounces) chocolate chips
- 1 cup cream or milk
- 1 teaspoon butter
- 3 cups rolled graham crackers
- 24 marshmallows
- 1 cup nutmeats

Place sugar, chips, and cream in a heavy-bottomed saucepan. Cook to soft ball stage. Stir in butter. In a large bowl, mix together crackers, marshmallows, and nut meats. Pour hot chocolate mixture over, and stir until ingredients are well mixed. Drop by spoonful onto waxed paper.

Bernice Bachman
Gridley, Illinois
Illinois MCC Relief Sale

Desserts and Sweets

Coconut Kisses

- ½ cup egg whites
- 1¼ cups sugar
- ½ teaspoon salt
- ½ teaspoon vanilla
- 2½ cups moist coconut

Beat the egg whites until stiff. Gradually add the sugar, salt, and vanilla. Fold in the coconut. Drop by spoonful onto ungreased brown paper on an ungreased cookie sheet. Bake at 325° for 20 minutes. Slide paper onto a wet towel to rest for a minute before removing cookies.

Custard Cream Bars

Custard:
- ½ cup butter
- ¼ cup sugar
- 5 tablespoons cocoa
- 1 teaspoon vanilla
- 2 eggs
- 2 cups graham wafer crumbs
- 1 cup coconut
- ½ cup walnuts

Icing:
- ¼ cup butter
- 3 tablespoons milk
- 2 tablespoons vanilla custard powder
- 2 cups powdered sugar, sifted

Place softened butter, sugar, cocoa, vanilla, and eggs in top of double boiler. Mix well and set over boiling water. Stir until the mixture resembles custard. Combine wafer crumbs, coconut, and nuts. Add cooked mixture. Pack evenly in a 9-inch greased square pan. Prepare icing by creaming butter. Combine milk and custard powder and add to butter. Blend in sifted powdered sugar. Spread over custard base and let stand 15 minutes. Melt 4 squares semisweet chocolate with 1 tablespoon butter and spread over icing. When set, cut into bars.

DANISH APPLE SQUARES

- 2½ cups flour
- 1 cup shortening
- ½ teaspoon salt
- 1 egg yolk plus enough milk to measure ⅔ cup
- 1 cup crushed corn flakes
- 6 cups sliced apples
- 1 cup sugar
- 1 teaspoon cinnamon
- 1 egg white, stiffly beaten

Glaze:
- 1 cup icing sugar
- 1-2 tablespoons water
- 1 teaspoon vanilla

Mix together flour, shortening, salt, and egg-milk mixture to make a dough. Divide dough in half. Roll out 1 portion into a 10½x15-inch rectangle to fit a cookie sheet. Spread rectangle on cookie sheet. Sprinkle with corn flakes, cover with apples, then sprinkle with sugar and cinnamon. Roll out other portion of dough, place on top, and seal edges. Brush top crust with beaten egg white. Bake at 400° for 30-40 minutes or until golden brown. Mix glaze ingredients. Drizzle over hot pastry when you take it from oven. Cut cooled pastry into squares to serve.

Alice Klassen
Alberta MCC Relief Sale, Coaldale

DATE PINWHEELS

- ½ cup butter
- ½ cup brown sugar
- ½ cup white sugar
- 1 egg
- ½ teaspoon vanilla
- 2 cups pastry flour
- ⅛ teaspoon salt
- ¼ teaspoon soda

Filling:
- 7-8 ounces dates, cut
- ⅓ cup water
- ¼ cup sugar
- ⅛ teaspoon salt
- 1 cup nuts

Cream butter. Add sugars, egg, and vanilla in order given. Sift flour, salt, and soda together and add to butter mixture. Chill until firm enough to roll. Simmer all filling ingredients (except nuts) 5 minutes, stirring often. Add nuts and cool. If desired, add grated rind from 1 lemon or 1 tablespoon lemon juice. Roll cookie dough to 9x12-inch rectangle. Spread with cooled filling. Roll up tightly and wrap in wax paper. Chill or freeze overnight for easier slicing. Slice ⅛ inch thick. Bake on greased cookie sheet at 350°-375° for 10 minutes. Store in airtight container. Rolls may be kept in freezer and sliced for baking as needed.

Ginger Snaps

- ¾ cup melted butter or ½ cup melted margarine
- 1 cup sugar
- 1 egg, beaten
- 3 tablespoons molasses
- About 2 cups flour
- 1½ teaspoons baking soda
- 1 teaspoon cinnamon
- ½ teaspoon cloves
- ½ teaspoon ginger

Cream butter and sugar. Add egg and molasses. Sift together dry ingredients. Add to creamed mixture. Form into small balls and roll in sugar. Bake at 350° for 10-12 minutes

Makes about 3 dozen cookies.

Lorraine Deckert
Dolton, South Dakota

IT IS BETTER TO SUFFER WRONG THAN TO DO IT,
AND HAPPIER TO BE SOMETIMES CHEATED THAN
TO NEVER TRUST.

Glazed Apple cookies

- 1 cup shortening
- 2½ cup brown sugar
- 2 eggs
- 4 cups flour
- 2 teaspoons baking soda
- 1 teaspoon salt
- 2 teaspoons cloves
- 1 teaspoon nutmeg
- 1 cup nuts
- 2 cups raisins
- ½ cup apple juice or milk
- 2 cups chopped raw apples
- 2 teaspoons cinnamon

Mix ingredients and bake.

R. Beiler
Quarryville, Pennsylvania

HONEY COOKIES

- ❖ 1 cup sugar
- ❖ 1 scant cup butter or lard
- ❖ 2 eggs
- ❖ ½ cup sour cream
- ❖ 1 cup honey
- ❖ 2 teaspoons baking soda
- ❖ Flour (approximately 5 cups)
- ❖ Lemon or orange flavoring

Mix all ingredients together well. Roll out immediately and cut into squares. Bake on greased baking sheet at 350° for 10 minutes or until lightly browned.

Caroline (Birky) Stutzman
Contributed by Adella (Stutzman) Gingrich
Albany, Oregon
Oregon MCC Fall Festival, Albany

KIFLI COOKIES

- ❖ 1 cup butter at room temperature
- ❖ 1 cup (8 ounces) cream-style cottage cheese
- ❖ 2 cups all-purpose flour

Cinnamon-Nut Filling:
- ❖ 2 unbeaten egg whites
- ❖ ½ cup sugar
- ❖ 2 cups finely chopped nuts
- ❖ 2 tablespoons ground cinnamon

Beat together butter and cottage cheese until light and fluffy. Add flour, beating until dough forms a ball. Divide dough into 3 equal portions. Wrap each portion separately and refrigerate until firm (several hours or overnight). To bake cookies, preheat oven to 375°. Prepare filling (mix the ingredients together) and set aside. On floured surface, roll out dough, one portion at a time, into a 10-inch circle. Spread circle with a third of the filling, covering dough to within ½ inch of the edge. Cut circle into 24 pie-shaped wedges. Beginning at the outer edge, roll up each wedge lightly. Place, point side down, on greased cookie sheet. Bake 13-15 minutes (watch carefully). Remove cookies from sheet and cool on rack. Frost with a mixture of powdered sugar, butter, and milk.

Makes 6 dozen cookies.

Laura Ann Belsley
Morton, Illinois
Bethel Mennonite Church, Pekin
Illinois MCC Relief Sale, Peoria

Layer Bars

- ¼ pound butter
- 1 cup crushed graham crackers
- 1 cup flaked coconut
- 1 package (16 ounces) chocolate chips
- 1 package (16 ounces) butterscotch chips
- 1 cup chopped nuts
- 1 can (14 ounces) sweetened condensed milk

Melt butter in a 9x13-inch pan. Layer remaining ingredients in pan in order given. Bake at 350° for 30 minutes. Cool and cut into bars to serve.

Lemon Cookies

- 1 box lemon cake mix
- 1 egg
- 1 8-ounce container of Cool Whip
- ¼ cup flour

Mix ingredients together. Take scoops the size of a teaspoon and roll in confectioner's sugar to make balls. Place on cookie sheet and bake at 350°.

R. Beiler
Quarryville, Pennsylvania

Lemon Poppyseed Cookies

- 2 cups flour
- ¾ teaspoon salt
- ⅓ cup poppyseeds
- ½ pound (2 sticks) butter or margarine
- ½ cup sugar
- 2 tablespoons grated lemon zest (yellow skin from about 3 lemons)
- 1 egg
- ¼ teaspoon vanilla

Combine flour, salt, and poppyseeds. Set aside. Cream butter, sugar, and lemon zest. Beat in egg and vanilla. Gradually add flour mixture to creamed mixture and beat. Cover and refrigerate at least 30 minutes. Form chilled dough into logs 2 inches in diameter. Refrigerate or freeze for 30 minutes. Heat oven to 350°. Cut the logs into thick slices (about ¼ inch thick). Bake on ungreased cookie sheets for 9-10 minutes or until edges are brown.

Makes about 40 cookies.

Mrs. Dennis (Shirley) Ries
Freeman, South Dakota
Minn-Kota MCC Relief Sale
Sioux Falls, South Dakota

Lemon Squares

Crumbs:
- ❖ 1 cup soda cracker crumbs
- ❖ ½ cup butter
- ❖ 1 cup brown sugar
- ❖ 1 cup coconut
- ❖ ½ teaspoon baking soda
- ❖ 1 cup flour

Filling:
- ❖ 1 cup white sugar
- ❖ 2 tablespoons cornstarch, rounded
- ❖ 2 eggs, slightly beaten
- ❖ 1 cup cold water
- ❖ ¼ cup butter, melted
- ❖ ½ teaspoon vanilla
- ❖ 1 lemon and rind

Combine ingredients to make crumbs. Press three-fourths of crumbs in bottom of 9x9-inch pan. Bake 25 minutes in slow oven at 325°. Combine filling ingredients and spread over baked crumbs. Sprinkle with remaining crumbs. Bake 20 minutes longer.

Marmalade Nut Cookies

- ❖ ½ cup butter or margarine
- ❖ ⅔ cup brown sugar
- ❖ 1 egg
- ❖ 1 teaspoon vanilla
- ❖ 1¾ cups all-purpose flour
- ❖ 2 teaspoons baking powder
- ❖ ½ teaspoon salt
- ❖ ½ teaspoon soda
- ❖ 1 cup chopped walnuts
- ❖ ½ cup marmalade

Sift together flour, baking powder, salt, and soda. Mix together butter, sugar, egg, and vanilla. Combine with dry ingredients. Add walnuts and marmalade. Drop on greased cookie sheet and bake at 350° for 10-12 minutes.

Marshmallow Delights

- ½ cup butter
- ¾ cup brown sugar
- ½ cup chopped walnuts
- 2 eggs, beaten
- ¼ cup coconut
- 3 cups colored miniature marshmallows
- 2½ cups graham wafer crumbs

Melt butter in top of double boiler. Add eggs, sugar, and coconut and set over simmering water. Cool to lukewarm. Blend in crumbs, nuts, and marshmallows. Pack into buttered pan 12x8x2 inches. Ice with butter icing. Cut in squares. Can be used without icing if preferred.

Melting Moments

- 1 cup butter
- ¾ cup brown sugar
- 1 egg
- 1 teaspoon vanilla
- 1¾ cup all-purpose flour, sifted
- ½ teaspoon cream of tartar
- ½ teaspoon soda
- Pecans

Cream the butter, brown sugar, egg, and vanilla. Add the flour, cream of tartar, and soda. Make into little balls. Press a pecan on top of each.

Mexican Wedding Cakes

- 1 cup margarine
- ½ cup sugar
- ½ teaspoon salt
- 2 teaspoons vanilla
- 2 cups flour
- 1 cup chopped walnuts

Cream margarine and sugar. Add salt, vanilla, flour, and nuts. Mix well. Chill dough. Shape into balls and flatten with bottom of a design tumbler dipped in flour. Bake at 325° until lightly browned. Rub tops of cookies in powdered sugar.

Ester V. Mishler
Johnstown, Pennsylvania
MCC Quilt Auction and Relief Sale, Johnstown

Mint Chocolate Sticks

❖ Brownies

Icing:
❖ 2 tablespoons soft butter
❖ 1 cup powdered sugar, sifted
❖ 1 tablespoon cream
❖ ¾ teaspoon peppermint

Glaze:
❖ 1 square unsweetened chocolate
❖ 1 tablespoon butter

Make brownies using your favorite recipe or the one on page 242. Make icing by working the butter into the powdered sugar. Add the cream and peppermint. Stir until smooth. Cover brownies with icing and refrigerate while making glaze. Make glaze by melting the chocolate and butter together. Drizzle over cool firm icing. Tilt pan back and forth until glaze covers surface. Refrigerate. Cut into strips 2½x¾ inches.

Molasses Krinkles

❖ 2½ cups sifted pastry flour
❖ 2 teaspoons soda
❖ ½ teaspoon salt
❖ 1-2 teaspoons ginger to taste
❖ 1-2 teaspoons cinnamon to taste
❖ ¾ cup shortening
❖ 1 cup white sugar
❖ 1 egg, unbeaten
❖ 4 tablespoons molasses

Sift flour once. Add soda and spices. Sift 3 times. Cream shortening. Add sugar and egg. Beat thoroughly. Add molasses, then add flour mixture gradually. Roll into 1¼-inch balls after dough is well chilled and roll in sugar. Bake on ungreased pan at 350° for 15-20 minutes.

To make Raisin Ginger Cookies, add 1½ cups raisins to this recipe.

Monster Cookies

❖ 6 eggs
❖ 1 pound brown sugar
❖ 2 cups white sugar
❖ 1½ teaspoons vanilla
❖ 4 teaspoons baking soda
❖ ½ pound (2 sticks) margarine
❖ 1½ pounds peanut butter
❖ 1½ teaspoons corn syrup (Karo)
❖ 9 cups quick-cooking rolled oats
❖ ½ pound chocolate chips
❖ 1 cup coconut

Mix ingredients in order given. Drop on cookie sheets, using ice cream scoop. Flatten with a fork. Bake at 325° for 10-12 minutes.

Esther V. Mishler
Johnstown, Pennsylvania
MCC Quilt Auction and Relief Sale, Johnstown

New Year's Cookies

- 1 cake yeast dissolved in ¼ cup water
- 2 cups milk, scalded and cooled
- ¼ cup sugar
- 3 eggs, well beaten
- 1¼ teaspoons salt
- ¼ cup butter, melted
- ¾ pound raisins
- About 4-5 cups flour

Add dissolved yeast to the milk. Add sugar, eggs, salt, and butter. Plump raisins in hot water for a minute or two. Drain and add to milk mixture. Stir in enough flour to make a soft dough. Let rise until doubled. Heat oil in kettle or deep fat fryer to 350°-375°. Dip spoon in hot fat, then into dough. Drop dough by spoonful into oil. Turn to fry to a golden brown. Drain and roll in granulated or powdered sugar as for doughnuts, or dip in sugar as they are eaten.

Nebraska MCC Relief Sale, Aurora

New Year's Cookies (Portzelky)

- 12 cups raisins
- ⅓ cup yeast
- 2 tablespoons sugar
- 2 cups warm water
- 10 cups water
- 3½ cups powdered milk
- 1 cup soft margarine
- 4 cups sugar
- 2 tablespoons (⅛ cup) salt
- 18 well-beaten eggs
- 22 cups flour

Pour boiling water over raisins and set aside until other ingredients are mixed, then strain and add. Dissolve yeast and the 2 tablespoons sugar in the 2 cups warm water. Let set until foamy. Combine the 10 cups water, powdered milk, and margarine. Heat to lukewarm. Stir in sugar, salt, eggs, and yeast mixture. Gradually stir in flour. Let batter stand for 1 hour before frying.

Edith Warkentin
Kelowna, British Columbia, Relief Sale

A HANDFUL OF PATIENCE IS WORTH MORE
THAN A BUSHEL OF BRAINS.

OATMEAL RAISIN COOKIES

- 1¾ cups sifted all-purpose flour
- 1 teaspoon baking powder
- 1 teaspoon soda
- ½ teaspoon salt
- 2 eggs
- 1¼ cups white sugar
- ½ cup shortening
  (or part butter and lard)
- 6 tablespoons molasses
- 1 teaspoon vanilla
- 2 cups quick oatmeal
- ½ cup raisins, chopped
- ⅓ cups walnuts, chopped

Sift flour, baking powder, salt, sugar, and soda into mixing bowl. Add unbeaten eggs, shortening, molasses, and vanilla. Stir with wooden spoon until smooth (1½ minutes) or beat with mixer until smooth. Add rolled oats, raisins, and walnuts. Drop 4 inches apart on greased cookie sheet. Bake at 325° for 12-15 minutes. Baked cookies should be approximately 2¾ inches in diameter.

OATMEAL-WALNUT COOKIES

Dough:
- 1 cup shortening
- 1 cup brown sugar
- 1 cup white sugar
- ½ teaspoon vanilla
- 2 eggs
- 1¼ cups flour
- 1 teaspoon soda
- ½ teaspoon cinnamon

Cream shortening, sugar, vanilla, and eggs together in order given. Add flour, soda, and cinnamon.

Make the following additions if desired:

- Fold in 3 cups oatmeal and ½ cup (or more) black walnuts.

- Fold in 2 cups oatmeal, 1 cup coconut, and 2 cups cornflakes.

- Fold in 3 cups oatmeal, ½ cup chopped walnuts, and omit the spices.

Drop by teaspoon on greased cookie sheet. Bake at 350°-375° for 10-15 minutes.

OH HENRY BARS

- 1 cup sugar
- 1 cup white corn syrup
- 1¼ cup crunchy peanut butter
- 6 cups Rice Krispies
- 1 cup chocolate chips

Bring sugar and syrup to a boil. Add peanut butter. Stir well. Combine cereal and chips. Pour hot syrup over dry mixture. Mix well. Spread in a buttered 9x13-inch pan, patting out evenly. Let cool, then cut into bars to serve.

Amy Hofer
Carpenter, South Dakota
Minn-Kota Country Auction and Relief Sale
Sioux Falls, South Dakota

OLD-FASHIONED RAISIN BARS

- 1 cup seedless raisins
- 1 cup water
- ½ cup salad oil
- 1 cup sugar
- 1 slightly beaten egg
- 1¾ cups flour
- ¼ teaspoon salt
- 1 teaspoon soda
- 1 teaspoon cinnamon
- ½ teaspoon nutmeg
- ½ teaspoon ground allspice
- 1 teaspoon cloves
- ½ cup walnuts

Combine raisins and water. Bring to boil and remove from heat. Stir in salad oil. Cool to lukewarm. Stir in sugar and egg. Sift together dry ingredients and beat into raisin mixture. Stir in nuts. Pour into greased 13x9x2-inch pan. Bake at 375° for 20 minutes. When cool, cut into bars. Dust with powdered sugar.

OUR FAVORITE CHOCOLATE CHIP COOKIES WITH OATMEAL

- 8 eggs
- 6 cups brown sugar
- 4 cups lard
- 4 teaspoons soda and 4 teaspoons vanilla dissolved in ½ cup hot water
- 8 cups quick oats
- 4 cups small semisweet chocolate pieces
- 7-8 cups flour

Mix ingredients together in order given, stirring well after each ingredient. Use 7 cups of flour and then bake several test cookies. Add more flour to final mixture if needed.

Malinda King
Honey Brook, Pennsylvania

PEPPERMINT COOKIES

- 2 cups cream
- 1 cup butter
- 3 cups sugar
- 5 eggs
- Oil of peppermint to taste
- 3 tablespoons baking ammonia dissolved in ¼ cup boiling water
- 5 teaspoons baking powder
- 8½ cups flour

Mix together cream and butter. Add sugar and eggs. Cream, adding flavoring when almost creamed. Stir in baking ammonia mixture, baking powder, and flour. Chill dough overnight. The next day, roll out dough and cut into desired shapes. Bake at 375° for 10-15 minutes (depending on size of cookies).

From the Mennonite Treasury of Recipes
MCC British Columbia Relief Sale, Kelowna

PEPPERMINT COOKIES WITH MILK

- 1 cup milk
- 2 tablespoons baking ammonia or baking powder
- 1 cup shortening
- 12 drops oil of peppermint
- 1 cup cold milk
- 9 cups all-purpose flour
- 2 ½ cups sugar

Bring 1 cup milk to a boil. Dissolve the baking ammonia or baking powder in hot milk. Add shortening and stir to dissolve. Add oil of peppermint and cold milk. Stir this liquid into a mixture made of the flour and the sugar. (Dough should be soft.) Refrigerate for a few hours. Roll dough ¼ inch thick and cut with cookie cutter. Bake at 375° until done.

PEPPERNUTS

- 2 cups (4 sticks) margarine
- 8 cups brown sugar
- 8 eggs
- 2 teaspoons anise oil
- 2 teaspoons baking soda dissolved in ¼ cup hot water
- 9 cups flour
- 2 teaspoons cream of tartar
- 2 teaspoons cinnamon
- 2 teaspoons nutmeg
- 2 teaspoons ground cloves

Cream margarine and sugar in a large bowl. Add eggs and anise oil. Mix well. Add dissolved soda. Mix together 4 cups of the flour with the cream of tartar, cinnamon, nutmeg, and cloves. Add to the creamed mixture. Gradually add remaining flour. Roll into long thin rolls and freeze. To bake, cut frozen rolls into thin slices. Place on greased cookie sheets. Bake at 350° for 8-10 minutes.

Frank Yoder
Iowa MCC Relief Sale, Iowa City

CHRISTMAS PEPPERNUTS

- ½ cup vegetable oil
- 1 cup brown sugar
- 2 eggs
- 1 tablespoon vanilla
- 2 cups flour
- 1 teaspoon baking soda
- 1 teaspoon baking powder
- 1 cup raisins
- 1 cup nuts (preferably walnuts)
- 1 cup coconut

Cream together oil and sugar. Beat in eggs and vanilla. Stir in flour, baking soda, and baking powder. Mix well. In a food chopper, grind raisins, nuts, and coconut. (To keep raisins from sticking together, wash them in hot water just before grinding.) Mix into dough. Chill dough for 1 hour. Roll on lightly floured board into rolls about ½ inch thick. Cut with floured knife. Bake at 325° for 8 minutes.

Makes about 2 quarts peppernuts.

Mary B. Duerksen
Mountain Lake, Minnesota
Minn-Kota MCC Relief Sale
Sioux Falls, South Dakota

FRUIT AND SPICY PEPPERNUTS

- ½ cup butter
- 1½ cups sugar
- 2 eggs
- ½ cup raisins, ground
- 4 teaspoons buttermilk
- 3 cups flour
- 1 teaspoon baking soda
- ½ teaspoon salt
- 1 teaspoon nutmeg
- ½ teaspoon cinnamon
- ½ teaspoon cloves
- 1 cup coconut
- 1 cup chopped nuts

Cream butter, sugar, and eggs until fluffy. Add raisins and buttermilk. Sift together all dry ingredients and add to creamed mixture. Add coconut and nuts. Mix well. Store in tightly covered container in the refrigerator overnight. (This helps dough to season and flavors to blend.) To bake, roll dough in pencil-like ropes and cut in ½-inch pieces with sharp knife, or scissors, that has been dipped in flour. Place pieces separately on cookie sheet and bake at 375° for 8-10 minutes or until golden brown.

Makes ½-¾ gallon peppernuts.

Erna Sallaska
Balko, Oklahoma
Oklahoma Mennonite Relief Sale, Fairview

PRIDE OF IOWA COOKIES

- 1 cup shortening (part butter)
- 1 cup white sugar
- 1 cup brown sugar
- 2 eggs, beaten
- 1 cup coconut
- 1 cup nuts and/or raisins
- 1 package (12 ounces) chocolate chips
- 1 teaspoon vanilla
- 2¼ cups sifted flour
- 1 teaspoon baking powder
- ½ teaspoon salt
- 1 teaspoon baking soda
- 2 cups uncooked rolled oats

Cream shortening and sugars. Add beaten eggs. Add coconut, nuts, chips, and vanilla. Add flour, baking powder, salt, soda, and oatmeal. Roll dough into balls the size of a large walnut. Bake at 350° for 9 minutes or until golden brown.

Mrs. Wilbert (Alice) Graber
Parker, South Dakota
Minn-Kota MCC Relief Sale
Sioux Falls, South Dakota

RASPBERRY SQUARES

Dough:
- 1 cup flour
- 1 teaspoon baking powder
- ⅛ teaspoon salt
- ½ cup butter
- 1 tablespoon milk
- 1 egg, beaten

Topping:
- 1 cup white sugar
- 1 beaten egg
- ¼ cup melted butter
- 2 cups coconut
- 1 teaspoon vanilla

Mix ingredients for dough. Roll and put in pan. Spread on raspberry jam in thin layer. Mix topping ingredients and spread over jam. Bake in moderate oven for 25 minutes.

Refrigerator Norwegian Cookies

- 1 cup lard
- 1 cup butter
- 1 cup white sugar
- 1 cup brown sugar
- 3 eggs
- 4½ cups all-purpose flour
- 1 teaspoon baking soda
- 1 teaspoon cinnamon
- 1 teaspoon salt
- 1 cup nut meats

Cream shortening and sugar until fluffy. Add stiffly beaten eggs. Sift together flour, baking soda, cinnamon, and salt. Work dry ingredients, then nuts, into dough. Knead to form a roll. Chill overnight. Cut into slices and bake at 350° for 8-10 minutes or until lightly browned.

Iris Frank
East Peoria Mennonite Church
Illinois MCC Relief Sale, Peoria

ENJOY THESE COOKIES WITH A BOWL OF ICE CREAM.

Roderkuchen (Bow Ties)

- 1 cup egg yolks
- 1 cup sour cream
- 1½ cups sugar
- Flour

Mix together egg yolks, sour cream, and sugar. Add enough flour to make a stiff dough. Roll out dough about ¼ inch thick. Using a fluted wheel, cut dough into rectangular pieces. Make a small slit in the center of each piece, then pull one end of the rectangle through the slit to form a "bow tie." Fry in deep fat heated to 350°.

Erna Marie Reimer
Beatrice, Nebraska
First Mennonite Church
Nebraska MCC Relief Sale, Aurora

Rocky Road Squares

- ½ cup butter or margarine
- 1 cup powdered sugar
- 1 6-ounce package butterscotch chips
- 1 beaten egg
- 2 cups miniature marshmallows
- Graham wafers

Heat first 4 ingredients in double boiler until melted. Cool slightly. Add miniature marshmallows. Pour into 8x8-inch pan lined with whole graham wafers. Refrigerate.

ଓ

SHORTBREAD

- 1 pound butter
- ½ cup brown sugar
- ½ cup powdered sugar
- 1 teaspoon vanilla
- ⅛ teaspoon salt
- 4 cups all-purpose flour

Using an electric beater, cream the butter until very light. While still beating, add the brown sugar, powdered sugar, vanilla, and salt. Beat 5 minutes. Add the flour, using beater at first, then hands. (The heat of the hands helps the process.) These may be pressed into shapes from a press or they may be chilled, rolled, and cut into shapes. Decorate. Bake at 325° for 7 minutes.

Make Almond or Filbert Shortbread by adding ½-1 cup crushed almonds or filberts to above recipe.

Makes 75 cookies.

OATMEAL SHORTBREAD

- 1 cup butter
- ½ cup brown sugar
- ½ cup powdered sugar
- ½ teaspoon vanilla
- 1½ cups oatmeal
- 1 cup all-purpose flour
- 1 teaspoon baking powder
- Chocolate sprinkles

Cream the first 4 ingredients very well in order given. Add the oatmeal and the flour, sifted with the baking powder. Shape into small balls and flatten, or make into a roll about 8 inches long and 1½ inches in diameter, roll in sprinkles, chill, and slice. Bake at 325° for 7-10 minutes.

Makes 75 cookies.

Sour Cream Raisin Bars

- 2 cups raisins
- ¾ cup butter
- 1½ cups water
- 1½ cups rolled oats
- 1½ cups flour
- 1 teaspoon baking soda
- ¾ cup brown sugar

Filling:

- 1 cup sugar
- 1½ cups sour cream
- 3 eggs
- 3 tablespoons cornstarch

Cook raisins in water until soft and plump. Drain and cool. In a large bowl, combine flour, oats, sugar, butter, and baking soda. Mix until crumbly. Press 3 cups of mixture into a 9x13-inch pan. Keep 1½ cups of mixture aside. Combine filling ingredients and water from raisins and cook over low heat. Stir until mixture comes to a boil. Boil for 1 minute. Remove from heat and stir in raisins. Spread over crumb crust. Sprinkle with remaining crust mixture. Bake at 350° for 30-35 minutes.

Strawberry Cookies

- 1 can sweetened condensed milk
- ½ package strawberry gelatin
- 1 heaping tablespoon powdered sugar
- 2 cups fine coconut
- ½ cup almonds, finely chopped or ground
- Icing

Mix ingredients and let chill overnight. Shape into berry shapes and roll in remaining gelatin powder. Attach small leaves of green-colored icing.

CB

SUGAR COOKIES

- 1 cup shortening
- 1 cup butter
- 1 cup white sugar
- 1 cup brown sugar
- 4 eggs, well beaten
- 5 cups all-purpose flour
- 2 teaspoons soda
- 4 teaspoons cream of tartar
- 1 teaspoon salt
- 2 teaspoons vanilla

Cream shortening and butter. Add sugar, creaming thoroughly. Add well-beaten eggs and mix again. Sift together flour, soda, cream of tartar, and salt. Add to shortening mixture. Add vanilla. Chill dough in refrigerator several hours or overnight. Roll about ⅛ inch thick and sprinkle with sugar. Use soup can as cookie cutter (2½-inch diameter). Bake 8 minutes at 350°.

To make Ice Cream Cookies, use above recipe, adding the following filling to make sandwich cookies: 1 cup sweet cream, 6 tablespoons brown sugar, 1 tablespoon butter, and 2 teaspoons vanilla. Boil until thick. Fill cookies while warm. Chill.

BUTTERMILK SUGAR COOKIES

- 2 tablespoons baking soda
- 1 quart buttermilk
- 6 cups sugar
- 1 pound solid vegetable shortening, melted
- ½ pint sour thick cream
- 1½ tablespoons vanilla
- 13½ cups all-purpose flour

Dissolve soda in buttermilk. Add sugar, hot melted shortening, cream, and vanilla. Add 7½ cups of the flour. Mix well. Add the remaining 6 cups flour and mix by hand. Bake at 400° for 8-10 minutes. Let cool. Frost.

Makes about 135 medium-sized cookies.

Mary Kilmer Horning and
Anna Horning Zimmerman
Contributed by Mrs. Harold
(Irene) Zimmerman

MOLASSES SUGAR COOKIES

- ¾ cup shortening
- 1 cup sugar
- ¼ cup light molasses
- 1 egg
- 2 cups flour
- 2 teaspoons baking soda
- 1 teaspoon cinnamon
- ½ teaspoon cloves
- ½ teaspoon ginger
- ½ teaspoon salt

Cream shortening and sugar. Add molasses and egg. Beat well. Sift in remaining ingredients. Form dough into balls and roll in sugar. Bake at 375° for 8-10 minutes.

Mel Long
Sterling, Illinois
Science Ridge Mennonite Church
Illinois MCC Relief Sale, Peoria

STAY-SOFT SUGAR COOKIES

- 2 cups white sugar
- 1 cup butter-flavored solid vegetable shortening
- 4 eggs
- 1 cup milk
- ½ teaspoon vanilla
- 1 teaspoon baking soda
- 4 tablespoons baking powder
- 4 cups flour

Cream together sugar, shortening, eggs, milk, and vanilla. Add remaining ingredients. Mix well. Drop by teaspoon onto greased cookie sheets. Bake at 350° for 12-15 minutes or until edges are golden brown. (If you'd rather roll the dough for cutout cookies, increase the flour to 5½ cups.)

Makes 4 dozen cookies.

Tillie Janzen
Mountain Lake, Minnesota
Minn-Kota MCC Relief Sale
Sioux Falls, South Dakota

SWEDISH CREAMS

- 1 cup margarine
- ⅓ cup whipping cream
- 2 cups flour
- Granulated sugar

Filling:
- ¼ cup margarine
- 1 egg yolk
- 1 teaspoon vanilla
- ¾ cup powdered sugar

Mix together the 1 cup margarine, cream, and flour. Chill dough 1 hour. Roll dough ⅛ inch thick and cut into donut hole shape. Roll in granulated sugar, place on greased cookie sheets, and prick with a fork. Bake at 375° for 7-9 minutes. Mix ingredients for filling. When cookies are cool, spread filling on half the cookies. Top each with one of the plain cookies to make a sandwich.

Eunice Chupp
Goshen, Indiana
Pleasant View Mennonite Church
Indiana MCC Relief Sale, Goshen

Swirl Chocolate Bars

- ❖ 1 package German chocolate cake mix
- ❖ ½ cup sugar
- ❖ 1 egg
- ❖ 1 package (8 ounces) cream cheese
- ❖ ½ cup chocolate chips

Prepare cake batter following package directions. Pour into a greased and floured jelly roll pan. Mix sugar, egg, and cream cheese well. Stir in chips. Drop by teaspoon all over cake batter. Take a knife and swirl through batter to swirl filling. Bake at 350° for 25-30 minutes. Cool and cut into bars to serve.

Amy Hofer
Carpenter, South Dakota
Minn-Kota Country Auction and Relief Sale
Sioux Falls, South Dakota

Tempters

- ❖ ½ cup shortening
- ❖ 1 cup white sugar
- ❖ 1 beaten egg
- ❖ 1 teaspoon vanilla
- ❖ ¼ teaspoon almond extract
- ❖ 2 tablespoons milk
- ❖ 2 cups pastry flour
  (or 1¾ cups all-purpose)
- ❖ 1½ teaspoons baking powder
- ❖ ½ teaspoon salt
- ❖ ½ cup nuts (optional)
- ❖ ½ cup chocolate chips
- ❖ 1 cup coconut

Cream shortening. Blend in sugar, egg, flavorings, and milk. Mix in dry ingredients one-third at a time. Mix in nuts, chocolate chips, and coconut. Drop by teaspoon onto greased cookie sheet. Press with wet fork. Bake at 350° for 12 minutes.

Tropical Bars

- 1 cup sifted all-purpose flour
- ¼ teaspoon salt
- ¼ cup brown sugar, packed
- ¼ cup butter
- 1 egg
- 1 cup brown sugar, packed
- 1 teaspoon rum extract
- ½ cup sifted all-purpose flour
- ½ teaspoon baking powder
- ¼ teaspoon salt
- 1 cup flaked coconut
- ¼ cup cut-up maraschino cherries
- ½ cup well-drained crushed pineapple

Heat oven to 350°. Lightly grease a 9-inch square cake pan. Sift 1 cup flour and ¼ teaspoon salt into bowl. Add ¼ cup sugar and blend lightly. Add butter, working into dry ingredients first with a fork, then with fingers until mixture is crumbly. Press firmly into bottom of prepared pan. Bake 15 minutes. Remove from oven. Beat egg thoroughly. Add 1 cup sugar gradually, beating well after each addition. Beat in rum extract. Sift ½ cup flour, baking powder, and ¼ teaspoon salt into mixture and stir to blend. Stir in coconut, cherries, and pineapple. Spread over hot pastry layer and return to oven. Bake about 35 minutes or until well browned. Cool in pan and cut in bars.

$250 Cookies

- 2 cups butter
- 2 cups granulated sugar
- 2 cups brown sugar
- 4 eggs
- 2 teaspoons vanilla
- 4 cups flour
- 5 cups quick-cooking rolled oats, blended in blender
- 1 teaspoon salt
- 2 teaspoons baking powder
- 2 teaspoons baking soda
- 24 ounces chocolate chips
- 1 milk chocolate bar (8 ounces), grated
- 3 cups chopped nuts

Cream together butter and sugars. Add eggs and vanilla. Mix well. Add flour, oats, salt, baking powder, and soda. Stir in chips, grated chocolate, and nuts. Roll dough into balls or drop by spoonful onto greased cookie sheets. Bake at 375° for 10 minutes.

Makes about 112 cookies.

Helen Klassen
MCC British Columbia Relief Sale, Kelowna

☙

BUTTERSCOTCH BROWNIES

- ❖ ¼ cup butter or butter-flavored vegetable shortening
- ❖ 1 cup packed light brown sugar
- ❖ 1 egg
- ❖ ¾ cup flour
- ❖ 1 teaspoon baking powder
- ❖ ½ teaspoon salt
- ❖ ½ teaspoon vanilla
- ❖ ½ cup chopped nuts

Preheat oven to 350°. Melt butter over low heat. Remove from heat and blend in sugar. Cool and stir in egg. Blend in flour, baking powder, and salt. Mix in vanilla and nuts. Spread in a well-greased 8-inch square pan. Bake 25 minutes. Cut into bars while still warm.

Sally Ann Reddecliff
Johnstown, Pennsylvania
MCC Quilt Auction and Relief Sale, Johnstown

CAKE FLOUR BROWNIES

- ❖ ½ cup butter
- ❖ 1 cup sugar
- ❖ 2 eggs
- ❖ 2 squares baking chocolate, melted
- ❖ 1 cup cake flour, sifted
- ❖ ½ teaspoon baking powder
- ❖ ½ teaspoon salt
- ❖ ½ cup nutmeats
- ❖ ½ teaspoon vanilla

Cream butter with sugar. Add eggs one at a time, beating well after each addition. Add cooled melted chocolate. Sift dry ingredients together and add to creamed mixture. Add nutmeats and vanilla. Bake at 350° for 25-30 minutes. Cool and cut into bars to serve.

Delicious Brownies

- ¾ cup butter or margarine
- ½ cup brown sugar
- ½ cup white sugar mix
- 3 eggs, separated
- 1 teaspoon vanilla
- 1 teaspoon baking powder
- 1 teaspoon salt
- ¼ teaspoon baking soda
- 2 cups all purpose flour
- Nuts, butterscotch bits, or chocolate chips (optional)

Combine butter and sugars. Add egg yolks, vanilla, baking powder, stalt, baking soda, and flour. Spread in pan. Beat egg white until frothy. Add 1 cup brown sugar and make stiff. Combine with brownie batter. Sprinkle with nuts, butterscotch bits, or chocolate chips. Bake at 350° for 30-40 minutes.

Aaron and Sadie Smucker
New Providence, Pennsylvania

Speedy Brownies

- 2 cups brown sugar
- 1¾ cups all-purpose flour
- ½ teaspoon salt
- 5 eggs
- 1 cup vegetable oil
- 1 teaspoon vanilla
- 1 cup chocolate chips
- Confectioners' sugar

Mix the first 6 ingredients. Beat well and pour into a cake pan. Sprinkle with chocolate chips and confectioners' sugar. Bake at 350° for 30 minutes.

Amish Cook
Lancaster, Pennsylvania

CB

CHERRY PIE

- 2 ¾ cups cherries and juice (fresh or frozen and thawed, no sugar)
- 1 cup sugar
- 3 tablespoons quick-cooking tapioca
- 3 drops almond flavoring
- Few drops red coloring

Cover top completely with pastry or pastry strips. Bake at 425° for 10 minutes or 375° for 30 minutes. Best results are if tapioca stands on cherries before putting into pie.

PEACH PIE

- 2 ¾ cups peaches and juice (fresh or frozen and thawed, no sugar)
- 1 cup sugar
- 3 tablespoons quick-cooking tapioca
- 3 drops almond flavoring

Make same as cherry pie, above.

BLUEBERRY OR ELDERBERRY PIE

- 2 ¾ cups blueberries or elderberries and juice (fresh or frozen and thawed, no sugar)
- ⅓ cup finely cut rhubarb
- 3 tablespoons lemon juice
- 1 cup sugar
- 3 tablespoons quick-cooking tapioca
- 3 drops almond flavoring

Make same as cherry pie, above. Rhubarb and lemon juice will give the needed tartness.

ELDERBERRY PIE

- 1 cup applesauce
- 1 unbaked pie shell
- 1½ cups elderberries
- 1 cup sugar

Spread applesauce over the bottom of the unbaked pie shell, and then add the elderberries and sugar.

BAKE ALL OF THE ABOVE AT 425° FOR 10 MINUTES OR 375° FOR 30 MINUTES.

Brown Sugar Pie Pastry

- 5 cups flour
- 3 tablespoons brown sugar
- 1 teaspoon baking powder
- 1 teaspoon salt
- 1 pound lard
- 1 egg
- 2 tablespoons vinegar
- Water
- Milk
- Granulated sugar

Sift flour, brown sugar, baking powder, and salt into a bowl. Work in lard. Measure the egg and vinegar into a measuring cup. Stir only to blend, then fill cup to ⅞ line with water. Mix well with flour mixture. Store in refrigerator in a tight plastic dish. When making crusts, cut top pastry cover smaller than pie plate, leaving about 1 inch fruit showing when cover is put on pie. Steam can escape and pie will not boil out into oven. Brush cover with milk and sprinkle with sugar.

Makes 8 single crusts.

Classic Pie Pastry

- 1 pound lard
- 1 cup boiling water
- 6 cups pastry flour
- 2 teaspoons sugar
- 2 teaspoons baking powder
- 2 teaspoons salt

Cut lard into a narrow bowl. Add boiling water and stir well. Sift the pastry flour, sugar, baking powder, and salt into a large bowl. Add lard mixture. Stir with wooden spoon. Store in refrigerator bowl or heavy plastic. (Can be frozen.)

Makes 9 single crusts.

Ice Water Pie Pastry

- 2 ½ cups pastry flour
- 1 teaspoon salt
- ½ teaspoon baking powder
- ¾ cup corn oil
- 1 tablespoon vinegar
- Ice water

Sift together the pastry flour, salt, and baking powder. Measure the corn oil into a cup. Add the vinegar and fill with ice water. Blend all with a fork. Roll on wax paper.

Makes 3 crusts.

SIMPLE PIE PASTRY

- ❖ 14 cups flour
- ❖ 1 pound lard
- ❖ 1 pound shortening
- ❖ 2 teaspoons salt
- ❖ Water

Blend flour, lard, shortening, and salt with cutter or hands. Store in airtight container. For 1 pie shell, use 1¼ cups mix sprinkled with 3 tablespoons water. Mix until it stays in ball. Roll.

CRUMBS FOR FRUIT PIES

- ❖ ¼ cup butter
- ❖ ½ cup brown sugar
- ❖ 1 cup flour
- ❖ ½ teaspoon soda

Using fingertips, work the butter thoroughly into the brown sugar, flour, and soda. This amount covers the thickened fruit of 3 pies, serving as a cover.

ADOPT THE PACE OF NATURE;

HER SECRET IS PATIENCE.

APPLE BUTTER PIE

- ❖ ½ cup apple butter
- ❖ 2 eggs
- ❖ ½ cup brown sugar
- ❖ 1½ teaspoons cornstarch
- ❖ 1 teaspoon cinnamon
- ❖ 2 cups milk

Beat apple butter, eggs, brown sugar, cornstarch, and cinnamon. Add milk and beat slowly. Pour into unbaked 10-inch pie shell. It may be covered with strips of pastry laid in lattice fashion. Bake at 425° for 10 minutes and at 350° for 30 minutes.

Dutch Apple Pie

Filling:
- Apples, sliced into wedges
- ½ cup sour cream, ¼ cup milk, or ¼ cup water
- 2 tablespoons lemon juice
- Butter

Crumbs:
- 1 cup brown sugar
- ⅓ cup flour
- ½ teaspoon cinnamon
- Unbaked pie pastry

Mix the ingredients for the crumbs. Spread one-third of the mixture over the bottom of the pie pastry. Cover this with layers of the apple wedges. The top layer may be arranged in a design, i.e. sixths in a circle. Cover with the remaining crumbs. Spoon the sour cream, milk, or water and the lemon juice over the apples. If milk or water are used, dot with butter for additional glaze. Bake at 450° for 10 minutes, then at 375° for 40 minutes.

Tart Apple Pie

- ⅓ cup white sugar
- ⅓ cup brown sugar
- ½ teaspoon cinnamon
- 1 cup applesauce
- 2 cups sliced apples
- 1 unbaked 9-inch pie shell

Topping:
- ¾ cup flour
- ⅓ cup brown sugar
- 6 tablespoons butter

Combine sugars, cinnamon, applesauce, and apples. Place in pie shell. For topping, combine flour and brown sugar. Cut in butter. Spread crumbled mixture over top of pie. Bake until filling is hot and bubbly and crust is browned.

Bernice Lehman
Johnstown, Pennsylvania
MCC Quilt Auction and Relief Sale, Johnstown

GIVE EVERY MAN YOUR EAR, BUT FEW YOUR VOICE. TAKE
EACH MAN'S CENSURE, BUT RESERVE YOUR JUDGMENT.

Big Valley Half Moon Pies

Pie Crust:
- ❖ 1 cup shortening
- ❖ 2½ cups flour
- ❖ ½ teaspoon baking powder
- ❖ 1 teaspoon salt
- ❖ 1 egg
- ❖ 1 teaspoon vinegar
- ❖ Cold water

Filling:
- ❖ 6 cups cooked snitz (dried apples)
- ❖ 2 cups brown sugar
- ❖ 1 cup white sugar
- ❖ 4 teaspoons cinnamon
- ❖ ½ cup flour
- ❖ 3 teaspoons lemon juice
- ❖ ¼ teaspoon salt

Mix dry ingredients for pie crust. In a cup, beat the egg and vinegar. Fill the cup half full with cold water and add to dry ingredients. To make the filling, cook the apples until soft with as little water as possible, then mash. Add remaining ingredients. Form pie dough into balls the size of a large walnut. Roll each ball into a round flat shape. On one half, make several holes with a pie crimper. On the other half, add a heaping tablespoon of cooled apple filling. Fold the half with holes over the filled side. Press edges together firmly and trim around the edges with a pie crimper. Bake at 375° for 20 minutes.

Betty Hartzler
Belleville, Pennsylvania

Boysenberry Pie

Pie Crust (full recipe):
- ❖ 16 cups flour
- ❖ 3 cups shortening
- ❖ 4 cups milk
- ❖ 2 tablespoons salt

Boysenberry Filling (per pie):
- ❖ 4 cups berries
- ❖ ¾ cup sugar
- ❖ 2 tablespoons cornstarch
- ❖ 2 tablespoons raspberry-flavored gelatin

Make pastry. Roll into bottom and top crusts and set aside. Mix filling ingredients thoroughly and pour into crust. Top with a second crust. Pinch edges to seal. Spray top crust with milk from a spray bottle. Sprinkle with sugar.

Kathy Heinrichs Weist
Kingsburg, California

BROWNIE PIE

Crust:
- 3 egg whites
- Pinch of salt
- ¾ cup sugar
- ¾ cup chocolate wafers or graham crackers, coarsely crushed
- ½ cup chopped walnuts
- ½ teaspoon vanilla
- ½ teaspoon almond extract

Filling:
- 1 package lemon pie filling, prepared
- 1 cup whipping cream, whipped

Note: Ingredients listed will make one pie crust, but enough filling for two pies

To make the crust, beat egg whites and salt until frothy. Gradually add sugar, beating until whites form very stiff peaks. Fold in crumbs and walnuts, then vanilla and almond extracts. Turn into a well-greased pie tin, spreading evenly. Bake at 325° for 35 minutes. Remove from oven and cool completely. To make the filling, prepare lemon pie filling according to package directions. Fold whipped cream into cooled filling. Fill pie crusts.

Serves 8.

Minn-Kota MCC Relief Sale
Sioux Falls, South Dakota

BUTTERMILK PIE

- 1 cup sugar
- 2 tablespoons flour
- ½ teaspoon soda
- 2 tablespoons melted butter
- 2 eggs
- 1 teaspoon lemon juice
- 2 cups buttermilk

Combine the sugar, flour, and soda. Beat the melted butter, eggs, and lemon juice. Add the sugar mixture and buttermilk. Pour into unbaked 10-inch pie shell. Bake at 425° for 10 minutes and at 350° for 35 minutes.

COCONUT PIE

- 1 envelope unflavored gelatin
- ¼ cup sugar
- ⅛ teaspoon salt
- 3 eggs, separated
- 1 ¾ cups milk
- 1 teaspoon vanilla
- ¾ cup flaked coconut
- ¼ cup sugar

Mix the gelatin, ¼ cup sugar, and salt in top of double boiler. Beat together the egg yolks and milk. Add to gelatin mixture. Cook, stirring constantly, until gelatin dissolves. Remove from heat and stir in vanilla. Chill, stirring occasionally, until mixture mounds. Stir in the coconut. Make a meringue of the egg whites and ¼ cup sugar. Fold into gelatin mixture and pile in baked 9-inch pie shell. Chill. Top can be garnished with maraschino cherries or fresh fruits in season.

CUSTARD PIE

- 4 eggs
- ½ cup sugar
- ¼ teaspoon salt
- 2½ cups milk
- ½ teaspoon vanilla
- Pinch nutmeg
- 1 unbaked pie shell

Beat eggs slightly. Mix in sugar, salt, milk, vanilla, and nutmeg. Pour into unbaked pie shell. Bake at 400° for 25-30 minutes.

Bernice Schroll
Contributed by N. Elizabeth Graber
Wayland, Iowa
Iowa MCC Relief Sale, Iowa City

GRANDMA'S EGG CUSTARD PIE

- 3 large eggs
- ½ cup sugar
- ½ teaspoon salt
- 2⅔ cups milk
- 1 teaspoon vanilla
- 1 unbaked pie shell

Beat eggs slightly. Beat in sugar, salt, milk, and vanilla. Pour into pastry-lined pie pan. Bake at 350° for 15 minutes. Reduce heat to 325° and bake 25 minutes more or just until silver knife inserted in custard comes out clean. Serve cold.

Ethel P. Thomas
Johnstown, Pennsylvania
MCC Quilt Auction and Relief Sale, Johnstown

ENGLISH WALNUT PIE

- 1 rounded tablespoon flour
- ¼ cup sugar
- ⅛ teaspoon salt
- 3 eggs, well beaten
- ¼ cup water
- 1 cup King syrup (you choose type)
- 2 tablespoons butter, melted (do not use margarine)
- 1 cup chopped walnut meats
- 1 unbaked 9-10 inch pie shell

Combine flour, sugar, and salt. Add beaten eggs. Combine water, syrup, and butter. Mix well with eggs. Spread walnuts over bottom of pie shell. Pour filling over nuts. Bake at 425° for 10 minutes. Reduce heat to 350° and bake 35 minutes longer. If crust browns too quickly, cover edges with aluminum foil halfway through baking time.

Erma Kauffman
Cochranville, Pennsylvania
Gap Relief Sale
Gap, Pennsylvania

FRESH PEACH PIE

- 8 cups fresh sliced peaches (about 11 large peaches)
- 2 cups sugar, divided
- 4 tablespoons flour
- 2 eggs
- 1 teaspoon vanilla
- 1 teaspoon salt
- 2 cups sour cream

Topping:
- ⅔ cup brown sugar
- ⅔ cup flour (double if desired)
- ¼ cup butter
- 1 teaspoon cinnamon

Slice peaches and place in a bowl. Sprinkle with ½ cup sugar and let stand. Combine 1½ cups sugar, flour, eggs, and salt. Fold in sour cream and vanilla. Stir into peaches. Pour into 3 9-inch baking pans. Bake at 400° for 15 minutes, then reduce heat to 350° until done (about 1½ hours). Mix topping ingredients and pour over top.

Makes about 5 regular pies.

Amish Cook
Paradise, Pennsylvania

NO ONE IS USELESS IN THIS WORLD WHO LIGHTENS THE BURDEN OF IT FOR SOMEONE ELSE.

GRAPE PIE

Pie:
- ❖ Grapes
- ❖ 1 egg
- ❖ 1 cup sugar
- ❖ 2 tablespoons flour
- ❖ 1 tablespoon butter
- ❖ 1 tablespoon lemon juice

Crumbs:
- ❖ ¼ cup flour
- ❖ ¼ cup sugar
- ❖ 2 tablespoons butter

Topping:
- ❖ 1 egg white, beaten
- ❖ 2 tablespoons sugar

Wash the desired amount of grapes and squeeze the pulp from the skins. Cook pulp 5 minutes and press through a sieve to separate the seeds. Beat the egg. Add the sugar, flour, butter, and lemon juice. Add the skins and the pulp. Pour into unbaked pie shell and cover with a lattice top of pastry strips or top with crumbs, made by combining the listed ingredients. Bake. Combine ingredients for topping and serve with pie.

GRASSHOPPER PIE

- ❖ 24 cream-filled chocolate cookies, crushed
- ❖ ¼ cup margarine, melted
- ❖ ¼ cup milk
- ❖ Few drops peppermint extract
- ❖ Few drops green food coloring
- ❖ 1 jar marshmallow creme
- ❖ 2 cups heavy cream, whipped

Combine cookie crumbs and margarine. Press into 9-inch spring pan, reserving ½ cup of mixture for topping. Gradually add milk, extract, and food coloring to marshmallow creme. Mix until well blended. Fold in whipped cream. Pour into pan and sprinkle with remaining crumbs. Freeze. Remove 30 minutes before serving.

GROUND CHERRY PIE

- ❖ 1½ cups cooked ground cherries
- ❖ ¾ cup sugar
- ❖ 3 tablespoons Minute tapioca
- ❖ Pastry for double-crust pie

Mix filling ingredients. Pour into a pastry-lined pie pan. Add upper crust and bake 45 minutes.

Mrs. Helen Schmidt
Marion, South Dakota

∞

LEMON SPONGE PIE

- 2 egg yolks
- Grated rind and juice of 1 lemon
- 1 cup sugar
- 3 tablespoons flour
- 3 tablespoons butter
- ¼ teaspoon salt
- 1 cup milk
- 2 beaten egg whites

Beat all the ingredients, except the egg whites, together in order given. Then add the egg whites. Pour into unbaked pie shell. Preheat oven to 425°. Put pies in and reduce to 250° for 40 minutes.

MAPLE WALNUT OR PECAN PIE

- 3 eggs
- ¾ cup brown sugar
- 2 tablespoons flour
- 1¼ cups maple syrup (mix with corn syrup if you wish)
- ¼ cup melted butter
- 1½ cups coarsely cut walnuts or pecans (or more)

Beat eggs and add brown sugar, flour, maple syrup, and butter. Stir in the walnuts or pecans. Pour into an unbaked 10-inch pie shell. Sprinkle remaining nuts on top. Bake at 400° for 10 minutes, then 375° for 30 minutes.

MONTGOMERY COUNTY OR LEMON DROP PIE

Sauce:
- Juice and rind of 2 lemons
- 2 cups sugar
- 2 tablespoons flour
- 3 beaten eggs
- 4 cups milk

Dough:
- ½ cup butter
- 1 cup sugar
- ½ cup sweet milk
- 1 teaspoon soda
- 1¼ cups flour

Make the sauce by cooking the juice and rind of the lemons with the sugar, flour, eggs, and milk in a double boiler (sauce should be thin). Make the dough by creaming the butter and sugar. Add the milk and soda, which has been sifted into the flour. Mix until it forms a soft dough. Divide sauce evenly into 3 9-inch pie plates. Drop spoonfuls of dough evenly on each plate. Do not stir. Bake at 425° for 10 minutes and at 350° for 30 minutes.

MINCEMEAT

- 1½ pounds beef
- 1½ pounds pork
- ½ pound suet
- 2 pounds seedless raisins
- 2 pounds currants
- 2 pounds granulated sugar
- 1 pound brown sugar
- 2 oranges
- 2 lemons
- ½ pound citron peel
- 2 quarts peeled and cored apples
- 1 cup molasses
- 2 teaspoons ground cloves
- 3 teaspoons cinnamon
- 3 teaspoons nutmeg
- 1 cup cider

Cook beef, pork, and suet until tender. Mince fine or put through chopper. Put the apples, oranges, and lemons through chopper. Mix all ingredients thoroughly. Bring to a boil and simmer 12 minutes. Put in jars and seal while hot.

PEACH COBBLER

Bottom Layer:
- 5 cups sliced peaches
- ¾ cup sugar
- 2 tablespoons flour
- ½ teaspoon cinnamon
- ¼ teaspoon salt
- 1 teaspoon vanilla
- 1 tablespoon butter

Upper Layer:
- 1 cup flour
- 1 cup sugar
- 1 teaspoon baking powder
- ½ teaspoon salt
- 4 tablespoons butter
- 2 eggs, slightly beaten

Mix ingredients for bottom layer together and pour into a 9x13-inch pan. Mix together ingredients for upper layer and pour over ingredients in pan. Bake at 350° for 30-35 minutes.

Amish Cook
New Providence, Pennsylvania

Peanut Butter Pie

- 2 egg yolks
- 1½ cups scalded milk
- 1 cup brown sugar
- 3 tablespoons peanut butter
- 1 tablespoon flour or 1½ teaspoons cornstarch
- ¼ teaspoon salt
- 1 baked pie shell

Combine egg yolks, milk, sugar, peanut butter, flour, and salt. Cook until thickened, stirring often. Cool slightly. Pour into baked pie shell. Top with your favorite meringue. Place in a hot oven just long enough to brown meringue.

Bernice Schroll
Contributed by N. Elizabeth Graber
Wayland, Iowa
Iowa MCC Relief Sale, Iowa City

Perischke

- 9 cups flour
- 4½ cups shortening, at room temperature
- ½ teaspoon baking powder
- 1 tablespoon salt
- 2 tablespoons vinegar
- 3 eggs
- 2 cups milk
- Sugar/cinnamon mixture

Mix dough ingredients as you would for a pie dough. Roll out. Cut into 5-inch squares. Prepare a filling by cooking dried apricots, prunes, raisins, peaches, or any combination of dried fruits with just enough water and sugar to make a jam-like filling. Put several tablespoons of filling in the center of each square. Fold corners into middle and seal. Bake at 375°-400° for about 25 minutes. Make a fresh apple filling, if desired, by spreading sliced apples in center of dough square. Sprinkle with sugar and cinnamon.

Makes enough dough for 40-50 pies.

Minn-Kota MCC Relief Sale
Sioux Falls, South Dakota

Poppy Seed Pie

- 1 cup poppy seeds
- 4 egg yolks
- 3 cups milk
- 2 cups cream
- 2 cups sugar
- 1 teaspoon vanilla
- 2 tablespoons cornstarch
- 2 tablespoons flour
- 3 baked pie shells

Mix together all filling ingredients. Cook until thick. Divide evenly among the 3 baked pie shells. Make your favorite egg white meringue to spread over each pie. Brown meringue in hot oven.

Pant Hofer
Carpenter, South Dakota

PUMPKIN PIE

- ❖ 1½ cups cooked pumpkin
- ❖ 1 teaspoon flour
- ❖ 1 cup sugar
- ❖ 1 teaspoon cinnamon
- ❖ 1 teaspoon ginger
- ❖ ⅛ teaspoon nutmeg
- ❖ ½ teaspoon mace
- ❖ ¼ teaspoon salt
- ❖ 3 eggs, well beaten
- ❖ ½ cup milk
- ❖ Pastry for deep-dish single-crust pie

Mix pumpkin, flour, sugar, spices, and salt. Combine beaten eggs and milk. Add to pumpkin mixture. Stir it all together. Pour into a deep pie plate lined with a good rich pastry. Bake in a moderate oven (350°) for about 35 minutes.

Altoona Women's Institute Cookbook
(contributed by Mrs. P. L. Dick)
Ben Sawatzky
Winnipeg, Manitoba
MCC Manitoba Relief Sale

CUSTARD PUMPKIN PIE

- ❖ 1 cup cooked pumpkin
- ❖ 3 eggs, separated
- ❖ ½ cup white sugar
- ❖ ½ cup brown sugar
- ❖ 1 tablespoon cornstarch
- ❖ ½ teaspoon salt
- ❖ ¼ teaspoon ginger
- ❖ ¼ teaspoon cloves
- ❖ 1 teaspoon cinnamon
- ❖ 2 cups milk, scalded
- ❖ 1 unbaked 9-inch pie shell

Add beaten egg yolks, sugars, cornstarch, salt, and spices to pumpkin. Gradually add scalded milk, mixing thoroughly. Fold in stiffly beaten egg whites. Pour mixture into unbaked pie shell. Bake at 425° for 10 minutes. Reduce heat to 350° and bake for 30 minutes more.

Mrs. Lovell Franks
East Peoria, Illinois
East Peoria Mennonite Church
Illinois MCC Relief Sale, Peoria

EASY PUMPKIN PIE

- ❖ 1 cup sugar
- ❖ 1-2 eggs
- ❖ 1 cup pumpkin
- ❖ 1 tablespoon flour
- ❖ 1 cup milk
- ❖ 1 egg white
- ❖ Nutmeg
- ❖ Cinnamon

Beat the first 4 ingredients and add the milk. Moisten the unbaked pie shell with the egg white, then add the remainder to the filling. Sprinkle the moist shell with nutmeg. Sprinkle a generous coating of cinnamon over top of pie. Bake at 425º for 10 minutes and reduce to 325º for 25 minutes.

SUGAR-FREE PUMPKIN PIE

- ½ cup baking mix
- 2 beaten eggs or 1 carton egg substitute
- 1 can (16 ounces) pumpkin
- ½ scant cup Sugar Twin or other sugar substitute
- 1 can (12 ounces) evaporated skim milk
- ¼ teaspoon nutmeg
- 1 teaspoon cinnamon
- 2½ teaspoons vanilla

Combine all ingredients. Pour into a greased pie pan. Bake at 350° (325° for a glass pie plate) for 1 hour.

Rosalie R. Forrester
Bloomington, Illinois
Faith Evangelical Mennonite Church
Illinois MCC Relief Sale, Peoria

PINEAPPLE BAVARIAN PIE

Crust:
- 1½ cups graham cracker crumbs
- ¼ cup butter
- ¼ cup brown sugar

Filling:
- 1¼ cups crushed pineapple
- 1 package lemon gelatin
- ½ cup sugar
- ½ teaspoon lemon rind
- 3 teaspoons lemon juice
- 1 cup chilled evaporated milk

Combine ingredients for crust, press into 9-inch plate, and bake 10 minutes at 350°. To make the filling, bring the pineapple to a boil. Add the gelatin, sugar, lemon rind, and 2 teaspoons lemon juice. Stir until all is dissolved. Cool until it thickens slightly. Add 1 tablespoon lemon juice to the milk. Beat until stiff. Fold into chilled pineapple mixture. Chill slightly. Pour into graham cracker shell and chill until time to serve.

RASPBERRY CREAM PIE

- ¾ quart raspberries (frozen may be used)
- 3 tablespoons flour
- ¾ cup brown sugar
- ½ cup white sugar
- Milk
- Sour cream

Line a 9-inch pie dish with dough. Pour berries in and sprinkle with flour and sugar. Add milk until the dish is almost full. Pour sour cream around the top of the berries. Bake at 400° for 10 minutes, then at 350° until done.

Frances H. Martin
Quarryville, Pennsylvania

℃

RHUBARB PIE WITH MERINGUE

- ❖ 1 10-inch pastry shell
- ❖ 3 cups finely cut strawberry and rhubarb
- ❖ 1¼ cups sugar
- ❖ 3 tablespoons flour
- ❖ 1 tablespoon lemon or orange rind and juice
- ❖ 1½ teaspoons salt
- ❖ 2 eggs, separated
- ❖ 3 tablespoons sugar
- ❖ ½ teaspoon cornstarch
- ❖ ¼ teaspoon baking powder

Fill the pastry shell with the rhubarb/strawberry mixture. Mix together the sugar, flour, lemon rind and juice, salt, and egg yolks. Pour this over the rhubarb and bake at 425° for 10 minutes, then at 375° for 30 minutes. When the pie is nearly baked, beat the reserved egg whites stiff. Add the sugar, cornstarch, and baking powder. Pour over baked pie and brown in the oven until golden peaks appear. The above meringue can be used on any pie.

SHOOFLY PIE

Pie Filling:
- ❖ ⅔ teaspoon soda
- ❖ ¼ cup hot water
- ❖ 1 cup maple syrup (mix with corn syrup if you wish)
- ❖ ¾ cup cold water

Crumb Mixture:
- ❖ 1 cup pastry flour
- ❖ ⅔ cup brown sugar
- ❖ ¼ teaspoon salt
- ❖ 2 tablespoons butter

Dissolve the soda in the hot water. Mix with maple syrup and cold water. Make the crumb mixture by working the butter into the flour, sugar, and salt with fingertips. Remove about ⅔ cup crumbs and mix the rest with the pie filling. Pour into the pie shell. Sprinkle the reserved crumbs over top. Bake at 425° for 20 minutes and at 325° for 20 minutes.

Sour Cream Elderberry Pie

- 1 cup sugar
- 2 tablespoons flour
- 1 cup sour cream
- 2 cups elderberries

Combine the sugar, flour, sour cream, and elderberries. Pour into 9-inch pie shell and bake at 425° for 15 minutes, then at 350°-375° for 30 minutes.

Strawberry Pie

- 1 quart strawberries
- ½ cup water
- 3 tablespoons cornstarch
- 1 cup sugar
- 1 tablespoon butter
- 1 tablespoon lemon juice
- Few grains salt

Sort the strawberries into 2 equal parts. Crush the part that has the less perfect berries. Cut the remaining berries into quarters or halves depending on size. Add the water mixed with the cornstarch to the crushed berries. Cook until thick and clear. Add the sugar, butter, lemon juice, and a few grains salt. Cool. Add reserved cut berries. Pour into baked shell. Chill. Serve with whipped cream.

Vanilla Pie

Filling:
- 2 cups brown sugar
- 5 tablespoons flour
- 1 cup maple syrup
- 4 cups hot water
- 2 teaspoons vanilla
- 3 unbaked pie shells

Crumbs:
- 2 cups flour
- 1 cup brown sugar
- 1 teaspoon soda
- 1 teaspoon cream of tartar
- 1 cup butter

To make the filling, mix the brown sugar and the flour. Add the maple syrup and hot water. Cook until starch is cooked and is syrupy. Cool and add the vanilla. Make the crumb mixture by using fingertips to blend the flour, brown sugar, soda, cream of tartar, and butter. Divide the filling into 3 unbaked pie shells. Divide the crumbs and sprinkle over the 3 pies. Bake at 425° for 10 minutes and reduce to 325° for 25 minutes.

ANHALTSKUCHEN (LOAF CAKE TOPPED WITH ALMONDS)

- 1 cup butter
- 2 cups sugar
- 6 eggs
- 2 cups enriched flour, sifted
- ¼ teaspoon almond extract
- 1 package (2¼ ounces) slivered almonds or ½ cup

Cream butter and sugar well. Add eggs and beat until light and fluffy. Add flour and almond extract. Mix well. Spoon into greased 5½x9-inch loaf pan. Smooth batter to sides, leaving the center somewhat hollowed out so that loaf will be level after baking. Sprinkle almonds over batter. Bake at 325° for about 1 hour or until golden brown. Cool on rack. To serve, cut into slices.

Makes about 16 slices.

Mrs. Lawrence (Ann) Reimer
Beatrice, Nebraska

ALMOND TORTE

Batter:
- ½ pound unblanched almonds, finely ground
- 1 cup sugar
- 6 whole eggs
- 5 egg whites, beaten stiff
- 1 teaspoon baking powder
- 1 cup fine dry bread crumbs

Filling:
- 1 cup milk
- 1 cup triple strength coffee
- 1 package vanilla pudding
- 1 package unflavored gelatin
- 1 cup whipping cream

To prepare batter, beat sugar into whole eggs. Add almonds, crumbs, and baking powder. Fold in egg whites. Pour into shallow cake pan. Bake at 325° until done. Cool completely. To prepare filling, add milk and coffee to pudding. Mix and bring to boil. During boiling, soak gelatin in cold water. Add to pudding, stirring occasionally to avoid lumps. Cool completely. Whip whipping cream and fold into pudding. Slice cake and spread mixture between layers and on top. Garnish with finely grated chocolate.

Angel Food Cake

- 2 cups egg whites
  (1 dozen jumbo eggs)
- 2 teaspoons cream of tartar
- ½ teaspoon salt
- 2 cups sugar
- 2 cups cake flour sifted
  with ½ cup sugar
- 2 teaspoons vanilla

Beat egg whites until foamy. Add cream of tartar and beat just until stiff enough to stand in peaks. Add salt. Slowly add the 2 cups sugar, continuing to beat until stiff peaks form. Fold in flour-sugar mixture and, finally, vanilla. Put in tube pan and into cold oven. Turn heat to 350° for 20 minutes, then to 350°-375° for 10-15 minutes. Invert cake to cool.

Ethel P. Thomas
Johnstown, Pennsylvania
MCC Quilt Auction and Relief Sale, Johnstown

Sauce for Angel Food Cake

- ½ cup white sugar
- 2 tablespoons cornstarch
- 1 egg
- 1 cup pineapple juice
  or diluted lemon juice
- 1 envelope prepared whipped
  topping mix

Cook over low heat until mixture thickens. Remove from heat and cool. Mix with whipped topping.

Banana Cake

- ⅔ cup soft shortening
- 2½ cups cake flour
- 1⅔ cups sugar
- 1¼ teaspoons baking powder
- 1 teaspoon soda
- 1 teaspoon salt
- 1¼ cups mashed bananas
- ⅓ cup buttermilk
- 2 eggs

Measure shortening into a large mixing bowl. Sift flour, sugar, baking powder, soda, and salt. Add to shortening. Add mashed bananas. Use beater to blend all, then beat 2 minutes on medium speed. Add buttermilk and eggs. Beat 2 minutes longer. Bake at 350° in 2 9-inch layer pans or a 9x13-inch pan.

Black Chocolate Cake with Mocha Icing

Batter:
- ❖ 2 cups sifted cake flour
- ❖ 1 cup white sugar
- ❖ 2 teaspoons soda
- ❖ ½ teaspoon salt
- ❖ ¼ cup cocoa
- ❖ 1 cup cold water
- ❖ 1 cup salad dressing
- ❖ 1 teaspoon vanilla

Icing:
- ❖ 2 tablespoons butter
- ❖ 2 tablespoons cocoa
- ❖ ½ cup powdered sugar
- ❖ 3 tablespoons strong hot coffee
- ❖ ¼ teaspoon vanilla
- ❖ Pinch of salt

Mix dry ingredients. Blend in wet ingredients. Do not beat. Bake at 350° for at least 45 minutes or until the center springs back when touched. Cool. Mix icing ingredients and spread over cake.

BLACK FOREST TORTE

Batter:
- 1 cup flour
- 2 teaspoons baking powder
- ½ teaspoon salt
- ⅓ cup dry cocoa
- 3 eggs
- 1 teaspoon vanilla
- 1 cup sugar
- ½ cup boiling water

Filling Ingredients:
- Butter Cream (instructions below)
- 1 can cherry pie filling
- 1½ cups whipping cream or
  3 packages whipped topping mix
- Maraschino cherries in juice
- 1 square semisweet chocolate

Butter Cream:
- 1 package chocolate pudding mix
- 2 cups milk
- ⅔ cup soft butter

Combine flour, baking powder, salt, and cocoa. Stir well to blend and set aside. Beat eggs and vanilla until thick. Add sugar gradually and continue beating. Add dry ingredients with mixer at low speed. Add boiling water. Mix well. Pour batter into 2 large round cake pans. Bake at 400° for 20 minutes. Prepare butter cream by cooking pudding. Cool. Cream butter and beat in cooled pudding. If necessary, refrigerate until butter cream reaches spreading consistency. After cake cools, split each layer in half. Place bottom layer on large cake plate. Cover with a layer of butter cream, then one-third can of cherry pie filling. Continue in this way until all but 1 cake layer is used. Whip cream and add 2 tablespoons cherry juice. Spread one-fourth of cream on cake. Top with last layer. Cover entire cake with cream. Chill for several hours. At serving time, place some maraschino cherries around top of cake and sprinkle with grated chocolate.

CHOCOLATE APPLESAUCE CAKE

- ½ cup shortening
- 2 unbeaten eggs
- 2 cups applesauce
- 2 cups flour
- 1½ cups sugar
- 1½ teaspoons baking soda
- 2 tablespoons cocoa
- ½ teaspoon cinnamon
- ½ teaspoon ground allspice
- ½ teaspoon ground cloves
- ½ teaspoon ground nutmeg
- ½ cup chopped nuts
- 1 package (6 ounces)
  chocolate chips
- 2 tablespoons sugar

Beat together shortening, eggs, and applesauce. Add flour, the 1½ cups sugar, baking soda, cocoa, and spices. Spread batter in greased and floured 9x13-inch pan. Top batter with nuts, chocolate chips, and the 2 tablespoons sugar. Bake at 350° for 40 minutes.

Linda King
Roanoke, Illinois
Metamora Mennonite Church
Illinois MCC Relief Sale, Peoria

GRANDMOTHER CRESSMAN'S APPLESAUCE CAKE

- ❖ ½ cup plus 1 tablespoon shortening
- ❖ 1 cup brown sugar
- ❖ 1 egg, beaten
- ❖ 2 cups sifted pastry flour
- ❖ 1 teaspoon soda
- ❖ 3 tablespoons cocoa
- ❖ ½ teaspoon salt
- ❖ 1 teaspoon cinnamon
- ❖ ¼ teaspoon cloves
- ❖ 1 cup applesauce (unsweetened preferred)
- ❖ 1 cup chopped raisins, slightly floured

Cream shortening and add sugar gradually. Beat until light. Add beaten egg and beat again. Add sifted dry ingredients alternately with applesauce. Fold in raisins. Bake in loaf, square, or cupcake pan at 350°.

'BAKED-ON' FROSTING FOR AN APPLESAUCE CAKE

- ❖ 1 egg white
- ❖ ¼ teaspoon baking powder
- ❖ ¾ cup brown sugar
- ❖ ¼ cup chopped nuts

Beat egg white until frothy. Add baking powder and beat until stiff. Gradually add brown sugar and beat until creamy. Spread over hot (baked) cake. Sprinkle with nuts. Return cake to 350° oven and bake just until topping bubbles and turns light brown.

Margarete (Claassen, Goertz) Penner
Contributed by Faye Claassen
Albany, Oregon
Oregon MCC Fall Festival, Albany

IF YOU WANT GOOD ADVICE,
CONSULT AN OLD MAN.

CHRISTMAS CAKE

- 2 pounds raisins
- ½ pound glazed cherries
- ½ pound candied pineapple, diced
- 1½ pounds dates
- 1 pound gumdrops
- 1 pound mixed peel
- 1 pound mixed fruit
- ½ pound almonds
- ½ cup corn syrup
- 1 teaspoon each of cinnamon, cloves, nutmeg, ground allspice, and salt
- 12 eggs, separated
- 1 pound white sugar
- 1 pound butter
- 1 teaspoon soda
- 3¼ cups flour

Cream butter, sugar, egg yolks, and corn syrup. Add half of flour to fruit. Add remaining flour, soda, and spices. Mix all together. Add stiff egg whites. Bake 2 hours (1 hour at 350° and 1 hour at 300°). Add pan of water to oven while baking.

CRANBERRY CAKE

- 2 cups flour
- ½ teaspoon salt
- 2 teaspoons baking powder
- 1½ cups sugar
- ¼ cup soft butter or margarine
- 1 cup milk
- 3 cups whole raw cranberries

Butter Sauce:
- ½ cup butter
- 1 cup sugar
- 1 tablespoon cornstarch
- ½ cup whipping cream
- 1 teaspoon vanilla

Mix cake ingredients, adding cranberries last. Pour into greased 13x9-inch pan. Bake at 375°. Mix all sauce ingredients (except vanilla) and bring to a boil. Remove from heat and stir in vanilla. Serve warm over cake.

Serves 12-15.

Arlene Dick
Mountain Lake, Minnesota
Minn-Kota MCC Relief Sale
Sioux Falls, South Dakota

DOWN-SIDE UP FUDGE CAKE

- ❖ 1 tablespoon solid vegetable shortening
- ❖ ¾ cup white sugar
- ❖ ½ cup milk
- ❖ 1 teaspoon vanilla
- ❖ 1 cup flour
- ❖ 1½ tablespoons cocoa
- ❖ 1 teaspoon baking powder
- ❖ ½ teaspoon salt

Topping:
- ❖ ½ cup chopped nuts
- ❖ ¼ cup cocoa
- ❖ ½ cup white sugar
- ❖ ½ cup brown sugar
- ❖ 1¼ cups boiling water

To make the cake batter, cream shortening and sugar. Stir in milk and vanilla. Sift together flour, cocoa, baking powder, and salt. Add to creamed mixture, mixing thoroughly. Pour into greased 8-inch square pan. Top batter with nuts. Combine cocoa and sugars and sprinkle evenly over nuts. Pour the boiling water (be sure it's boiling) over batter and topping. Bake at 350° for 35 minutes. Cool 15 minutes, then invert cake onto serving plate. Serve plain or with whipped topping. You can decrease the amount of cocoa, if desired, and omit the nuts.

E.A.F.
MCC Quilt Auction and Relief Sale
Johnstown, Pennsylvania

FRUIT COCKTAIL CAKE

Batter:
- ❖ 2 large eggs
- ❖ 1½ cups white sugar
- ❖ 2 cups unsifted all-purpose flour
- ❖ 2 teaspoons soda

Topping:
- ❖ ¼ pound butter
- ❖ 1 cup white sugar
- ❖ ½ cup evaporated milk
- ❖ 1 cup coconut
- ❖ 1 teaspoon vanilla
- ❖ ¾ cup chopped nuts

To prepare batter, beat eggs and sugar. Sift together flour and soda. Add dry ingredients to first mixture alternately with 1 can (14 ounces) fruit cocktail (include syrup). Bake at 350° in 9x13-inch pan. To prepare topping, mix all ingredients in a small saucepan. Boil together 2 minutes and spread on warm cake.

Graham Wafer Cake

Batter:
- 1 cup white sugar
- ½ cup shortening or butter
- l egg
- 2 cups graham wafer crumbs, rolled fine
- 2 tablespoons flour
- 1½ teaspoons baking powder
- 1 cup coconut
- 1 cup milk
- Vanilla
- Pinch of salt

Topping:
- 2 cups brown sugar
- 4 tablespoons butter or margarine
- 2 tablespoons flour
- 6 tablespoons cream or milk
- Vanilla

Beat sugar, shortening, and egg. Add milk and dry ingredients. Bake 45 minutes at 350°. (Graham wafers can be substituted with vanilla wafers.) Cook topping ingredients (except vanilla) until they boil. Boil 1 minute and remove from heat. Add vanilla and beat until shine begins to disappear. Spread quickly over cake.

Grandma's Cocoa Cake

- l egg
- 1 cup sugar
- ½ cup lard
- 1 teaspoon salt
- 5 heaping teaspoons cocoa
- 1 cup sour milk
- 1 teaspoon soda
- 2 cups (scant) flour
- 1 teaspoon vanilla

Mix in order given. Bake in a slow oven.

GRANNY CAKE

- ❖ 1½ cups white sugar
- ❖ 2 teaspoons baking soda
- ❖ 2 cups flour
- ❖ ½ teaspoon salt
- ❖ 2 eggs, beaten
- ❖ 1 can (20 ounces) crushed pineapple
- ❖ ½ cup brown sugar
- ❖ ½ cup chopped nuts

Glaze:
- ❖ ½ cup sugar
- ❖ 1 stick (½ cup) margarine
- ❖ 1 cup evaporated milk
- ❖ 1 teaspoon vanilla

Stir together the white sugar, baking soda, flour, and salt. Add eggs and pineapple. Mix well. Pour into a 13x9-inch pan. Sprinkle brown sugar and nuts over batter. Bake at 350° for 35-40 minutes. About 20 minutes before cake is finished baking, prepare glaze. Combine sugar, margarine, and milk in a saucepan. Bring to a boil and boil 15 minutes. Remove from heat and stir in vanilla. Pour glaze over hot cake when you take it from oven.

Makes 24 servings.

Sherry Troyer
Mio, Michigan

GREAT-GRANDMOTHER TROYER'S EGGLESS WONDER SPICE CAKE

- ❖ 1¾ cups granulated sugar
- ❖ ⅓ cup margarine or ¼ cup lard
- ❖ 3 cups all-purpose flour
- ❖ ½ teaspoon salt
- ❖ 1½ teaspoons cinnamon
- ❖ ½ teaspoon ground nutmeg
- ❖ ¼ teaspoon ground cloves
- ❖ 2 cups buttermilk
- ❖ 2 teaspoons baking soda

Topping/Filling:
- ❖ ⅔ cup granulated sugar
- ❖ 3 tablespoons cornstarch
- ❖ 1¼ cups apple juice
- ❖ 1 cup raisins, plumped
- ❖ 2 tablespoons margarine or butter

Cream together sugar and margarine. Sift together flour, salt, and spices. Stir together buttermilk and baking soda. Add buttermilk and flour mixtures alternately to the creamed mixture, beating well after each addition. Pour batter into 2 greased and floured 8-inch round cake pans. Bake at 350° for 30-35 minutes or until toothpick inserted in center comes out clean. To make topping/filling, combine sugar and cornstarch. Add juice and raisins. Cook over medium heat, stirring frequently, until thick. Add margarine and remove from heat. Cool slightly. Spread between layers and over top of cake (topping will drizzle down sides of cake). For a chocolate version of this cake, reduce flour to 2½ cups, add ½ cup cocoa, and omit the spices.

Topping developed by
great-granddaughter Janelle Claassen
Newberg, Oregon
Oregon MCC Fall Festival, Albany

Jelly Roll

- 6 eggs, separated
- 1 cup sugar
- 1 cup white flour
- 1 teaspoon baking powder
- 1 teaspoon vanilla
- 1 can lemon pie filling or jar strawberry jam

Beat egg whites until very stiff. Add sugar. Beat egg yolks and mix into beaten whites. Add flour, baking powder, and vanilla. Mix well. Line a rimmed cookie sheet with waxed paper or spray with cooking spray. Spread batter over sheet. Bake at 325°-350° for 10-15 minutes. Remove from cookie sheet immediately after baking and place on counter, which has been spread with sugar. (This coats the outside of the jelly roll with sugar.) Spread pie filling or jam on cake. Roll up.

Mary B. Duerksen
Mountain Lake, Minnesota
Minn-Kota MCC Relief Sale
Sioux Falls, South Dakota

Karovei

- 2 cups cream
- 2 cups sugar
- Half a stick (¼ cup) butter
- ¼ cup lard
- 2½ teaspoons salt
- 3 large eggs
- 2 cups flour
- 3 packages yeast
- Additional flour (to make a soft dough)

Mix cream, 1½ cups of the sugar, butter, lard, and salt. Bring to a boil. Remove from heat and let cool to lukewarm. Beat eggs and mix in remaining ½ cup sugar. Let stand. Make a sponge of the 2 cups flour, yeast, and enough lukewarm water to make a fairly thick batter. Let sponge rise until cream mixture is lukewarm. Stir cream and egg mixtures into sponge. Stir in enough additional flour to make a soft dough. Knead dough twice at 25 minute intervals. Let rise in a warm place for about 3 hours. Divide dough among 10-12 pie pans, spreading to cover bottom of pan. Let rise until double in size (about 3 hours). Bake at 325°-350° for 20 minutes. Cool. Ice with your favorite frosting. Decorate with candy corn, another decorative candy, or with colored sugar.

Makes 10-12 cakes.

Mid-Kansas MCC Relief Sale, Hutchinson

LAZY DAISY OATMEAL CAKE

Batter:
- ❖ 1¼ cups boiling water
- ❖ 1 cup oatmeal
- ❖ ½ cup shortening
- ❖ 1 cup white sugar
- ❖ 1 cup brown sugar, packed
- ❖ 1 teaspoon vanilla
- ❖ 2 eggs
- ❖ 1½ cups sifted flour
- ❖ 1 teaspoon soda
- ❖ ½ teaspoon salt
- ❖ ¾ teaspoon cinnamon
- ❖ ¼ teaspoon nutmeg

Topping:
- ❖ ¼ cup melted butter
- ❖ ½ cup brown sugar
- ❖ 3 tablespoons cream
- ❖ ⅓ cup chopped nutmeats
- ❖ ¾ cup coconut

Pour water over oatmeal. Cover and let stand 20 minutes. Beat shortening until creamy. Gradually add sugars and beat until fluffy. Blend in vanilla and eggs. Add oat mixture. Mix well. Sift together dry ingredients and add to creamed mixture. Mix well. Pour into greased and floured 9-inch pan. Bake at 350° for 50 minutes. Combine all topping ingredients and spread over warm cake. Broil until frosting becomes bubbly and lightly browned.

MARBLE CHIFFON CAKE

- ❖ ½ cup cocoa
- ❖ ¼ cup white sugar
- ❖ ¼ cup boiling water
- ❖ ¼ teaspoon red food coloring
- ❖ 2¼ cups cake flour
- ❖ 1½ cups sugar
- ❖ 1 teaspoon salt
- ❖ 3 teaspoons baking powder
- ❖ ½ cup corn oil
- ❖ 5 unbeaten egg yolks
- ❖ ¾ cup cold water
- ❖ 2 teaspoons vanilla
- ❖ ½ teaspoon cream of tartar
- ❖ 1 cup egg whites

Combine cocoa, white sugar, boiling water, and food coloring. Stir until smooth and set aside. Measure and sift flour, sugar, salt, and baking powder into small bowl. Make a well and add in order corn oil, egg yolks, cold water, and vanilla. Beat until smooth. Measure cream of tartar and egg whites into a large bowl. Beat until very stiff. Pour egg yolk mixture gradually over egg whites. Gently fold just until blended. Do not stir. Place half of batter into another bowl. Pour cocoa mixture over it and blend. Immediately pour alternate layers of dark and white batter into ungreased tube pan. Bake at 325° for 55 minutes.

Maple-Nut Chiffon Cake

Batter:
- 2 cups sifted cake flour
- 1½ cups white sugar
- 3 teaspoons baking powder
- 1 teaspoon salt
- ½ cup salad oil
- 6 egg yolks
- ¾ cup cold water
- 2 teaspoons maple flavoring
- 6 egg whites
- 1 cup ground walnuts
- ½ teaspoon cream of tartar

Icing:
- 1 egg
- ¼ cup butter
- ¼ cup milk
- 1 teaspoon maple flavoring
- 1 pound powdered sugar

Sift first 4 batter ingredients together. Add the next 4 ingredients in order given. Beat until smooth. Combine egg whites and cream of tartar in a large bowl. Beat until very stiff peaks form. Pour egg yolk batter in thin stream over egg whites. Gently fold in until blended. Fold in nuts. Bake in a 10-inch ungreased tube pan at 350° for 60-65 minutes. To prepare icing, beat first 4 icing ingredients until fluffy. Add powdered sugar. Spread on cake.

Miracle Whip Cake

- 2 cups flour
- 1 cup sugar
- ½ cup cocoa
- ¼ teaspoon (level) baking soda
- ½ teaspoon baking powder
- 1 cup Miracle Whip
- 1 cup water
- 1 teaspoon vanilla

Combine all ingredients. Bake at 350° for 30 minutes.

Rosalie R. Forrester
Bloomington, Illinois
Faith Evangelical Mennonite Church
Illinois MCC Relief Sale, Peoria

POOR MAN CAKE

- ❖ 2 cups sugar
- ❖ 4 cups flour
- ❖ 1 teaspoon baking soda
- ❖ 1 teaspoon salt
- ❖ 1 teaspoon cinnamon
- ❖ 1 teaspoon ground nutmeg
- ❖ 1 teaspoon ground cloves
- ❖ 1 box (16 ounces) raisins
- ❖ 2 cups cold water
- ❖ ½ cup solid vegetable shortening
- ❖ 1 cup cold water

In a large mixing bowl, mix together sugar, flour, baking soda, salt, and spices. Place raisins and the 2 cups cold water in a saucepan and boil for 15 minutes. Add shortening and 1 cup cold water. Stir until shortening melts. Pour raisin mixture into dry ingredients and mix well. Bake at 350° for 40-60 minutes for a 13x9-inch pan or 30 minutes for 2 8-inch square pans. (You can also bake the cake in 2 bread/loaf pans.) Test with a toothpick to determine when it is done.

MCC Quilt Auction and Relief Sale
Johnstown, Pennsylvania

PUMPKIN ROLL

- ❖ 3 eggs
- ❖ ⅔ cup cooked pumpkin
- ❖ 1 teaspoon baking powder
- ❖ ¾ cup flour
- ❖ 1 cup sugar
- ❖ 1 teaspoon salt
- ❖ ½ teaspoon cinnamon

Filling:
- ❖ 1 package (8 ounces) cream cheese, softened
- ❖ 2 tablespoons butter, softened
- ❖ 1 teaspoon vanilla
- ❖ 1 cup powdered sugar

Mix all cake ingredients in a bowl with a spoon. Grease a jelly roll pan and line with waxed paper. Spread batter over bottom of pan. Bake at 375° for 15 minutes. Sprinkle powdered sugar on a clean tea towel. Turn pan over on tea towel to remove cake. Roll up as for jelly roll. Let cool. While cake is cooling, prepare filling by beating all ingredients until smooth. Unroll cooled cake and spread filling over inside. Roll back up. Refrigerate until serving time.

Grace Cable
Hollsopple, Pennsylvania
MCC Quilt Auction and Relief Sale, Johnstown

PREACH NOT TO OTHERS WHAT THEY SHOULD EAT,
BUT EAT AS BECOMES YOU, AND BE SILENT.

Queen Elizabeth Cake

Batter:
- ❖ 1 cup boiling water
- ❖ 1 cup chopped dates
- ❖ 1 teaspoon baking soda
- ❖ ¼ cup shortening
- ❖ 1 cup white sugar
- ❖ 1 egg
- ❖ 1 teaspoon vanilla
- ❖ ½ cup walnuts
- ❖ 1½ cups flour
- ❖ 1½ teaspoons baking powder
- ❖ ¼ teaspoon salt

Topping:
- ❖ ¼ cup melted butter
- ❖ ½ cup brown sugar
- ❖ 3 tablespoons cream
- ❖ ⅓ cup chopped nutmeats
- ❖ ¾ cup coconut

Add soda to dates. Pour boiling water over and let cool. Cream shortening. Add sugar and cream well. Beat in egg, vanilla, and salt. Add flour, baking powder, and nuts alternately with date mixture. Bake at 350° for 1 hour in an 8x12-inch pan. Combine all topping ingredients and spread over warm cake. Broil until frosting becomes bubbly and lightly browned.

Raw Apple Cake

- ❖ 3 eggs
- ❖ 2 cups sugar
- ❖ 1½ cups oil
- ❖ 3 cups flour
- ❖ 1 teaspoon soda
- ❖ 1 teaspoon salt
- ❖ 2 teaspoons vanilla
- ❖ 3 cups chopped apples
- ❖ 1½ cups nuts

Topping:
- ❖ 1 cup brown sugar
- ❖ ¼ cup milk
- ❖ ½ cup butter

Mix together eggs, sugar, and oil. Combine flour, soda, salt, vanilla, apples, and nuts. Add to first mixture. Pour into greased angel food cake pan. Bake at 325° for 1 hour 15 minutes. Combine topping ingredients while cake is baking and boil for 2½-3 minutes. While cake is still warm, make holes with a fork and pour topping over top.

Ammon and Rebecca Stoltzfoos
New Providence, Pennsylvania

SAUERKRAUT CAKE

- 2¼ cups all-purpose flour
- ½ cup cocoa
- 1 teaspoon baking powder
- 1 teaspoon soda
- ¼ teaspoon salt
- ⅔ cup sauerkraut (drained and rinsed)
- ⅔ cup butter
- 1½ cups sugar
- 3 large eggs
- 1 teaspoon vanilla
- 1 cup strong cooled coffee or water

Combine first 5 ingredients. Cream butter and sugar. Add in 1 egg at a time. Add vanilla, liquid, and dry ingredients alternately, beginning and ending with flour. Stir in sauerkraut and bake at 350° for 20-25 minutes in a 9x13-inch pan or layer cake pans.

SCHICHTKUCHIN (LAYER CAKE)

- 1 cup butter
- 1½ cups sugar
- 4 eggs
- 3 cups flour
- 3 teaspoons baking powder
- 1 cup milk
- Filling of choice

Cream butter and sugar. Add eggs and beat well. Mix flour and baking powder. Add to creamed mixture alternately with milk. Spreading only a thin layer of batter in each pan, divide batter evenly among 9 greased 8-inch, or 8 greased 9-inch, round cake pans. Bake at 350° for about 10 minutes. Cool. Fill with chocolate, lemon, almond paste, or fruit filling.

Etna Marie Reimer
Nebraska MCC Relief Sale, Aurora

SOUR CREAM COCOA CAKE

- 2½ cups flour
- 2 cups sugar
- 6 tablespoons cocoa
- 2 teaspoons baking soda
- ½ teaspoon salt
- ½ teaspoon cinnamon
- 4 eggs, well beaten
- 2 cups thick sour cream
- 1 teaspoon vanilla

Sift dry ingredients together 3 times. Mix eggs, sour cream, and vanilla. Add to dry ingredients and beat well. Bake at 375° for 35 minutes.

Lanna Waltner
Hurley, South Dakota
Minn-Kota MCC Relief Sale
Sioux Falls, South Dakota

SOUR CREAM SPICE CAKE

- 1 cup brown sugar
- 1 egg
- 1 cup sour cream
- ½ cup raisins
- 1½ cups sifted flour
- ½ teaspoon cream of tartar
- ½ teaspoon salt
- 1 teaspoon cinnamon
- ½ teaspoon ground cloves
- 1 teaspoon baking soda

Beat sugar and egg. Stir in sour cream, then raisins. Add dry ingredients. Spread evenly in greased 9x9-inch pan. Bake for 25 minutes at 350°.

TEXAS CHOCOLATE CAKE

- 2 cups flour
- 2 cups sugar
- 2 sticks (1 cup) margarine
- 3 tablespoons cocoa
- 1 cup water
- ½ cup buttermilk
- 2 eggs
- 1 teaspoon baking soda
- 1 teaspoon vanilla
- ½ teaspoon cinnamon

Icing:
- 3 tablespoons cocoa
- 1 stick (½ cup) butter
- 6 tablespoons milk
- 1 box powdered
  sugar (approximately)
- 1 teaspoon vanilla
- 1 cup chopped nuts (optional)

Sift together flour and sugar. Combine margarine, cocoa, and water and bring to a boil. Pour over flour-sugar mixture. Mix well. Add remaining ingredients. Mix well. Pour into greased and floured 13x9-inch pan. Bake at 350° for 30 minutes. Cool about 15 minutes before icing. About 5 minutes after taking cake from oven, combine cocoa, butter, and milk in a saucepan. Bring to a boil. Remove from heat and beat in powdered sugar in batches until icing is of desired consistency. Add vanilla and nuts toward end. Beat well. Spread icing on warm cake.

Missouri MCC Relief Sale, Harrisonville

WACKY CAKE

- ❖ 3 cups flour
- ❖ 2 cups sugar
- ❖ ½ cup cocoa
- ❖ 2 teaspoons soda
- ❖ 1 teaspoon salt
- ❖ 2 tablespoons vinegar
- ❖ 2 teaspoons vanilla
- ❖ ⅔ cup salad oil
- ❖ 2 cups water

Sift the first 5 ingredients into an ungreased 9x12-inch pan. Mix and make three holes. Pour vinegar, vanilla, and salad oil into holes. Pour water over top and mix until all ingredients are blended. Bake at 350° for 30-35 minutes.

ICING

- ❖ 1 cup milk
- ❖ 5 tablespoons flour
- ❖ ½-1 cup shortening
- ❖ 1 cup sugar
- ❖ Salt
- ❖ Vanilla

Mix milk and flour. Boil until very thick. Cool. Beat shortening. Add sugar and beat until fluffy. Add this slowly to cooked mixture. Beat for 15 minutes. Add salt and vanilla. This will keep in refrigerator for weeks and is ready to use any time.

CHOCOLATE ICING

- ❖ ¼ cup butter
- ❖ ¼ cup cocoa
- ❖ ¼ cup milk
- ❖ Vanilla to taste
- ❖ Powdered sugar to taste

Melt the butter and cocoa in a pan. Move mixture to a small mixing bowl. Start beater and add alternately the milk, vanilla to taste, and enough powdered sugar to create desired consistency.

Maple Cream Icing

- 1 cup brown sugar
- 3 tablespoons milk
- 1 tablespoon butter
- Powdered sugar
- Vanilla or maple flavoring

Mix sugar, milk, and butter in pan. Bring to boil. Remove from heat. Add powdered sugar to make a spreading consistency. Add vanilla or maple flavoring.

Foamy Rum Sauce

- 1 egg, separated
- ½ cup corn syrup
- 2 teaspoons rum extract

Beat the egg white until stiff. Gradually add ¼ cup corn syrup, beating constantly. Beat the egg yolk until lemon colored. Gradually add ¼ cup corn syrup and the rum extract. Fold egg yolk mixture into stiffly beaten egg white mixture and serve.

CB

APPLE BUTTER PUDDING

- ❖ 2 eggs
- ❖ 1 cup brown sugar
- ❖ 3 tablespoons apple butter
- ❖ 1 cup sour cream
- ❖ 2 cups pastry flour
- ❖ 1 teaspoon soda
- ❖ ½ teaspoon cloves
- ❖ ¼ teaspoon nutmeg
- ❖ 1 teaspoon cinnamon
- ❖ ¾ cup raisins, lightly floured

Beat the eggs, brown sugar, apple butter, and cream well in order given. Sift together and add the flour, soda, cloves, nutmeg, and cinnamon. Add the raisins. Pour into greased casserole, cover with wax paper, and steam 1½ hours. Serve with milk (sweetened).

APPLE CRISP

- ❖ 3¾ gallons (16 pounds) apples, pared and sliced
- ❖ ⅓ cup lemon juice
- ❖ 2 cups water
- ❖ 1 quart rolled wheat or 1 quart plus ¾ cup rolled oats
- ❖ 6 pounds brown sugar
- ❖ 1½ quarts flour
- ❖ 2⅔ tablespoons cinnamon
- ❖ 2 teaspoons salt
- ❖ 2½ pounds butter or margarine

Divide apples evenly among 4 greased baking pans (each about 20x12x2 inches). Mix lemon juice and water. Pour over apples. Thoroughly combine wheat, sugar, flour, cinnamon, and salt. Mix in butter until crumbly. Cover apples with topping (use about 2 quarts per pan). Bake at 350° for 40-60 minutes or until apples are soft and top crust is browned and slightly cracked. Let cool before cutting. Serve while still warm, topped with whipped topping or ice cream.

Serves 100.

Martha Tschetter
Freeman, South Dakota
Minn-Kota MCC Relief Sale
Sioux Falls, South Dakota

Apple Dumplings

- 2 cups flour
- 2 teaspoons baking powder
- 1 teaspoon salt
- ½ cup shortening
- ½ cup milk
- Half or whole apples, cored

Sauce:
- 2 cups brown sugar
- 2 cups water
- ½ teaspoon cinnamon

Sift together the flour, baking powder, and salt. Add the shortening and blend as for pastry. Add the milk and blend. Pat into a ball, roll out, and cut into squares large enough to cover a half or whole cored apple (pie pastry may also be used). Place half or whole apples on dough squares. Bring corners of dough together at apple top and pinch together. Combine ingredients for sauce. Cook and simmer for 5 minutes. Pour sauce into baking dish. Place apple dumplings on top. Bake at 425° for 10 minutes, then at 375° until apples are soft (about 30 minutes).

Apple Pudding

- ½ cup butter
- 1 cup sugar
- 2 eggs, beaten
- 1 cup sour cream
- 2 cups sifted flour
- 1 teaspoon baking powder
- 1 teaspoon baking soda
- ½ teaspoon salt
- 1 teaspoon vanilla
- 2-3 apples, peeled and cored
- ¼ cup sugar
- ½ teaspoon cinnamon

Cream together the butter and 1 cup sugar. Add the eggs and sour cream. Sift together and add the flour, baking powder, baking soda, and salt. Beat until batter is light and add the vanilla. Slice the apples and toss in a mixture of ¼ cup sugar and the cinnamon. Pour more than half the batter into a warm and greased pan (9-inch square). Arrange apple slices evenly over batter and top with remaining batter. Bake at 350° for 30 minutes. Reduce heat to 325° and continue to bake 14 minutes longer. Sprinkle additional sugar and cinnamon over top of cake and serve warm with milk.

THE GEM CANNOT BE POLISHED WITHOUT FRICTION,
NOR THE MAN PERFECTED WITHOUT TRIALS.

BAVARIAN CREAM

- 1 envelope unflavored gelatin
- ¼ cup sugar
- ⅛ teaspoon salt
- 2 egg yolks
- 1¼ cups milk
- 1 teaspoon vanilla
- 2 egg whites
- ¼ cup sugar
- 1 cup heavy cream, whipped

In top of double boiler, mix gelatin, ¼ cup sugar, and salt. Beat together egg yolks and milk. Add to gelatin mixture. Place over boiling water and stir constantly until gelatin dissolves (about 5 minutes). Add vanilla. Chill until consistency of egg whites. Beat egg whites until stiff. Gradually add ¼ cup sugar while beating. Fold gelatin mixture into the stiffly beaten egg whites. Fold this mixture into heavy cream. Pour into 6-cup mold or into 6 individual molds.

BOHNE BEROGGAE

Filling:
- 2 cups dried pinto beans
- 1 teaspoon salt
- 1⅓ cups sugar

Dough:
- Your own favorite recipe for sweet yeast dough

Sauce:
- 1 quart half-and-half or 2 cups milk mixed with 2 cups cream
- 1 cup sugar
- 3 tablespoons cornstarch

Cook dried beans. Drain and mash. Stir in salt and sugar. When dough is ready to shape, form it into 48 balls the size of a large walnut. Let rise about 10 minutes. One by one, pull balls apart. Place 1 rounded teaspoon bean mixture on half the dough. Reseal with other half by pinching edges together. Place in greased pans. Let rise about 30 minutes. Bake in moderate oven about 25 minutes. Prepare sauce by cooking half-and-half with the sugar and cornstarch 2-3 minutes or until thickened. Serve hot over the beroggae.

Makes 4 dozen.

Mid-Kansas MCC Relief Sale, Hutchinson

Desserts and Sweets

ॐ

BUTTERFINGER DESSERT

- 2½ cups graham cracker crumbs
- 1½ cups crushed Rice Krispies
- ½ cup melted margarine
- 2 packages (3½ ounces each) instant vanilla pudding mix
- 2 cups milk
- 1 quart vanilla ice cream
- 1 container (8 ounces) non-dairy whipped topping, thawed
- 2 Butterfinger candy bars

Combine crumbs, crushed cereal, and margarine. Spread two-thirds of the crumbs over the bottom of a 9x13-inch cake pan. Reserve remaining crumbs. Combine pudding mix and milk. Mix until smooth. Blend in ice cream. Pour mixture over crumbs in pan. Let set in refrigerator. Spread whipped topping over top. Crush candy bars and mix with remaining crumbs. Sprinkle mixture over whipped topping. Serve chilled. You may keep this dessert in the freezer if desired, but thaw slightly before serving.

Serves 12.

Marie Hofer
Freeman, South Dakota
Minn-Kota Relief Sale
Sioux Falls, South Dakota

CARAMEL KRISP

- 1 7-ounce package caramels
- 2 tablespoons water in double boiler
- ½ cup nuts
- Pinch of salt
- 7 cups cornflakes or crisp rice cereal

Melt caramels over hot water. Add nuts and salt after caramel is melted. Add cornflakes. Put on greased cookie sheet. Let set until cool.

CARAMEL PUDDING

- 2 tablespoons butter
- 1 cup brown sugar
- 4 cups cold milk
- 3 tablespoons cornstarch
- ⅓ cup milk
- 1 teaspoon vanilla

Heat the butter and brown sugar until golden brown. Add the milk. Continue to heat on medium heat. Mix the cornstarch and ⅓ cup milk to make a paste. Add to brown sugar mixture just before it reaches the boiling point. Stir constantly until it boils. Turn off heat and cover for 3 minutes to cook starch completely. Add vanilla and cool.

CHEESECAKE

- 2 cups crushed graham wafers
- ½ cup melted butter
- 1 package lemon-lime gelatin
- ¾ cup boiling water
- 8 ounces cream cheese
- 1 large can evaporated milk
- 1 cup white sugar

Mix together graham wafers and melted butter. Pack in buttered pan, saving ¼ cup crumbs for top. Dissolve gelatin in boiling water. Allow to partially jell. Beat together cream cheese, milk, and sugar. Add to gelatin mixture and pour over crumb crust. Top with remaining crumbs.

COOKIE SALAD

- 1 package instant pudding mix
- 1 cup buttermilk
- 1 small can crushed pineapple
- 1 container (8 ounces) non-dairy whipped topping, thawed
- Half a package fudge-striped cookies, broken into small pieces

Mix ingredients in order given. Chill.

Serves 8.

CREAM CHEESE GRAPES

- 1 package (8 ounces) cream cheese, softened
- 1½ cups powdered sugar
- 1 cup sour cream
- 1 tablespoon lemon juice
- 1 container (8 ounces) non-dairy whipped topping, thawed
- 4 pounds seedless grapes
- 2 bananas, sliced (optional)

Mix cream cheese, sugar, sour cream, and lemon juice thoroughly. Add whipped topping and mix well. Add grapes and bananas. Chill.

Serves 6-8.

Cut Glass Cake

Crumb Crust:
- 1½ cups graham wafer crumbs
- ¼ cup brown sugar
- ¼ cup melted butter

Filling:
- 1 package each of lime, strawberry, cherry, and lemon gelatin
- 1 extra package lemon gelatin
- ½ cup hot pineapple juice
- ¼ cup sugar
- Cold water
- 2 packages whipped topping mix

Mix together ingredients for crumb crust. Pat into 9x13-inch pan, reserving ¼ cup for top. Bake at 300° for 15 minutes. Cool. Dissolve 1 package of each gelatin flavor in 1 cup hot water. Add ½ cup cold water to each flavor. Pour gelatin mixtures into separate square pans and allow to jell overnight. Dissolve extra package lemon gelatin in pineapple juice. Add sugar and cold water. Chill until it begins to jell. Prepare whipped topping mix according to directions on package. Fold partly jelled lemon gelatin into whipped topping and refrigerate. Cut the pans of set gelatin into squares and mix into whipped topping mixture. Pour into crumb crust and top with reserved crumbs. Chill and cut into squares to serve.

Frozen Dessert

Base:
- 1 cup flour
- ½ cup margarine
- ¼ cup brown sugar
- ½ cup chopped nuts

Topping:
- 1 package (16 ounces) frozen strawberries, thawed
- 1 cup sugar
- 2 egg whites
- 1 tablespoon lemon juice
- ½ teaspoon vanilla
- 1 cup whipping cream, whipped

Prepare base by combining all ingredients and placing in a 400° oven for 15 minutes, stirring regularly, until brown. Sprinkle the crumbs over the bottom of a 9x13-inch pan, saving some of them to top the dessert. Do not press the crumbs down. Prepare topping by beating strawberries, sugar, egg whites, lemon juice, and vanilla for 10 minutes. Fold in whipped cream. Spoon topping over crumbs and garnish with reserved crumbs. Put in freezer. Thaw slightly and cut in squares to serve.

Anne Neufeld
Coaldale, Alberta
Alberta MCC Relief Sale, Coaldale

DUMP CAKE

- 1 19-ounce can crushed pineapple
- 1 19-ounce can strawberry or cherry pie filling
- 1 box yellow cake mix
- Butter

Pour pineapple (including juice) into a greased 9x13-inch pan. Pour cherries or strawberries on top. Sprinkle with dry cake mix and dot with butter. Bake at 350° for 1 hour.

FOUR-LAYER DESSERT

- 1½ cups flour
- ¾ cup soft margarine
- 1 cup chopped nuts
- 1 package (8 ounces) cream cheese, softened
- 1 cup powdered sugar
- 2 containers (8 ounces each) non-dairy whipped topping, thawed
- 2 packages (3½ ounces each) instant chocolate or lemon pudding mix
- 3 cups milk

Prepare crust by combining flour, margarine, and ¾ cup of the chopped nuts. Press over bottom of a 9x13-inch pan. Bake at 375° for 15-20 minutes. Cool. Combine cream cheese and powdered sugar. Mix in 1 container of the whipped topping. Spread over crust. Prepare pudding mix using the 3 cups milk, as directed on package. Pour over cream cheese layer. Spread remaining container of whipped topping over dessert. Sprinkle with remaining ¼ cup chopped nuts. Refrigerate.

Serves 12-15.

Mrs. Allan (Doris) Bachman
Putnam, Illinois
Willow Springs Mennonite Church, Tiskilwa
Illinois MCC Relief Sale, Peoria

FROZEN BERRY FLUFF

- 2 egg whites
- 1 tablespoon lemon juice
- 1½ cups sugar
- 2 cups sliced fresh strawberries
- 1 cup whipped cream or whipped topping

Beat the egg whites and lemon juice slightly in large bowl. Gradually add the sugar and strawberries. Beat at high speed for 12-15 minutes until mixture is fluffy and has large volume. Fold in whipped cream or whipped topping and freeze.

FRUIT PIZZA DESSERT

Crust:
- ½ cup margarine
- ½ cup solid vegetable shortening (Crisco)
- 1½ cups sugar
- 2 eggs
- 2 teaspoons cream of tartar
- 1 teaspoon baking soda
- ¼ teaspoon salt
- 2¾ cups flour

Topping 1:
- 1 package (8 ounces) cream cheese, softened
- ½ cup sugar
- 2 tablespoons fruit juice

Topping 2:
- 1 can pineapple chunks
- 1 can mandarin orange segments
- 2 bananas, sliced
- Fresh strawberries, sliced
- 3 tablespoons cornstarch

Make crust by mixing shortenings, sugar, and eggs. Add remaining ingredients. Mix thoroughly. Press into large jelly roll pan. Bake at 400° for 8-10 minutes. Cool. Make Topping 1 by beating all ingredients together. Spread on cooled crust. Make Topping 2 by draining canned fruits (reserve juice). Arrange canned and fresh fruit over cream cheese layer. Combine a little of the fruit juice with the cornstarch to make a smooth paste. Bring reserved juice to a boil, add cornstarch paste, and cook until thick and clear. Cool and pour sauce over fruit layer. Chill pizza before serving.

Serves 12-16.

GRAHAM CRACKER FLUFF

- 2 egg yolks
- ½ cup sugar
- ⅔ cup milk
- 1 package gelatin (1 tablespoon)
- ½ cup cold water
- 2 egg whites
- 1 cup whipping cream
- 1 teaspoon vanilla
- 3 tablespoons melted butter
- 3 tablespoons sugar
- 12 graham crackers

Beat egg yolks and add sugar and milk. Cook in top of double boiler until slightly thickened. Soak gelatin in the cold water. Pour hot mixture over softened gelatin and stir until smooth. Chill until slightly thickened. Add stiffly beaten egg whites, vanilla, and whipped cream to chilled mixture. Combine melted butter, cracker crumbs, and sugar to make crumbs. Sprinkle half of the crumbs in bottom of serving dish. Add mixture and top with remaining crumbs. Let cool in refrigerator until set.

Makes 6-8 servings.

HOMEMADE ICE CREAM

- ❖ 6 eggs, separated
- ❖ 2½ cups whipping cream
- ❖ 1 cup sugar
- ❖ Flavoring

Beat cream until stiff and add ⅓ cup sugar. Beat egg yolks, remaining sugar, and flavoring until stiff and lemon colored. Gently fold together and add stiffly beaten egg whites last. Freeze, stirring gently 3 times, once every hour, to keep liquid from forming at the bottom. If desired, add 1 cup of blueberries or any fresh fruit (mashed if necessary) at third stirring.

Makes half a gallon.

BUTTERSCOTCH TOPPING

- ❖ 1 cup brown sugar
- ❖ 2 tablespoons corn syrup
- ❖ ¼ cup rich milk
- ❖ 3 tablespoons butter

Combine all ingredients. Stir until boiling and simmer for 3 minutes.

From Amish Cooking, *published by Pathway Publishers Corporation*

ORANGE-PINEAPPLE ICE CREAM

- ❖ 9 eggs, beaten (fewer eggs may be used)
- ❖ 3¾ cups white sugar
- ❖ ½ package orange Kool-Aid
- ❖ 1 13-ounce can crushed pineapple or juice
- ❖ 1 quart rich milk
- ❖ Additional cream or milk
- ❖ 3 dissolved junket tablets

Beat eggs and sugar together thoroughly. Add the Kool-Aid and pineapple. Pour into a plastic container. Heat the milk. Pour into container. Add additional cream or milk until the container is filled up to several inches from the top. Add the junket tablets. Stir. Let set 15 minutes, then freeze.

Variations: Omit pineapple and Kool-Aid and use vanilla or lemon flavoring. Brown sugar may also be used instead of white.

Makes 6 quarts.

From Amish Cooking, *published by Pathway Publishers Corporation*

Lemon Fluff Dessert

- 1 package lemon gelatin
- Juice and rind of 1 lemon
- ½ cup white sugar
- 1½ cups boiling water
- 1 large can evaporated milk, chilled

Crumbs:
- 12 double graham wafers, crushed
- ⅓ cup melted butter
- ½ cup white sugar

Combine the crumb ingredients. Pack half into a 9x13-inch pan. Mix together the gelatin, lemon juice and rind, ½ cup white sugar, and boiling water. Chill until partly set. Whip the milk until very stiff. Beat gelatin mixture slightly and fold into whipped milk. Pour into pan and top with remaining crumbs. Chill 24 hours.

My Mother's Date Pudding

- ½ cup white sugar
- ½ cup brown sugar
- Shortening the size of an egg
- 1½ cups flour
- 1 cup boiling water
- 1 cup dates, finely chopped
- 1 teaspoon soda
- 1 cup nuts
- Pinch of salt

Pour boiling water over dates, soda, and salt. Mix with remaining ingredients and bake at 350°. Break into pieces and layer with banana slices and whipped cream with a final layer of whipped cream on top.

Amish Cook
York, Pennsylvania

BEAR IN MIND THAT YOU SHOULD CONDUCT
YOURSELF IN LIFE AS AT A FEAST.

☙

ORANGE DELIGHT DESSERT

Cake:
- ❖ 1 box angel food cake mix

Filling and Frosting:
- ❖ 1 cup sugar
- ❖ 4 tablespoons cornstarch
- ❖ 1 tablespoon grated orange rind
- ❖ 1½ tablespoons lemon juice
- ❖ ½ teaspoon salt
- ❖ 1 cup orange juice
- ❖ 2 egg yolks
- ❖ ¼ cup butter
- ❖ 1 package whipped topping mix
- ❖ Maraschino cherries

Prepare cake mix according to directions. Bake in 10-inch tube pan and cool. In heavy pot, mix sugar, cornstarch, orange rind, lemon juice, salt, orange juice, and egg yolks. Cook until thick. Remove from heat and stir in butter. Cool to room temperature. Prepare whipped topping according to directions and fold into cooled filling. Cut cake in half crosswise to make 2 layers. Place 1 layer on large cake plate and cover with a quarter of the filling mixture. Top with second cake layer. Frost sides and top with remaining filling mixture. Garnish with maraschino cherries. Cover and store in cool place for 24 hours.

PRUNE PUDDING

- ❖ ½ pound prunes
- ❖ 2 cups boiling water
- ❖ ¾ cup sugar
- ❖ 1 stick cinnamon (optional)
- ❖ 1¼ cups boiling water
- ❖ ¼ cup cornstarch
- ❖ ½ cup water

Cover the prunes with 2 cups boiling water. Cover and boil 5 minutes. Cool and remove stones. Add the sugar, cinnamon, and an additional 1¼ cups boiling water. Bring to boil and simmer 5 minutes. Mix the cornstarch with ½ cup water. Add to prune mixture and simmer 5 minutes. Serve cold with whipped cream.

Raspberry Cobbler

- ⅔ cup sugar
- 1 tablespoon cornstarch
- 1 cup boiling water
- 2 cups raspberries, blueberries, or blackberries
- 1¾ cups flour
- 2 teaspoons baking powder
- ½ teaspoon salt
- ¼ cup soft shortening
- ¾ cup sugar
- 1 egg
- ¾ cup milk
- 1 teaspoon vanilla

In a small saucepan, mix together the ⅔ cup sugar and the cornstarch. Add the boiling water and boil 1 minute. Spread berries over bottom of baking pan. Pour mixture over berries. Mix together flour, baking powder, and salt. Add shortening, the ¾ cup sugar, egg, milk, and vanilla. Beat with beater or spoon until mixed well. Spoon dough over berries. Bake at 350° for 25-30 minutes. Serve warm with or without milk.

Grace Cable
Hollsopple, Pennsylvania
MCC Quilt Auction and Relief Sale, Johnstown

Rice Fluff

- 1 3-ounce package orange or lemon gelatin
- 1 cup boiling water
- ½ cup pineapple juice
- ½ cup white sugar
- 1 cup drained pineapple
- 1½ cups cooked rice
- 1 cup whipped cream

Dissolve the gelatin in the boiling water. Add the pineapple juice and sugar. When mixture begins to jell, whip until fluffy and add the pineapple and rice. Fold whipped cream. Chill.

7¢ Pudding

- 1 cup brown sugar
- Butter ball the size of an egg
- 1 cup sweet milk
- 2 cups flour
- 1 teaspoon soda
- ½ teaspoon cream of tartar
- ¼ teaspoon nutmeg
- ½ cup raisins

Mix the brown sugar with the butter. Add alternately the sweet milk, the flour sifted with the soda, the cream of tartar, and the nutmeg. Add the raisins. Pour into bowl and steam 3 hours.

Spicy Fudge Pudding

- ❖ 11 cups sifted all-purpose flour
- ❖ 2 teaspoons baking powder
- ❖ ¾ cup granulated sugar
- ❖ ⅛ teaspoon salt
- ❖ 2 tablespoons cocoa
- ❖ ¾ teaspoon cinnamon
- ❖ ¼ teaspoon cloves
- ❖ ½ cup milk
- ❖ ½ teaspoon vanilla
- ❖ 2 tablespoons melted butter or margarine
- ❖ ½ cup firmly packed brown sugar
- ❖ ½ cup white sugar
- ❖ 1 cup cold water

Sift together the flour, baking powder, sugar, salt, cocoa, cinnamon, and cloves into a mixing bowl. Combine the milk, vanilla, and butter. Combine the 2 mixtures and stir just until smooth. Spread over bottom of buttered 8-inch square pan. Combine the brown and white sugars and sprinkle over batter. Pour the water over entire mixture. Do not stir. Bake at 325° for 40 minutes or until top is firm to a light touch.

Steamed Carrot Pudding

- ❖ 1 cup sugar
- ❖ ½ cup lard or suet
- ❖ 1 cup grated carrots
- ❖ 1 cup grated potatoes
- ❖ 1 cup raisins
- ❖ 1½ cups flour
- ❖ 1 teaspoon soda
- ❖ ½ teaspoon cloves
- ❖ ½ teaspoon cinnamon
- ❖ ½ teaspoon nutmeg
- ❖ Cherries and nuts

Sauce:
- ❖ 1 cup brown sugar
- ❖ 3 tablespoons butter
- ❖ 2 cups warm water
- ❖ 3 tablespoons cornstarch dissolved in ⅓ cup water
- ❖ 1 tablespoon vanilla

Blend the sugar and lard together. Add the carrots, potatoes, and raisins. Sift together and add the flour, soda, cloves, cinnamon, and nutmeg. Add cherries and nuts to taste. Steam 1½ hours. To make the sauce, caramelize the sugar and butter on low heat until rich golden brown. Add the water and stir. Slowly add the cornstarch mixture to the sauce. Cook until it thickens. Add the vanilla. Serve pudding hot with sauce or milk.

STEAMED PUDDING

- ¾ cup sugar
- 1 tablespoon butter
- 1 egg
- 1 tablespoon cocoa
- ½ cup milk
- 1½ cups flour
- 1 teaspoon baking powder
- 1 teaspoon vanilla

Mix all ingredients with electric mixer until very well blended. Pour into greased and floured pan that can safely be set in a pan of boiling water. Cover outer pan and steam pudding for about 50 minutes or until toothpick used as a tester comes out clean. Serve warm with whipped cream or non-dairy whipped topping.

Bernice Schroll
Contributed by N. Elizabeth Graber
Wayland, Iowa
Iowa MCC Relief Sale, Iowa City

STRAWBERRY ANGEL CAKE DESSERT

- Half an angel food cake
- 1 large package (6 ounces) instant vanilla pudding mix
- 1 cup cold milk
- 2 cups vanilla ice cream
- 1 large package (6 ounces) strawberry-flavored gelatin
- 2 cups boiling water
- 1 large box frozen strawberries, thawed
- Non-dairy whipped topping

Tear cake into bite-size pieces. Use to line a 13x9-inch glass baking dish. Whip together pudding mix and milk. Add ice cream and whip until smooth. Pour over cake in pan. Refrigerate 2-3 hours. Thoroughly mix gelatin and boiling water. Let cool. Stir in strawberries. Pour mixture over pudding-topped cake in pan. Refrigerate until set. Spread with whipped topping before serving.

Mary Ann Cashdollar
Morton, Illinois
First Mennonite Church, Morton
Illinois MCC Relief Sale, Peoria

GOOD FOOD ENDS WITH GOOD TALK.

STRAWBERRY CHANTILLY

- 1 cup flour
- ¼ cup brown sugar
- ½ cup margarine
- ¼ cup ground nuts
  or Grape-Nuts cereal
- 2 egg whites
- ⅔ cup granulated sugar
- 2 tablespoons lemon juice
- 1 pint strawberries, sliced
- 1 container (8 ounces) non-dairy
  whipped topping, thawed

Combine flour and brown sugar. Cut in margarine until blended. Stir in nuts. Spread on a rimmed cookie sheet. Bake at 325° for 20 minutes, stirring 3-4 times. Cool. Reserve ½ cup crumbs. Pat remainder over bottom of 9x13-inch pan. Beat egg whites, granulated sugar, and lemon juice until stiff. Add strawberries and beat until blended. Fold in whipped topping. Spread over crumbs in pan and top with reserved crumbs. Freeze. Let thaw for 20 minutes before serving. Cut in squares.

Bernice Lehman
Johnstown, Pennsylvania
MCC Quilt Auction and Relief Sale, Johnstown

STRAWBERRY PIZZA

Crust:
- 1 cup butter, softened
- 2 cups flour
- ½ cup powdered sugar

Topping 1:
- 1 package cream cheese, softened
- 1 cup powdered sugar
- 1 package Dream Whip whipped
  topping mix prepared according
  to package directions

Topping 2:
- 1 pint strawberries, crushed
- 1 cup granulated sugar
- 4 teaspoons cornstarch
- ¼ cup water
- 1 pint strawberries, sliced
  (reserve a few whole strawberries
  for garnish)

Prepare crust by mixing together butter, flour, and powdered sugar. Press into pizza pan. Bake at 350° for 20 minutes. Cool. Prepare Topping 1 by combining cream cheese, powdered sugar, and most of the whipped topping (reserve some to garnish top of pizza) until smooth. Spread over cooled crust. Chill. Prepare Topping 2 by combining crushed strawberries and granulated sugar. Bring to a boil and add paste of cornstarch and water. Cook until thick and clear. Cool thoroughly. Spread sliced strawberries over cream cheese layer. Pour cooled strawberry sauce over. Chill. Garnish with whipped topping and reserved whole strawberries before serving.

Serves 16.

Bernice Lehman
Johnstown, Pennsylvania
MCC Quilt Auction and Relief Sale, Johnstown

WHOOPIE PIES

Batter:
- ❖ 4 cups flour
- ❖ 2 cups sugar
- ❖ 2 teaspoons soda
- ❖ ½ teaspoon salt
- ❖ 1 cup shortening
- ❖ 1 cup cocoa
- ❖ 2 eggs
- ❖ 2 teaspoons vanilla
- ❖ 1 cup thick sour milk
- ❖ 1 cup cold water

Filling:
- ❖ 1 egg white, beaten
- ❖ 1 tablespoon vanilla
- ❖ 2 tablespoons flour
- ❖ 2 tablespoons milk
- ❖ 2 cups confectioners' sugar (or more as needed)
- ❖ ¾ cup vegetable shortening or margarine
- ❖ Marshmallow creme (optional).

To make the batter, cream together sugar, salt, shortening, vanilla, and eggs. Sift together flour, soda, and cocoa. Add this to the first mixture alternately with water and sour milk. Add slightly more flour if milk is not thick. Drop by teaspoons. Bake at 400°. To make filling, beat egg white, sugar, and vanilla. Then add the remaining ingredients. Beat well. A few drops peppermint flavor may be used in place of vanilla.

From Amish Cooking, *published by Pathway Publishers Corporation*

YOGURT

- ❖ 1 gallon milk
- ❖ 2 tablespoons unflavored gelatin
- ❖ ½ cup cold water
- ❖ ½ cup vanilla yogurt
- ❖ 1½ cups sugar
- ❖ Danish or pie filling of choice

Heat the milk to 180° or almost boiling. Cool slightly. Soak gelatin in water. Add gelatin mix, yogurt, and sugar to the milk. Beat well. Set in oven or a warm place for 8 hours. Skim off layer on top. Beat well. Stir in Danish or pie filling. Refrigerate. Stir well before serving.

Sarah King

☙

GRANDMA'S REMEDIES

BREAD AND MILK POULTICES

Heat milk in a pan. Put in a slice of white bread and leave until milk has soaked up and bread is quite warm. Place on infected sores or boils. Keep treatment up for at least 1 hour, using 2 or more pieces of bread and applying them directly to the sore. Keep bread as warm as the patient can stand it. This is highly recommended to bring boils to a head.

CLAIMS FOR HONEY

If you are run down, irritable, and always tired, try taking 3-4 teaspoons of honey a day for several months. It is good for insomnia, constipation, and poor blood.

If you scald or burn yourself, apply honey immediately. It will help the burn heal rapidly.

Twitching of the eyelids or the corner of the mouth can be cured by taking 2 teaspoons of honey at each meal.

Muscle cramps can be cured by taking 2 teaspoons of honey at each meal.

LILY WHISKEY

Fill a jar with the petals of the Madonna Lily. Get a bottle of good quality whiskey. Fill the jar so the petals are all covered. As they settle down, add more whiskey. This is especially good for burns and sores.

OLD-FASHIONED COUGH REMEDY

Boil one lemon slowly for 10 minutes. Cut in half and extract the juice with a squeezer. Put the juice into an ordinary drinking glass. Add 2 tablespoons of glycerin. Stir well, then fill up the glass with honey. Stir with a spoon before taking. Take 1 teaspoon when you have a coughing spell. Take 1 teaspoon every 3 hours if cough is severe.

Teas and What They Are Good For

Brew tea with ¼ cup of one of the ingredients below, 2 cups boiling water, and a little honey to cure common ailments.

Use chamomile flowers to treat diarrhea, boneset to treat cold and fever, thistle root for rheumatism, mullet leaves for anemia, burdock to treat kidney and bladder trouble, black strap molasses for arthritis, and sage to settle the stomach.

Uses for Cider Vinegar

Apply cider vinegar just as it comes from the bottle to infected part of skin six times a day (treats ringworm and shingles).

Mix equal parts cider vinegar and water. Apply to affected part of skin and allow to dry (treats poison ivy). Do this often.

Gargle with cider vinegar to sooth a sore throat.

CB

HAIR TONIC

- ½ cup sage leaves, pressed down
- 1 ounce glycerin
- 2 ounces bay rum

Make a pint of sage tea by mixing the sage leaves with the glycerin and rum. Apply to scalp daily.

COURAGE IS FEAR THAT HAS SAID ITS PRAYERS.

HOMEMADE LINIMENT

- 1 pint pure cider vinegar
- 3 eggs
- 3 ounces turpentine
- 3 ounces spirits of camphor

Beat eggs in a deep bowl for 10 minutes. Add turpentine, vinegar, and camphor slowly in order given, stirring constantly. Shake 2-3 times a day for 2 days.

MUSTARD PLASTER

- 1 tablespoon mustard
- 4 tablespoons flour
- Water to moisten

Mix ingredients and spread on clean white cotton. Place plaster over patient's lungs, which have been thoroughly covered with petroleum jelly or another grease. Watch very closely. Remove when skin is a rosy pink (a mustard plaster will burn).

Simple Ointment

- 2 ounces sulfur
- ½ pound melted lard

Mix thoroughly and allow to harden. Good for piles, itch, and skin diseases in general.

ය

Soap Making

How to Boil Soap

- 30 pounds soap grease (butcher scraps)
- 6 pounds caustic soda
- Water
- 5 pints salt
- 2 ounces oil of citronella (optional)

Boil the soap grease, soda, and 3 gallons of soft water for 3 hours. Add water from time to time until 5-6 additional gallons have been added. Add the salt. Stir well and put out fire. If you want scented soap, add 2 ounces of oil of citronella to every 60 pounds.

Relief Soap Recipe

- 1½ gallons water
- 3½ pounds lye
- 24 pounds grease

The day before you want to make soap, place the water in a large plastic or stainless steel (do not use aluminum) container. Carefully pour lye into water. Stir with a wooden spoon or spatula until lye is dissolved. Let mixture cool. The next day, heat clean grease to 110° in a large stainless steel (not aluminum) container. Carefully add lye solution, stirring with a wooden spoon or spatula until soap begins to thicken like honey. Pour into a heavy 5x16x22-inch cardboard box lined with plastic. Let set several hours until firm, but not solid. Cut into 4-inch squares. Let set in box for 3-4 days. Remove, dry, and cure. Soap will be ready to use in about 4-6 weeks.

Makes 40-50 pounds of soap.

Mary Wenger
Missouri MCC Relief Sale, Harrisonville

Cold Soap Recipe

- 5 pints cold water
- 4 tablespoons ammonia
- ½ cup borax
- 1 ounce oil of sassafras
- 1 box Tide (optional)
- 4 tablespoons white sugar
- ½ cup sal soda
- 2 ounces glycerin
- 2 cans lye

Combine all the listed ingredients. Let come to the right temperature (lukewarm). (It is heated by the lye.) Pour this mixture into 10 pounds melted lard. Be sure and pour the lye mixture into the lard. (Never pour the lard into the lye.) Stir until it is creamy. Let harden, but cut in pieces before it gets too hard. Use a granite or iron kettle to mix ingredients.

From Amish Cooking, *published by Pathway Publishers Corporation*

Before working in the garden, rub your fingernails over a piece of soap. Dirt can't get in, and soap washes out easily when washing.

DIRECTORY OF RELIEF SALES: UNITED STATES

For more information about the work of MCC, the history of relief sales, and the dates of the sales below, visit reliefsales.mcc.org.

STATE	CITY	NAME
California	Fresno	West Coast Mennonite Relief Sale and Auction
California	Upland	Southern California Festival and Sale for World Hunger and Relief
Colorado	Rocky Ford	Rocky Mountain Mennonite Relief Sale
Georgia	Perry	Peach Cobbler Mennonite World Relief Sale
Idaho	Nampa	Idaho Mennonite World Relief Sale
Illinois	Arthur	Arthur Mennonite Relief Sale
Illinois	Bloomington	Illinois Mennonite Relief Sale
Indiana	Goshen	Michiana Mennonite Relief Sale
Indiana	Odon	Daviess County Relief Sale
Iowa	Iowa City	Iowa Mennonite Relief Sale
Kansas	Hutchinson	Kansas Mennonite Relief Sale
Maryland	McHenry	TriState Relief Sale
Michigan	Fairview	Northern Michigan Relief Sale
Minnesota	Brooklyn Park	Festival for Sale for World Relief
Missouri	Harrisonville	Western Missouri Mennonite Relief Sale
Missouri	Versailles	Central Missouri MCC Relief Auction
Nebraska	Aurora	Nebraska MCC Relief Sale
North Dakota	Minot	Upper Midwest Relief Sale
Ohio	Kidron	Ohio Mennonite Relief Sale
Ohio	Wauseon	Black Swamp Benefit Bazaar
Oklahoma	Enid	Oklahoma Mennonite Relief Sale

State	City	Name
Oregon	Albany	Oregon Mennonite Festival for World Relief
Pennsylvania	Harrisburg	Pennsylvania Relief Sale
Pennsylvania	New Holland	Pennsylvania Heifer Relief Sale
Pennsylvania	Quarryville	Gap Relief Auction
South Dakota	Sioux Falls	Minn-Kota Festival for Mennonite World Relief
Texas	Edinburg	Rio Grande Valley Mennonite Relief Sale
Texas	Houston	Texas Mennonite Sale and Auction for World Relief
Virginia	Harrisonburg	Virginia Mennonite Relief Sale
Washington	Ritzville	Mennonite Country Auction

DIRECTORY OF RELIEF SALES: CANADA

Province	City	Name
Alberta	Coaldale	MCC Alberta Relief Sale
British Columbia	Abbotsford	Central Fraser Valley MCC Relief Sale, Auction and Festival
British Columbia	Black Creek	Black Creek MCC Relief Fair
British Columbia	Prince George	Mennonite Fall Fair
Manitoba	Brandon	Brandon MCC Relief Sale
Manitoba	Morris	Morris MCC Auction and Relief Sale
Ontario	Aylmer	MCC Charity Auction for Relief
Ontario	Hamburg	New Hamburg Mennonite Relief Sale
Ontario	Leamington	Leamington Mennonite Community Festival
Ontario	Listowel	Ontario Mennonite Relief Heifer Sale
Ontario	Toronto	Black Creek Pioneer Village Relief Sale
Saskatchewan	Saskatoon	Saskatoon MCC Relief Sale

MCC Relief Sales in the United States
reliefsales.mcc.org

MCC Thrift Shops in the United States
thrift.mcc.org

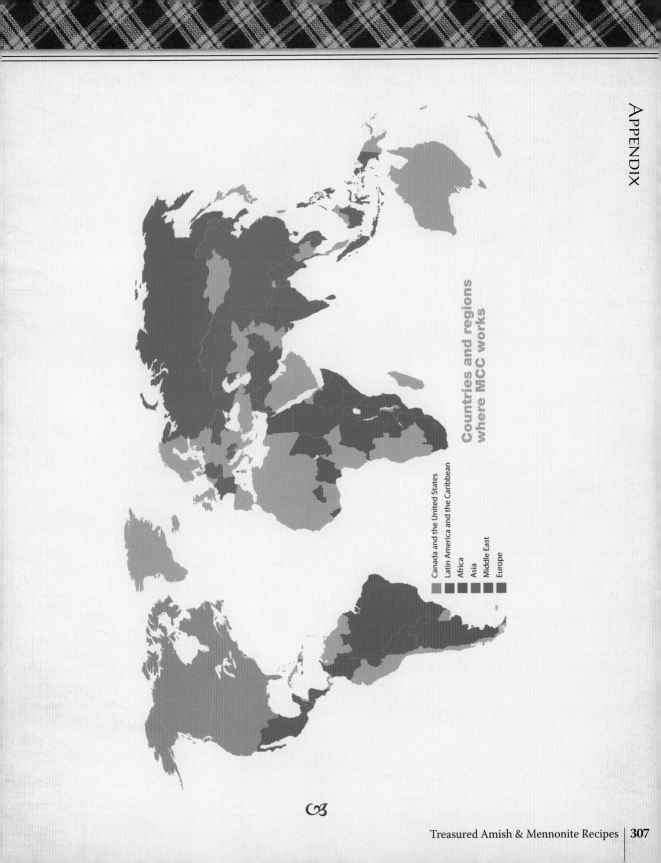

Countries and regions
where MCC works

Canada and the United States
Latin America and the Caribbean
Africa
Asia
Middle East
Europe

METRIC CONVERSION

U. S. MEASURE	METRIC
1 teaspoon (liquid)	4.93 milliliters
1 teaspoon (dry)	4.93 grams
1 tablespoon (liquid)	14.79 milliliters
1 tablespoon (dry)	14.79 grams
1 cup (liquid)	236.59 milliliters
1 cup (dry)	236 cubic centimeters*
1 pint	473.18 milliliters
1 quart (liquid)	946.35 milliliters
1 ounce (liquid)	29.57 milliliters
1 ounce (dry)	28.35 grams
1 pound	453.59 grams
1 inch	25.4 milliliters

*A cup is a measure of volume, while grams are a measure of mass. Dry ingredients vary in mass, so one cup of uncooked rice will not weigh the same as one cup of brown sugar. For this reason, no specific weight equivalent is given for the U. S. cup.

TEMPERATURE

To convert a temperature listed in degrees Fahrenheit to degrees Celsius, subtract 32 from the Fahrenheit temperature and divide the answer by 1.8. The resulting number is degrees Celsius. For example, 100°F minus 32 is 68. Sixty-eight divided by 1.8 is 37.78, or 37.78°C. Below are the temperature conversions for some of the oven settings found in this book.

FAHRENHEIT	CELSIUS
100°	37.78°
150°	65.56°
200°	93.33°
250°	121.11°
300°	148.89°
350°	176.67°
400°	204.44°
450°	232.22°

CB

ℭ𝔅

8

☙

Art of the Chicken Coop
A Fun and Essential Guide to Housing Your Peeps
By Chris Gleason

Hop on board the backyard chicken-raising trend! This fresh approach to designing and building chicken coops with seven stylish designs will keep your flock happy and your neighbors envious.

ISBN: 978-1-56523-542-7
$19.95 · 160 Pages

Know Your Chickens
By Jack Byard

Learn about 44 breeds of chicken like the lazy Barnvelder, and the friendly Belgian D'Uccle—sure to make a chicken enthusiast out of both young and old!

ISBN: 978-1-56523-612-7
$8.95 · 96 Pages

Also Available:
Know Your Pigs
ISBN: 978-1-56523-611-0
$8.95 · 64 Pages

Know Your Cows
ISBN: 978-1-56523-613-4
$8.95 · 96 Pages

Know Your Donkeys & Mules
ISBN: 978-1-56523-614-1
$8.95 · 78 Pages

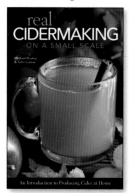

Real Cidermaking on a Small Scale
An Introduction to Producing Cider at Home
By Michael Pooley & John Lomax

Discover how easy it is to make hard cider from any kind of apple, whether from the backyard or the local market, and how mixing certain varieties will produce the best flavor.

ISBN: 978-1-56523-604-2
$12.95 · 112 Pages

You Bet Your Tomatoes
By Mike McGrath

From backyards to terraces, You Bet Your Tomatoes is a guide to growing heirloom tomatoes written by radio host and master gardener Mike McGrath.

ISBN: 978-1-56523-632-5
$12.95 · 96 Pages

Barns: A Close-Up Look
A Tour of America's Iconic Architecture Through Historic Photos and Detailed Drawings
Edited by Alan Giagnocavo

Take an in-depth tour of fourteen historic barns, each examined in detail with crisp black & white photography, scale drawings, elevations, and architectural plans.

ISBN: 978-56523-562-2
$19.95 · 128 pages

Also Available:
Lighthouses: A Close-Up Look
ISBN: 978-1-56523-560-1
$19.95 · 176 Pages

Covered Bridges: A Close-Up Look
ISBN: 978-1-56523-561-8
$19.95 · 160 Pages

Camp Cooking: The Black Feather Guide
Eating Well in the Wild
By Mark Scriver, Wendy Grater, and Joanna Baker

An indispensable guide for anyone who wants to eat well in the wild. The authors share their extensive knowledge, favorite recipes and proven methods so that you too can make your trip meals successful.

ISBN: 978-1-56523-644-8
$19.95 · 216 pages